CAMBRIDGE LIF

Books of end

CW01424453

Travel and Exploration

The history of travel writing dates back to the Bible, Caesar, the Vikings and the Crusaders, and its many themes include war, trade, science and recreation. Explorers from Columbus to Cook charted lands not previously visited by Western travellers, and were followed by merchants, missionaries, and colonists, who wrote accounts of their experiences. The development of steam power in the nineteenth century provided opportunities for increasing numbers of 'ordinary' people to travel further, more economically, and more safely, and resulted in great enthusiasm for travel writing among the reading public. Works included in this series range from first-hand descriptions of previously unrecorded places, to literary accounts of the strange habits of foreigners, to examples of the burgeoning numbers of guidebooks produced to satisfy the needs of a new kind of traveller - the tourist.

Travels to the Source of the Missouri River

The Lewis and Clark expedition of 1804–6 across America from Pittsburg to the Pacific and back was the third recorded transcontinental journey. President Jefferson had negotiated the Louisiana Purchase of over two million square kilometres from the French in 1803, and the aim of the expedition was to investigate the territory involved. He commissioned a Corps of Discovery as a scientific and military expedition to survey the acquisition, appointing his aide Meriwether Lewis (1774-1809) to lead it. It was hoped to discover that the Missouri and other rivers could be used for transcontinental communication and transport, and to assess the natural resources of the area. Some of the party returned east with specimens, reports and a map, while the remainder reached the Pacific in December 1805. Volume 2 covers the journey from Three Forks, Montana, the source of the Missouri, to the Pacific, and their winter quarters.

Cambridge University Press has long been a pioneer in the reissuing of out-of-print titles from its own backlist, producing digital reprints of books that are still sought after by scholars and students but could not be reprinted economically using traditional technology. The Cambridge Library Collection extends this activity to a wider range of books which are still of importance to researchers and professionals, either for the source material they contain, or as landmarks in the history of their academic discipline.

Drawing from the world-renowned collections in the Cambridge University Library, and guided by the advice of experts in each subject area, Cambridge University Press is using state-of-the-art scanning machines in its own Printing House to capture the content of each book selected for inclusion. The files are processed to give a consistently clear, crisp image, and the books finished to the high quality standard for which the Press is recognised around the world. The latest print-on-demand technology ensures that the books will remain available indefinitely, and that orders for single or multiple copies can quickly be supplied.

The Cambridge Library Collection will bring back to life books of enduring scholarly value (including out-of-copyright works originally issued by other publishers) across a wide range of disciplines in the humanities and social sciences and in science and technology.

Travels to the Source of the Missouri River

And Across the American Continent to the Pacific Ocean 1804, 1805, and 1806

VOLUME 2

MERIWETHER LEWIS
WIILLIAM CLARK
EDITED BY THOMAS REES

CAMBRIDGE
UNIVERSITY PRESS

CAMBRIDGE UNIVERSITY PRESS

Cambridge, New York, Melbourne, Madrid, Cape Town, Singapore,
São Paolo, Delhi, Dubai, Tokyo, Mexico City

Published in the United States of America by Cambridge University Press, New York

www.cambridge.org
Information on this title: www.cambridge.org/9781108023795

© in this compilation Cambridge University Press 2010

This edition first published 1815
This digitally printed version 2010

ISBN 978-1-108-02379-5 Paperback

This book reproduces the text of the original edition. The content and language reflect
the beliefs, practices and terminology of their time, and have not been updated.

Cambridge University Press wishes to make clear that the book, unless originally published
by Cambridge, is not being republished by, in association or collaboration with, or
with the endorsement or approval of, the original publisher or its successors in title.

TRAVELS

TO THE SOURCE OF

THE MISSOURI RIVER.

VOL. II.

TRAVELS

TO THE SOURCE OF

THE MISSOURI RIVER

AND ACROSS THE

AMERICAN CONTINENT

TO

THE PACIFIC OCEAN.

PERFORMED BY ORDER OF

THE GOVERNMENT OF THE UNITED STATES,

IN THE YEARS

1804, 1805, AND 1806.

BY CAPTAINS LEWIS AND CLARKE.

PUBLISHED FROM THE OFFICIAL REPORT,
AND ILLUSTRATED BY A MAP OF THE ROUTE,
AND OTHER MAPS.

A NEW EDITION, IN THREE VOLUMES.

VOL. II.

LONDON:
PRINTED FOR LONGMAN, HURST, REES, ORME, AND BROWN,
PATERNOSTER-ROW.
1815.

Printed by A. Strahan,
Printers-Street, London.

CONTENTS

OF

THE SECOND VOLUME.

a 3

CHAP. XIV.

Page

CHAP. XIX.

CHAP. XX.

CHAP. XXI.

xi

 CHAP. XXII.

 Page

A Party, headed by Captain Clarke, go in quest of a Whale driven on the Shore of the Pacific to obtain some of the Oil — They pass Clatsop River, which is described — The perilous Nature of this Jaunt, and the Grandeur of the Scenery described — In-dian mode of extracting Whale Oil — The Life of one of Captain Clarke's Party preserved by the Kindness of an Indian Woman — A short Account of the Chinnooks, of the Clatsops, Killamucks, the Lucktons, and an enumeration of several other Tribes — The Manner of Sepulchre among the Chinnooks, Clatsops, &c. — Description of their Weapons of War and Hunting — Their mode of building Houses — Their Manufactures and Cookery — Their mode of making Canoes — Their great Dexterity in managing that Vehicle   -   - 420

CHAP. XXIII.

An Account of the Clatsops, Killamucks, Chinnooks, and Cathlamahs — Their uniform Custom of flat-tening the Forehead — The Dress of these Savages, and their Ornaments described — The licensed Pros-titution of the Women, married and unmarried, of which a ludicrous instance is given — The Charac-ter of their Diseases — The common Opinion, that the Treatment of Women is the Standard by which the Virtues of an Indian may be known, combated and disproved by Examples — The Respect enter-tained by these Indians for old Age, compared with the different Conduct of those Nations who subsist by the Chase — Their mode of Government —

TRAVELS

UP

THE MISSOURI,

&c. &c.

CHAPTER XII.

MONDAY, July 15. We rose early, embarked all our baggage on board the canoes, which, though eight in number, are still heavily loaded, and at ten o'clock set out on our journey. At the distance of three miles we passed an island, just above which is a small creek coming in from the left, which we called Fort Mountain creek, the channel of which is ten yards wide, but now perfectly dry. At six miles we came to an island opposite to a bend, towards the north side; and reached at seven and a half miles the lower point of a woodland at the entrance of a beautiful river, which, in honour of the secretary of the navy, we called Smith's river. This stream falls into a bend on the south side of the Missouri, and is eighty yards wide. As far as we could discern its course, it wound through a charming valley, towards the south-east, in which many herds of buffaloe were feeding, till at the distance of twenty-five miles, it entered the rocky mountains, and was lost from our view. After dining near this place, we proceeded on four and three quarter miles, to the head of an island; four and a quarter miles beyond which is a second island on the left; three and a quarter miles further, in a bend of the river towards the north, is a wood, where we encamped for the night, after making nineteen and three quarter miles.

We find the prickly pear, one of the greatest beauties, as well as the greatest inconveniences of the plains, now in full bloom. The sun-flower too, a plant common on every part of the Missouri, from its entrance to this place, is here very abundant, and in bloom. The lamb's-quarter, wild cucumber, sandrush, and narrowdock, are also common. Two elk, a deer, and an otter, were our game to-day,

The river has now become so much more crooked than below, that we omit taking all its short meanders, but note only its general course, and lay down the small bends on our daily chart by the eye. The general width is from one hundred to one hundred and fifty yards. Along the banks are large beds of sand raised above the plains, as they always appear on the sides of the river opposite to the south-west exposure, seem obviously brought there from the channel of the river, by the incessant winds from that quarter : we find also more timber than for a great distance below the falls.

Tuesday, 16. There was a heavy dew last night. We soon passed about forty little booths, formed of willow bushes as a shelter against the sun. These seemed to have been deserted about ten days, and we supposed by the Snake Indians, or Shoshonees, whom we hoped soon to meet, as they appeared from the tracks to have a number of horses with them. At three and a quarter miles, we passed a creek or run, in a bend on the left side ; and four miles further, another run or small rivulet on the right. After breakfasting on a buffaloe shot by one of the hunters, Captain Lewis determined to go a-head of the party to the point where the river enters the Rocky mountains, and make the necessary observations before our arrival. He therefore set out with Drewyer, and two of the sick men, to whom he supposed the walk would be useful : he travelled on the north side of the river through a handsome level plain, which continued on the op-

posite side also, and at the distance of eight miles
passed a small stream, on which he observed a considerable quantity of the aspen tree. A little before twelve o'clock he halted on a bend to the
north, in a low ground covered with timber, about
four and a half miles below the mountains, and obtained a meridian altitude, by which we found the
latitude was 46° 46' 50" 2'''. His route then lay
through a high waving plain to a rapid, where the
Missouri first leaves the Rocky mountains, and here
he encamped for the night.

In the meantime we had proceeded after breakfast one mile to a bend in the left, opposite to
which was the frame to a large lodge situated in
the prairie, constructed like that already mentioned
above the Whitebear islands, but only sixty feet in
diameter; round it, were the remains of about
eighty leathern lodges, all which seemed to have
been built during the last autumn; within the next
fifteen and a quarter miles, we passed ten islands,
and on the last of which we encamped near the
right shore, having made twenty-three miles. The
next morning,

Wednesday, 17, we set out early, and at four
miles distance joined Captain Lewis at the foot of
the rapids, and after breakfast began the passage
of them : some of the articles most liable to be injured by the water were carried round. We then
double-manned the canoes, and with the aid of the
towing-line got them up without accident. For
several miles below the rapids the current of the

Missouri becomes stronger as you approach, and the spurs of the mountain advance towards the river, which is deep and more than seventy yards wide : at the rapids the river is closely hemmed in on both sides by the hills, and foams for half a mile over the rocks which obstruct its channel. The low grounds are now not more than a few yards in width, but they furnish room for an Indian road which winds under the hills on the north side of the river. The general range of these hills is from south-east to north-west, and the cliffs themselves are about eight hundred feet above the water, formed almost entirely of a hard black granite, on which are scattered a few dwarf-pine and cedar trees. Immediately in the gap is a large rock four hundred feet high, which on one side is washed by the Missouri, while on its other sides a handsome little plain separates it from the neighbouring mountains. It may be ascended with some difficulty nearly to its summit, and affords a beautiful prospect of the plains below, in which we could observe large herds of buffaloe. After ascending the rapids for half a mile we came to a small island at the head of them, which we called Pine island, from a large pine at the lower end of it, which is the first we have seen near the river for a great distance. A mile beyond Captain Lewis's camp we had a meridian altitude which gave us the latitude of 46° 42′ 14″ 7‴. As the canoes were still heavily loaded, all those not employed in working them walked on shore. The navigation is now very laborious. The river is deep but with little current, and from seventy to one hundred yards wide ; the low grounds are very narrow, with but little timber, and that chiefly the aspen tree. The cliffs are steep and hang over the river so much, that often we could not cross them, but were obliged to pass and repass from one side of the river to the other in order to make our way. In some places the banks are formed of rocks of dark black granite, rising perpendicularly to a great height, through which the river seems, in the progress of time, to have worn its channel. On these mountains we see more pine than usual, but it is still in small quantities. Along the bottoms which have a covering of high grass, we observe the sunflower blooming in great abundance. The Indians of the Missouri, and more especially those who do not cultivate maize, make great use of the seed of this plant for bread, or in thickening their soup. They first parch, and then pound it between two stones until it is reduced to a fine meal. Sometimes they add a portion of water, and drink it thus diluted : at other times they add a sufficient proportion of marrow grease to reduce it to the consistency of common dough, and eat it in that manner. This last composition we preferred to all the rest, and thought it at that time a very palatable dish. There is however very little of the broadleafed cottonwood on the side of the Falls, much the greater part of what we see being of the narrow-leafed species. There are also great quantities of red, purple, yellow, and black currants. The currants are very pleasant to the taste, and much preferable to those of our common garden. The bush rises to the height of six or eight feet; the stem simple, branching and erect. These shrubs associate in crops either in upper or timbered lands near the water courses. The leaf is petiolate, of a pale green, and in form resembles the red currant, so common in our gardens. The perianth of the fruit is one-leaved, five-cleft, abbreviated, and tubular. The corolla is monopetalous, funnel shaped, very long, and of a fine orange colour. There are five stamens and one pistillum of the first; the filaments are capillar, inserted in the corolla, equal and converging, the anther ovate and incumbent. The germ of the second species is round, smooth, inferior, and pedicelled : the style long and thicker than the stamens, simple, cylindrical, smooth, and erect. It remains with the corolla until the fruit is ripe; the stamen is simple and obtuse, and the fruit much the size and shape of our common garden currants, growing like them in clusters, supported by a compound footstalk. The peduncles are longer in this species, and the berries are more scattered. The fruit is not so acid as the common currant, and has a more agreeable flavour.

The other species differs in no respect from the yellow currant, excepting in the colour and flavour of the berries.

The serviceberry differs in some points from that of the United States. The bushes are small, sometimes not more than two feet high, and rarely ex-

ceed eight inches. They are proportionably small
in their stems, growing very thick, associated in
clumps. The fruit is of the same form, but for
the most part larger and of a very dark purple.
They are now ripe and in great perfection. There
are two species of gooseberry here, but neither of
them yet ripe: nor are the chokecherry, though in
great quantities. Besides, there are also at that
place the box-alder, red willow, and a species of
sumach. In the evening we saw some mountain
rams or big-horned animals, but no other game of
any sort. After leaving Pine island we passed a
small run on the left, which is formed by a large
spring rising at the distance of half a mile under
the mountain. One mile and a half above the
island is another, and two miles further a third
island, the river making small bends constantly
to the north. From this last island to a point
of rocks on the south side the low grounds become
rather wider, and three quarters of a mile beyond
these rocks, in a bend on the north, we encamped
opposite to a very high cliff, having made during
the day eleven and a half miles.

Thursday, 18. This morning early before our
departure we saw a large herd of the big-horned
animals, who were bounding among the rocks in
the opposite cliff with great agility. These inaccessible spots secure them from all their enemies, and
the only danger is in wandering among these precipices, where we should suppose it scarcely possible
for any animal to stand ; a single false step would

precipitate them at least five hundred feet into the water. At one mile and a quarter we passed another single cliff on the left; at the same distance beyond which is the mouth of a large river emptying itself from the north. It is a handsome, bold, and clear stream, eighty yards wide, that is nearly as broad as the Missouri, with a rapid current over a bed of small smooth stones of various figures. The water is extremely transparent, the low grounds are narrow, but possess as much wood as those of the Missouri: and it has every appearance of being navigable, though to what distance we cannot ascertain, as the country which it waters, is broken and mountainous. In honour of the secretary at war we called it Dearborn's river. Being now very anxious to meet with the Shoshonees or Snake Indians, for the purpose of obtaining the necessary information of our route, as well as to procure horses, it was thought best for one of us to go forward with a small party, and endeavour to discover them, before the daily discharge of our guns, which is necessary for our subsistence, should give them notice of our approach: if by an accident they hear us, they will most probably retreat to the mountains, mistaking us for their enemies who usually attack them on this side. Accordingly Captain Clarke set out with three men, and followed the course of the river on the north side; but the hills were so steep at first that he was not able to go much faster than ourselves. In the evening however he cut off many miles of the circuitous course of the river by crossing a mountain over which he found a wide Indian road, which in many places seems to have been cut or dug down in the earth. He passed also two branches of a stream which he called Ordway's creek, where he saw a number of beaver-dams extending in close succession towards the mountains as far as he could distinguish: on the cliffs were many of the big-horned animals. After crossing this mountain he encamped near a small stream of running water, having travelled twenty miles.

On leaving Dearborn's river we passed at three and a half miles a small creek, and at six beyond it an island on the north side of the river, which makes within that distance many small bends. At two and a half miles further is another island: three quarters of a mile beyond this is a small creek on the north side. At a mile and a half above the creek is a much larger stream thirty yards wide, and discharging itself with a bold current on the north side: the banks are low, and the bed formed of stones altogether. To this stream we gave the name of Ordway's creek, after sergeant John Ordway. At two miles beyond this the valley widens: we passed several bends of the river, and encamped in the centre of one on the south, having made twenty-one miles. Here we found a small grove of the narrow-leafed cottonwood, there being no longer any of the broad-leafed kind since we entered the mountains. The water of these rivulets which come down from the mountains is very cold, pure, and well tasted. Along their banks, as well as on the Missouri, the aspen is very common, but of a small kind. The river is somewhat wider than we found it yesterday; the hills more distant from the river and not so high: there are some pines on the mountains, but they are principally confined to the upper regions of them; the low grounds are still narrower and have little or no timber. The soil near the river is good, and produces a luxuriant growth of grass and weeds: among these productions the sunflower holds a very distinguished place. For several days past we have observed a species of flax in the low grounds, the leaf-stem and pericarp of which resemble those of the flax commonly cultivated in the United States: the stem rises to the height of two and a half or three feet, and springs to the number of eight or ten from the same root, with a strong thick bark apparently well calculated for use: the root seems to be perennial, and it is probable that the cutting of the stems may not at all injure it, for although the seeds are not yet ripe, there are young suckers shooting up from the root, whence we may infer that the stems which are fully grown and the proper stage of vegetation to produce the best flax, are not essential to the preservation or support of the root, a circumstance which would render it a most valuable plant. To day we have met with a second species of flax smaller than the first, as it seldom obtains a greater height than nine or twelve inches: the leaf and stem resemble those of the species just mentioned, except that the latter is rarely branched, and bears a single monopetalus bell-shaped blue flower, suspended with its limb downwards. We saw several herds of the big-horn, but they were in the cliffs beyond our reach. We killed an elk this morning and found part of a deer which had been left for us by Captain Clarke. He pursued his route,

Friday, 19, early in the morning, and soon passed the remains of several Indian camps formed of willow brush, which seemed to have been deserted this spring. At the same time he observed that the pine trees had been stripped of their bark about the same season, which our Indian woman says her countrymen do in order to obtain the sap and the soft parts of the wood and bark for food. About eleven o'clock he met a herd of elk and killed two of them, but such was the want of wood in the neighbourhood that he was unable to procure enough to make a fire, and he was therefore obliged to substitute the dung of a buffaloe, with which he cooked his breakfast. They then resumed their course along an old Indian road. In the afternoon they reached a handsome valley watered by a large creek, both of which extended a considerable distance into the mountain : this they crossed, and during the evening travelled over a mountainous country covered with sharp fragments of flint-rock : these bruised and cut their feet very much, but were

scarcely less troublesome than the prickly pear of
the open plains, which have now become so abundant that it is impossible to avoid them, and the
thorns are so strong that they pierce a double sole
of dressed deer skin : the best resource against
them is a sole of buffaloe hide in parchment. At
night they reached the river much fatigued, having
passed two mountains in the course of the day, and
having travelled thirty miles. Captain Clarke's
first employment on lighting a fire was to extract
from his feet the briars, which he found seventeen
in number.

In the mean time we proceeded on very well,
though the water appears to increase in rapidity as
we advance : the current has indeed been strong
during the day and obstructed by some rapids,
which are not however much broken by rocks, and
are perfectly safe : the river is deep, and its general width is from one hundred to one hundred
and fifty yards. For more than thirteen miles
we went along the numerous bends of the river,
and then reached two small islands; three and
three quarter miles beyond which is a small creek
in a bend to the left, above a small island on the
right side of the river. We were regaled about
ten o'clock P. M. with a thunder-storm of rain
and hail which lasted for an hour, but during
the day in this confined valley, through which we
are passing, the heat is almost insupportable; yet
whenever we obtain a glimpse of the lofty tops of
the mountains, we are tantalized with a view of

the snow. These mountains have their sides and summits partially varied with little copses of pine, cedar, and balsam fir. A mile and a half beyond this creek the rocks approach the river on both sides, forming a most sublime and extraordinary spectacle. For five and three quarter miles these rocks rise perpendicularly from the water's edge to the height of nearly twelve hundred feet. They are composed of a black granite near its base, but from its lighter colour above, and from the frag-ments we suppose the upper part to be flint of a yellowish brown and cream colour. Nothing can be imagined more tremendous than the frowning darkness of these rocks, which project over the river, and menace us with destruction. The river, of three hundred and fifty yards in width, seems to have forced its channel down this solid mass, but so reluctantly has it given way, that during the whole distance, the water is very deep even at the edges, and for the first three miles there is not a spot, except one of a few yards, in which a man could stand between the water and the towering perpendicular of the mountain: the convulsion of the passage must have been terrible, since at its outlet there are vast columns of rock torn from the mountain, which are strewed on both sides of the river, the trophies as it were of the victory. Se-veral fine springs burst out from the chasms of the rock, and contribute to increase the river, which has now a strong current, but very fortunately we are able to overcome it with our oars, since it would be impossible to use either the cord or the pole. We were obliged to go on some time after dark, not being able to find a spot large enough to encamp on, but at length, about two miles above a small island in the middle of the river we met with a spot on the left side, where we procured plenty of light-wood and pitchpine. This extraordinary range of rocks we called the Gates of the Rocky mountains. We had made twenty-two miles; and four and a quarter miles from the entrance of the Gates. The mountains are higher to-day than they were yesterday. We saw some big-horns, a few antelopes and beaver, but since entering the mountains have found no buffaloe: the otter are however in great plenty : the musquitoes have become less troublesome than they were.

Saturday, 20. By employing the tow-rope whenever the banks permitted the use of it, the river being too deep for the pole, we were enabled to overcome the current, which is still strong. At the distance of half a mile we came to a high rock in a bend to the left in the Gates. Here the perpendicular rocks cease, the hills retire from the river, and the vallies suddenly widen to a greater extent than they have been since we entered the mountains. At this place was some scattered timber, consisting of the narrow-leafed cotton-wood, the aspen, and pine. There are also vast quantities of gooseberries, serviceberries, and several species of currant, among which is one of a black colour, the flavour of which is preferable to

that of the yellow, and would be deemed superior
to that of any currant in the United States. We
here killed an elk, which was a pleasant addition
to our stock of food. At a mile from the Gates,
a large creek comes down from the mountains and
empties itself behind an island in the middle of a
bend to the north. To this stream, which is fifteen
yards wide, we gave the name of Potts's creek,
after John Potts, one of our men. Up this valley
about seven miles we discovered a great smoke, as
if the whole country had been set on fire; but
were at a loss to decide whether it had been done
accidentally by Captain Clarke's party, or by the
Indians as a signal on their observing us. We
afterwards learnt that this last was the fact; for
they had heard a gun fired by one of Captain
Clarke's men, and believing that their enemies
were approaching had fled into the mountains, first
setting fire to the plains as a warning to their
countrymen. We continued our course along several islands, and having made in the course of the
day fifteen miles, encamped just above an island,
at a spring on a high bank on the left side of the
river. In the latter part of the evening we had
passed through a low range of mountains, and the
country became more open, though still unbroken
and without timber, and the lowlands not very extensive : and just above our camp the river is again
closed in by the mountains. We found on the
banks an elk which Captain Clarke had left us,
with a note mentioning that he should pass the

mountains just above us and wait our arrival at some convenient place. We saw, but could not procure, some red-headed ducks and sand-hill cranes along the sides of the river, and a wood-pecker, about the size of the lark-woodpecker, which seems to be a distinct species : it is as black as a crow, with a long tail, and flies like a jay-bird. The whole country is so infested by the prickly pear, that we could scarcely find room to lie down at our camp.

Captain Clarke on setting out this morning had gone through the valley about six miles to the right of the river. He soon fell into an old Indian road which he pursued till he reached the Missouri, at the distance of eighteen miles from his last en-campment, just above the entrance of a large creek, which we afterwards called White-earth creek. Here he found his party so much cut and pierced with the sharp flint and the prickly pear, that he pro-ceeded only a small distance further, and then halted to wait for us. Along his track, he had taken the precaution to strew signals, such as pieces of cloth, paper and linen, to prove to the Indians, if by accident they met his track, that we were white men. But he observed a smoke some dis-tance a-head, and concluded that the whole coun-try had now taken the alarm.

Sunday, 21. On leaving our camp we passed an island at half a mile, and reached at one mile a bad rapid, at the place where the river leaves the mountain : here the cliffs are high and covered

with fragments of broken rocks, the current is also
strong, but although more rapid, the river is wider
and shallower, so that we are able to use the pole
occasionally, though we principally depend on the
towline. On leaving the rapid, which is about half
a mile in extent, the country opens on each side;
the hills become lower; at one mile is a large
island on the left side, and four and a half beyond
it, a large and bold creek twenty-eight yards wide,
coming in from the north, where it waters a handsome valley: we called it Pryor's creek after one
of the sergeants, John Pryor. At a mile above
this creek, on the left side of the Missouri, we
obtained a meridian altitude, which gave 46° 10'
32" 9''' as the latitude of the place. For the following four miles, the country, like that through which
we passed during the rest of the day, is rough and
mountainous, as we found it yesterday; but, at the
distance of twelve miles, we came, towards evening, into a beautiful plain, ten or twelve miles
wide, and extending as far as the eye could reach.
This plain, or rather valley, is bounded by two
nearly parallel ranges of high mountains, whose
summits are partially covered with snow, below
which the pine is scattered along the sides down
to the plain in some places, though the greater
part of their surface has no timber, and exhibits
only a barren soil, with no covering except dry
parched grass or black rugged rocks. On entering
the valley, the river assumes a totally different
aspect: it spreads to more than a mile in width,

and though more rapid than before, is shallow
enough in almost every part for the use of the pole,
while its bed is formed of smooth stones and some
large rocks, as it has been indeed since we entered
the mountains : it is also divided by a number of
islands, some of which are large near the northern
shore. The soil of the valley is a rich black loam,
apparently very fertile, and covered with a fine
green grass about eighteen inches or two feet in
height; while that of the high grounds is perfectly
dry, and seems scorched by the sun. The timber,
though still scarce, is in greater quantities in this
valley than we have seen it since entering the
mountains, and seems to prefer the borders of the
small creeks to the banks of the river itself. We
advanced three and a half miles in this valley, and
encamped on the left side, having made in all fifteen
miles and a half.

Our only large game to-day was one deer. We
saw, however, two pheasants of a dark brown
colour, much larger than the same species of bird
in the United States. In the morning too, we saw
three swans, which, like the geese, have not yet
recovered the feathers of the wing, and were unable
to fly : we killed two of them, and the third escaped
by diving and passing down the current. These
are the first we have seen on the river for a great
distance, and as they had no young with them, we
presume that they do not breed in this neighbourhood. Of the geese, we daily see great numbers,
with their young perfectly feathered, except on the

wings, where both young and old are deficient; the first are very fine food, but the old ones are poor and unfit for use. Several of the large brown, or sand-hill crane, are feeding in the low grounds on the grass, which forms their principal food. The young crane cannot fly at this season : they are as large as a turkey, of a bright reddish bay colour. Since the river has become shallow, we have caught a number of trout to-day, and a fish, white on the belly and sides, but of a bluish cast on the back, and a long pointed mouth opening somewhat like that of the shad.

This morning Captain Clarke wishing to hunt, but fearful of alarming the Indians, went up the river for three miles, when finding neither any of them nor of their recent tracks, returned, and then his little party separated to look for game. They killed two bucks and a doe, and a young curlew nearly feathered : in the evening, they found the musquitoes as troublesome as we did ; these animals attack us as soon as the labours and fatigues of the day require some rest, and annoy us till several hours after dark, when the coldness of the air obliges them to disappear ; but such is their persecution, that were it not for our biers, we should obtain no repose.

Monday, 22. We set out at an early hour. The river being divided into so many channels by both large and small islands, that it was impossible to lay it down accurately by following in a canoe any single channel ; Captain Lewis walked on shore, took the general courses of the river, and from the rising grounds laid down the situation of the islands and channels, which he was enabled to do with perfect accuracy, the view not being obstructed by much timber. At one mile and a quarter, we passed an island somewhat larger than the rest, and four miles further reached the upper end of another, on which we breakfasted. This is a large island, forming in the middle of a bend, to the north a level fertile plain, ten feet above the surface of the water, and never overflowed. Here we found great quantities of a small onion, about the size of a musket ball, though some were larger; it is white, crisp, and as well flavoured as any of our garden onions; the seed is just ripening, and as the plant bears a large quantity to the square foot, and stands the rigours of the climate, it will no doubt be an acquisition to settlers. From this production, we called it Onion island. During the next seven and three-quarter miles we passed several long circular bends, and a number of large and small islands, which divide the river into many channels, and then reached the mouth of a creek on the north side. It is composed of three creeks which unite in a handsome valley, about four miles before they discharge themselves into the Missouri, where it is about fifteen feet wide and eight feet deep, with clear transparent water. Here we halted for dinner, but as the canoes took different channels in ascending, it was some time before they all joined. Here we were delighted to find that the Indian woman recognises the country; she tells us that to this creek her countrymen make excursions to procure a white paint on its banks, and we therefore called it White-earth creek. She says also that the three forks of the Missouri are at no great distance, a piece of intelligence which has cheered the spirits of us all, as we hope soon to reach the head of that river. This is the warmest day, except one, we have experienced this summer. In the shade, the mercury stood at 80° above 0, which is the second time it has reached that height during this season. We encamped on an island, after making nineteen and three-quarter miles.

In the course of the day, we saw many geese, cranes, small birds common to the plains, and a few pheasants: we also observed a small plover or curlew of a brown colour, about the size of the yellow-legged plover or jack curlew, but of a different species. It first appeared near the mouth of Smith's river, but is so shy and vigilant that we were unable to shoot it. Both the broad and narrow-leafed willow continue, though the sweet willow has become very scarce. The rosebush, small honey-suckle, the pulpy-leafed thorn, southern-wood, sage and box-alder, narrow-leafed cotton-wood, red-wood, and a species of sumach, are all abundant. So too are the red and black goose-berries, service-berries, choke-cherry, and the black, red, yellow, and purple currant, which last seems to be a favourite food of the bear. Before encamp-

1

ing, we landed and took on board Captain Clarke, with the meat he had collected during this day's hunt, which consisted of one deer and an elk : we had ourselves shot a deer and an antelope. The musquitoes and gnats were unusually fierce this evening.

Tuesday, 23. Captain Clarke again proceeded with four men along the right bank. During the whole day, the river is divided by a number of islands, which spread it out sometimes to the distance of three miles ; the current is very rapid, and has many ripples ; and the bed formed of gravel and smooth stones. The banks along the low grounds are of a rich loam, followed occasionally by low bluffs of yellow and red clay, with a hard red slatestone intermixed. The low grounds are wide, and have very little timber, but a thick underbrush of willow, and rose and currant bushes : these are succeeded by high plains, extending on each side to the base of the mountains, which lie parallel to the river, about eight or twelve miles apart, and are high and rocky, with some small pine and cedar interspersed on them. At the distance of seven miles, a creek twenty yards wide, after meandering through a beautiful low ground on the left, for several miles, parallel to the river, empties itself near a cluster of small islands : the stream we called White-house creek, after Joseph Whitehouse, one of the party, and the islands, from their number, received the name of the " Ten islands." About ten o'clock we came up with

Drewyer, who had gone out to hunt yesterday,
and not being able to find our encampment, had
staid out all night: he now supplied us with five
deer. Three and a quarter miles beyond White-
house creek, we came to the lower point of an
island, where the river is three hundred yards wide,
and continued along it for one mile and a quarter,
and then passed a second island just above it. We
halted rather early for dinner, in order to dry some
part of the baggage which had been wetted in the
canoes: we then proceeded, and at five and a half
miles had passed two small islands. Within the
next three miles, we came to a large island, which,
from its figure, we called Broad island. From
that place we made three and a half miles, and encamped on an island to the left, opposite to a much
larger one on the right. Our journey to-day was
twenty-two and a quarter miles, the greater part of
which was made by means of our poles and cords,
the use of which the banks much favoured. During the whole time, we had the small flags hoisted
in the canoes to apprise the Indians, if there were
any in the neighbourhood, of our being white men
and their friends; but we were not so fortunate as
to discover any of them. Along the shores, we
saw great quantities of the common thistle, and
procured a further supply of wild onions, and a
species of garlic growing on the highlands, which
is now green and in bloom: it has a flat leaf, and
is strong, tough, and disagreeable. There was also
much of the wild flax, of which we now obtained

some ripe seed, as well as some bullrush and cattail flag. Among the animals, we met with a black snake about two feet long, with the belly as dark as any other part of the body, which was perfectly black, and which had one hundred and twenty-eight scuta on the belly, and sixty-three on the tail: we also saw antelopes, crane, geese, ducks, beaver, and otter; and took up four deer, which had been left on the water side by Captain Clarke. He had pursued, all day, an Indian road on the right side of the river, and encamped late in the evening at the distance of twenty-five miles from our camp of last night. In the course of his walk, he met, besides deer, a number of antelopes and a herd of elk, but all the tracks of Indians, though numerous, were of an old date.

Wednesday, 24. We proceeded for four and a quarter miles along several islands to a small run, just above which the low bluffs touch the river. Within three and a half miles further, we came to a small island on the north, and a remarkable bluff, composed of earth of a crimson colour, intermixed with strata of slate, either black or of a red resembling brick. The following six and three-quarter miles brought us to an assemblage of islands, having passed four at different distances; and within the next five miles we met the same number of islands, and encamped on the north, after making nineteen and a half miles. The current of the river was strong and obstructed, as indeed it has been for some days, by small rapids or ripples, which descend from one to three feet in the course of one hundred and fifty yards, but they are rarely incommoded by any fixed rocks, and, therefore, though the water is rapid, the passage is not attended with danger. The valley through which the river passes, is like that of yesterday; the nearest hills generally concealing the most distant from us; but when we obtain a view of them, they present themselves in amphitheatres, rising above each other as they recede from the river, till the most remote are covered with snow. We saw many otter and beaver to-day; the latter seems to contribute very much to the number of islands and the widening of the river. They begin by damming up the small channels of about twenty yards between the islands; this obliges the river to seek another outlet, and as soon as this is effected, the channel stopped by the beaver becomes filled with mud and sand. The industrious animal is then driven to another channel, which soon shares the same fate, till the river spreads on all sides, and cuts the projecting points of the land into islands. We killed a deer, and saw great numbers of antelopes, cranes, some geese, and a few red-headed ducks. The small birds of the plains, and the curlew, are still abundant: we saw, but could not come within gunshot of a large bear. There is much of the track of elk, but none of the animals themselves; and from the appearance of bones and old excrement, we suppose that buffaloe have sometimes strayed into the valley, though we have as yet seen no recent sign of them. Along the water are a number of snakes, some of a brown uniform colour, others black, and a third speckled on the abdomen, and striped with black, and a brownish yellow on the back and sides. The first, which are the largest, are about four feet long; the second is of the kind mentioned yesterday, and the third resembles in size and appearance the garter-snake of the United States. On examining the teeth of all these several kinds, we found them free from poison: they are fond of the water, in which they take shelter on being pursued. The musquitoes, gnats, and prickly pear, our three persecutors, still continue with us, and, joined with the labour of working the canoes, have fatigued us all excessively. Captain Clarke continued along the Indian road, which led him up a creek. About ten o'clock he saw, at the distance of six miles, a horse feeding in the plains. He went towards him, but the animal was so wild, that he could not get within several hundred paces of him: he then turned obliquely to the river, where he killed a deer and dined; having passed in this valley five handsome streams, only one of which had any timber; another had some willows, and was very much dammed up by the beaver. After dinner he continued his route along the river, and encamped at the distance of thirty miles. As he went along, he saw many tracks of Indians, but none of recent date. The next morning,

Thursday, 25, at the distance of a few miles he

arrived at the three forks of the Missouri. Here he found that the plains had been recently burnt on the north side, and saw the track of a horse, which seemed to have passed about four or five days since. After breakfast he examined the rivers, and finding that the north branch, although not larger, contained more water than the middle branch, and bore more to the westward, he determined to ascend it. He therefore left a note informing Captain Lewis of his intention, and then went up that stream on the north side for about twenty-five miles. Here Chaboneau was unable to proceed any farther, and the party therefore encamped, all of them much fatigued, their feet blistered, and wounded by the prickly pear.

In the meantime we left our camp, and proceeded on very well, though the water is still rapid and has some occasional ripples. The country is much like that of yesterday: there are however fewer islands, for we passed only two. Behind one of them is a large creek twenty-five yards wide, to which we gave the name of Gass's creek, from one of our sergeants, Patrick Gass: it is formed by the union of five streams, which descend from the mountains and join in the plain near the river. On this island we saw a large brown bear, but he retreated to the shore and ran off before we could approach him. These animals seem more shy than they were below the mountains. The antelopes have again collected in small herds, composed of several females with their young, attended

by one or two males, though some of the males
are still solitary or wander in parties of two
over the plains, which the antelope invariably
prefers to the woodlands, and to which it always
retreats if by accident it is found straggling
in the hills, confiding no doubt in its wonderful
fleetness. We also killed a few young geese,
but as this game is small and very incompetent to
the subsistence of the party, we have forbidden the
men any longer to waste their ammunition on them.
About four and a half miles above Gass's creek, the
valley in which we have been travelling ceases, the
high craggy cliffs again approach the river, which
now enters or rather leaves what appears to be a
second great chain of the Rocky mountains. About
a mile after entering these hills or low mountains
we passed a number of fine bold springs, which
burst out near the edge of the river under the
cliffs on the left, and furnished a fine freestone
water : near these we met with two of the worst
rapids we have seen since entering the mountains ;
a ridge of sharp pointed rocks stretching across
the river, leaving but small and dangerous channels for the navigation. The cliffs are of a lighter
colour than those we have already passed, and in
the bed of the river is some limestone which is
small and worn smooth, and seems to have been
brought down by the current. We went about a
mile further and encamped under a high bluff on
the right opposite to a cliff of rocks, having made
sixteen miles.

All these cliffs appeared to have been undermined

by the water at some period, and fallen down from
the hills on their sides, the strata of rock sometimes
lying with their edges upwards, others not detached
from the hills are depressed obliquely on the side
next the river as if they had sunk to fill up the
cavity formed by the washing of the river.

In the open places among the rocky cliffs are
two kinds of gooseberry, one yellow and the other
red. The former species was observed for the first
time near the Falls, the latter differs from it in no
respect, except in colour and in being of a larger
size : both have a sweet flavour, and are rather indifferent fruit.

Friday, 26. We again found the current strong
and the ripples frequent : these we were obliged to
overcome by means of the cord and the pole, the
oar being scarcely ever used except in crossing to
take advantage of the shore. Within three and
three quarter miles we passed seven small islands
and reached the mouth of a large creek which
empties itself in the centre of a bend on the
left side : it is a bold running stream fifteen yards
wide, and received the name of Howard creek after
John P. Howard one of the party. One mile beyond it is a small run which falls in on the same side
just above a rocky cliff. Here the mountains recede from the river, and the valley widens to the
extent of several miles. The river now becomes
crowded with islands of which we passed ten in
the next thirteen and three quarter miles, then at
the distance of eighteen miles we encamped on the
left shore near a rock in the centre of a bend

towards the left, and opposite to two more islands. This valley has wide low grounds covered with high grass, and in many with a fine turf of green sward. The soil of the islands is thin and meagre, without any covering except a low sedge and a dry kind of grass which is almost as inconvenient as the prickly pear. The seeds of it are armed with a long twisted hard beard at their upper extremity, while the lower part is a sharp firm point, beset at its base with little stiff bristles, with the points in a direction contrary to the subulate point to which they answer as a barb. We see also another species of prickly pear. It is of a globular form, composed of an assemblage of little conic leaves springing from a common root to which their small points are attached as a common centre, and the base of the cone forms the apex of the leaf which is garnished with a circular range of sharp thorns like the cochineal plant, and quite as stiff and even more keen than those of the common flat-leafed species. Between the hills the river had been confined within one hundred and fifty or two hundred yards, but in the valley it widens to two hundred or two hundred and fifty yards, and sometimes is spread by its numerous islands to the distance of three quarters of a mile. The banks are low, but the river never overflows them. On entering the valley we again saw the snow-clad mountains before us, but the appearance of the hills, as well as of the timber near us, is much as heretofore.

Finding Chaboneau unable to proceed, Captain

Clarke left him with one of the men, and accompanied by the other, went up the river about twelve miles to the top of a mountain. Here he had an extensive view of the river valley upwards, and saw a large creek which flowed in on the right side. He however discovered no fresh sign of the Indians, and therefore determined to examine the middle branch, and join us by the time we reached the forks: he descended the mountain by an Indian path which wound through a deep valley, and at length reached a fine cold spring. The day had been very warm, the path unshaded by timber, and his thirst was excessive; he was therefore tempted to drink: but although he took the precaution of previously wetting his head, feet, and hands, he soon found himself very unwell: he continued his route, and after resting with Chaboneau at his camp, resumed his march across the north fork near a large island. The first part was knee deep, but on the other side of the island the water came to their waists, and was so rapid, that Chaboneau was on the point of being swept away, and not being able to swim, would have perished if Captain Clarke had not rescued him. While crossing the island they killed two brown bear, and saw great quantities of beaver. He then went on to a small river which falls into the north fork, some miles above its junction with the two others: here, finding himself grow more unwell, he halted for the night, at the distance of four miles from his last encampment.

Saturday, 27. We proceeded on but slowly, the current being still so rapid as to require the utmost exertions of us all to advance, and the men are losing their strength fast in consequence of their constant efforts. At half a mile we passed an island, and a mile and a quarter further, again entered a ridge of hills which now approach the river, with cliffs apparently sinking like those of yesterday. They are composed of a solid limestone of a light lead colour when exposed to the air, though when freshly broken, it is of a deep blue, and of an excellent quality and very fine grain. On these cliffs were numbers of the bighorn. At two and a half miles we reached the centre of a bend towards the south, passing a small island, and at one mile and a quarter beyond this reached about nine in the morning, the mouth of a river seventy yards wide, which falls in from the south-east. Here the country suddenly opens into extensive and beautiful meadows and plains, surrounded on every side with distant and lofty mountains. Captain Lewis went up this stream for about half a mile, and from the height of a limestone cliff could observe its course about seven miles, and the three forks of the Missouri, of which this river is one. Its extreme point bore S. 65° E., and during the seven miles it passes through a green extensive meadow of fine grass, dividing itself into several streams, the largest passing near the ridge of hills on which he stood. On the right side of the Missouri, a high, wide, and extensive plain succeeds to this low meadow, which reaches the hills. In the meadow a large spring rises about a quarter of a mile from this south-east fork, into which it discharges itself on the right side, about four hundred paces from where he stood. Between the south-east and middle forks a distant range of snow-topped mountains spread from east to south, above the irregular broken hills nearer to this spot: the middle and south-west forks unite at half a mile above the entrance of the south-east fork. The extreme point at which the former can be seen, bears S. 15° E., and at the distance of fourteen miles, where it turns to the right round the point of a high plain, and disappears from the view. Its low grounds are several miles in width, forming a smooth and beautiful green meadow, and like the south-east fork it divides itself into several streams. Between these two forks, and near their junction with that from the south-west, is a position admirably well calculated for a fort. It is a limestone rock of an oblong form, rising from the plain perpendicularly to the height of twenty-five feet on three of its sides; the fourth towards the middle fork being a gradual ascent, and covered with a fine green sward, as is also the top, which is level, and contains about two acres. An extensive plain lies between the middle and south-west forks, the last of which, after watering a country like that of the other two branches, disappears about twelve miles off, at a point bearing south 30° west. It is also more divided and serpentine in its course than the other two, and possesses more timber in its meadows. This timber consists almost exclusively of the narrow-leafed cotton-wood, with an intermixture of box-alder and sweet-willow, the underbrush being thick and like that of the Missouri lower down. A range of high mountains partially covered with snow, is seen at a considerable distance, running from south to west; and nearly all around us are broken ridges of country like that below, through which those united streams appear to have forced their passage: after observing the country, Captain Lewis descended to breakfast. We then left the mouth of the south-east fork, which in honour of the secretary of the treasury, we called Gallatin's river; and at the distance of half a mile reached the confluence of the south-west and middle branch of the Missouris. Here we found the letter from Captain Clarke, and as we agreed with him that the direction of the south-west fork gave it a decided preference over the others, we ascended that branch of the river for a mile, and encamped in a level handsome plain on the left: having advanced only seven miles. Here we resolved to wait the return of Captain Clarke, and in the meantime make the necessary celestial observations, as this seems an essential point in the geography of the western world, and also to recruit the men and air the baggage. It was accordingly all unloaded and stowed away on shore. Near the three forks we saw many collections of the mud-nests of the small

martin attached to the smooth faces of the limestone rock, where they were sheltered by projections of the rock above it: and in the meadows
were numbers of the duck, or mallard, with their
young, who are now nearly grown. The hunters
returned towards evening with six deer, three otter
and a musk rat; and had seen great numbers of
antelopes, and much sign of the beaver and elk.

During all last night, Captain Clarke had a high
fever and chills, accompanied with great pain. He,
however, pursued his route eight miles to the middle branch, where not finding any fresh Indian
track, he came down it and joined us about three
o'clock, very much exhausted with fatigue and the
violence of his fever. Believing himself bilious, he
took a dose of Rush's pills, which we have always
found sovereign in such cases, and bathing the
lower extremities in warm water.

We are now very anxious to see the Snake Indians. After advancing for several hundred miles
into this wild and mountainous country, we may
soon expect that the game will abandon us. With
no information of the route, we may be unable to
find a passage across the mountains when we reach
the head of the river, at least such a one as will
lead us to the Columbia, and even were we so
fortunate as to find a branch of that river, the timber which we have hitherto seen in these mountains
does not promise us any fit to make canoes, so that
our chief dependence is on meeting some tribe from
whom we may procure horses. Our consolation is,

that this south-west branch can scarcely head with
any other river than the Columbia, and that if any
nation of Indians can live in the mountains, we
are able to endure as much as they, and have even
better means of procuring subsistence.

CHAPTER XIII.

SUNDAY, July 28. Captain Clarke continued very unwell during the night, but was somewhat relieved this morning. On examining the two streams, it became difficult to decide which was the larger or the real Missouri; they are each ninety yards wide, and so perfectly similar in character and appearance that they seem to have been

formed in the same mould. We were therefore
induced to discontinue the name of Missouri, and
gave to the south-west branch the name of Jefferson,
in honour of the president of the United States,
and the projector of the enterprise : and called the
middle branch Madison, after James Madison,
secretary of state. These two, as well as Gallatin
river, run with great velocity, and throw out large
bodies of water. Gallatin river is, however, the
most rapid of the three, and though not quite as
deep, yet navigable for a considerable distance.
Madison river, though much less rapid than the
Gallatin, is somewhat more rapid than the Jefferson ; the beds of all of them are formed of smooth
pebble and gravel, and the waters are perfectly
transparent. The timber in the neighbourhood
would be sufficient for the ordinary uses of an
establishment, which, however, it would be ad-
visable to build of brick, as the earth appears calculated for that purpose, and along the shores are
some bars of fine pure sand. The greater part of
the men, having yesterday put their deer skins in
water, were this day engaged in dressing them, for
the purpose of making clothing. The weather was
very warm, the thermometer in the afternoon was
at 90° above 0, and the musquitoes more than
usually inconvenient : we were, however, relieved
from them by a high wind from the south-west,
which came on at four o'clock, bringing a storm of
thunder and lightning, attended by refreshing
showers, which continued till after dark. In the

evening the hunters returned with eight deer and
two elk ; and the party who had been sent up the
Gallatin, reported that after passing the point,
where it escaped from captain Lewis's view yesterday, it turned more towards the east, as far as they
could discern the opening of the mountains, formed
by the valley which bordered it.   The low grounds
were still wide but not so extensive as near its
mouth, and though the stream is rapid and much
divided by islands, it is still sufficiently deep for
navigation with canoes.   The low grounds, although
not more than eight or nine feet above the water,
seem never to be overflowed, except a part on the
west side of the middle fork, which is stony and
seems occasionally inundated, are furnished with
great quantities of small fruit, such as currants and
gooseberries : among the last of which is a black
species, which we observe not only in the meadows
but along the mountain rivulets.   From the same
root rise a number of stems, to the height of five
or six feet, some of them particularly branched and
all reclining.   The berry is attached by a long
peduncle to the stem, from which they hang, of a
smooth ovate form, as large as the common garden
gooseberry, and as black as jet, though the pulp is
of a bright crimson colour.   It is extremely acid :
the form of the leaf resembles that of the common
gooseberry, though larger.   The stem is covered
with very sharp thorns or briars : the grass too is
very luxuriant, and would yield fine hay in parcels
of several acres.   The sand rushes will grow in

many places as high as a man's breast, and as thick
as stalks of wheat; it would supply the best food
during the winter to cattle of any trading or military post.

Sacajawea, our Indian woman, informs us that
we are encamped on the precise spot where her
countrymen, the Snake Indians, had their huts
five years ago, when the Minnetarees of Knife
river first came in sight of them, and from which
they hastily retreated three miles up the Jefferson,
and concealed themselves in the woods. The
Minnetarees, however, pursued and attacked them,
killed four men, as many women, and a number
of boys; and made prisoners of four other boys,
and all the females, of whom Sacajawea was one:
she does not, however, show any distress at these
recollections, nor any joy at the prospect of being
restored to her country; for she seems to possess
the folly or the philosophy of not suffering her
feelings to extend beyond the anxiety of having
plenty to eat and a few trinkets to wear.

Monday, 29. This morning the hunters brought
in some fat deer of the long-tailed red kind, which
are quite as large as those of the United States,
and are, indeed, the only kind we have found at
this place: there are numbers of the sand-hill
cranes feeding in the meadows; we caught a young
one of the same colour as the red deer, which
though it had nearly attained its full growth could
not fly; it is very fierce, and strikes a severe blow
with its beak. The kingfisher has become quite

common on this side of the Falls: but we have
seen none of the summer duck since leaving that
place. The mallard duck, which we saw for the
first time on the 20th instant, with their young,
are now abundant, though they do not breed on
the Missouri, below the mountains. The small
birds already described are also abundant in the
plains; here too, are great quantities of grass-
hoppers or crickets; and among other animals, a
large ant with a reddish brown body and legs, and
a black head and abdomen, who build little cones
of gravel, ten or twelve inches high, without a
mixture of sticks, and but little earth. In the
river we see a great abundance of fish, but we cannot tempt them to bite by any thing on our hooks.
The whole party have been engaged in dressing
skins, and making them into moccasins and leggings. Captain Clarke's fever has almost left him,
but he still remains very languid, and has a general soreness in his limbs. The latitude of our
camp, as the mean of two observations of the meridian altitude of the sun's lower limb with octant
by back observation, is N. 45° 24′ 8″ 5‴.

Tuesday, 30. Captain Clarke was this morning
much restored; and, therefore, having made all
the observations necessary to fix the longitude, we
reloaded our canoes, and began to ascend Jefferson river. The river now becomes very crooked,
and forms bends on each side; the current too is
rapid, and cut into a great number of channels,
and sometimes shoals, the beds of which consist of

coarse gravel. The islands are unusually numerous: on the right are high plains occasionally forming cliffs of rocks and hills; while the left was an extensive low ground and prairie intersected by a number of bayous or channels falling into the river. Captain Lewis, who had walked through it with Chaboneau, his wife, and two invalids, joined us at dinner, a few miles above our camp. Here the Indian woman said was the place where she had been made prisoner. The men being too few to contend with the Minnetarees, mounted their horses, and fled as soon as the attack began. The women and children dispersed, and Sacajawea as she was crossing at a shoal place, was overtaken in the middle of the river by her pursuers. As we proceeded, the low grounds were covered with cottonwood and a thick underbrush, and on both sides of the river, except where the high hills prevented it, the ground was divided by bayous, which are dammed up by the beaver, which are very numerous here. We made twelve and a quarter miles and encamped on the north side. Captain Lewis proceeded after dinner, through an extensive low ground of timber and meadow land intermixed; but the bayous were so obstructed by beaver dams, that in order to avoid them he directed his course towards the high plain on the right. This he gained with some difficulty, after wading up to his waist through the mud and water of a number of beaver dams. When he desired to rejoin the canoes he found the underbrush so thick, and the river so crooked, that this, joined to the difficulty of passing the beaver dams, induced him to go on and endeavour to intercept the river at some point where it might be more collected into one channel, and approach nearer to the high plain. He arrived at the bank about sunset, having gone only six miles in a direct course from the canoes: but he saw no traces of the men, nor did he receive any answer to his shouts nor the firing of his gun. It was now nearly dark; a duck lighted near him and he shot it. He then went to the head of a small island, where he found some driftwood, which enabled him to cook his duck for supper, and he laid down to sleep on some willow brush. The night was cool, but the driftwood gave him a good fire, and he suffered no inconvenience, except from the musquitoes.

Wednesday, 31. The next morning he waited till after seven o'clock, when he became uneasy lest we should have gone beyond his camp last evening, and determined to follow us. Just as he had set out with this intention, he saw one of the party in advance of the canoes; although our camp was only two miles below him, in a straight line, we could not reach him sooner, in consequence of the rapidity of the water and the circuitous course of the river. We halted for breakfast, after which Captain Lewis continued his route. At the distance of one mile from our encampment we passed the principal entrance of a stream on the left, which rises in the snowy mountains to the south-west, between Jefferson and Madison rivers, and discharges itself by seven mouths, five below, and one three miles above this, which is the largest, and

about thirty yards wide : we called it Philosophy
river. The water of it is abundant and perfectly
clear, and the bed, like that of the Jefferson, consists of pebble and gravel. There is some timber
in the bottoms of the river, and vast numbers of
otter and beaver, which build on its smaller mouths
and the bayous of its neighbourhood. The Jefferson continues as yesterday, shoaly and rapid,
but as the islands though numerous are small, it is
however more collected into one current than it
was below, and is from ninety to one hundred and
twenty yards in width. The low ground has a fertile soil of rich black loam, and contains a considerable quantity of timber, with the bullrush and
cattail flag very abundant in the moist parts, while
the drier situations are covered with fine grass,
tansy, thistles, onions, and flax. The uplands are
barren, and without timber : the soil is a light yellow clay intermixed with small smooth pebble and
gravel, and the only produce is the prickly-pear,
the sedge, and the bearded grass, which is as dry
and inflammable as tinder. As we proceeded, the
low grounds became narrower, and the timber
more scarce, till at the distance of ten miles the
high hills approach, and overhang the river on both
sides, forming cliffs of a hard black granite, like
almost all those below the limestone cliffs at the
three forks of the Missouri : they continue so for
a mile and three quarters, where we came to a point
of rock on the right side, at which place the hills
again retire, and the valley widens to the distance

of a mile and a half. Within the next five miles we passed four islands, and reached the foot of a mountain in a bend of the river to the left : from this place we went a mile and a quarter to the entrance of a small run discharging itself on the left, and encamped on an island just above it, after making seventeen and three quarter miles. We observe some pine on the hills on both sides of our encampment, which are very lofty. The only game which we have seen are one big-horn, a few antelopes, deer, and one brown bear, which escaped from our pursuit. Nothing was, however, killed to-day, nor have we had any fresh meat except one beaver for the last two days, so that we are now reduced to an unusual situation, for we have hitherto always had a great abundance of flesh.

Thursday, August 1. We left our encampment early, and at the distance of a mile, reached a point of rocks on the left side, where the river passes through perpendicular cliffs. Two and three quarter miles further we halted for breakfast under a cedar tree in a bend to the right : here as had been previously arranged, Captain Lewis left us, with Serjeant Gass, Chaboneau, and Drewyer, intending to go on in advance in search of the Shoshonees. He began his route along the north side of the river over a high range of mountains, as Captain Clarke, who ascended them on the 26th had observed from them a large valley spreading to the north of west, and concluded, that on leaving the mountain the river took that direction; but when he reached that valley, Captain Lewis found it to be the passage of a large creek falling just above the mountain into the Jefferson, which bears to the south-west. On discovering his error, he bent his course towards that river, which he reached about two in the afternoon, very much exhausted with heat and thirst. The mountains were very bare of timber, and the route lay along the steep and narrow hollows of the mountain, exposed to the mid-day sun, without air, or shade, or water. Just as he arrived there a flock of elk passed, and they killed two of them, on which they made their dinner, and left the rest on the shore for the party in the canoes. After dinner they resumed their march, and encamped on the north side of the river, after making seventeen miles; in crossing the mountains, Captain Lewis saw a flock of the black or dark brown pheasant, of which he killed one. This bird is one third larger than the common pheasant of the Atlantic States; its form is much the same. The male has not however the tufts of long black feathers on the sides of the neck, so conspicuous in the Atlantic pheasant, and both sexes are booted nearly to the toes. The colour is a uniform dark brown with a small mixture of yellow or yellowish brown, specks on some of the feathers, particularly those of the tail, though the extremities of these are perfectly black for about an inch. The eye is nearly black, and the iris has a small dash of yellowish brown; the feathers of the tail are somewhat longer than those of our pheasant, but the same in number, eighteen, and nearly equal in size, except that those of the middle are somewhat the longest; their flesh is white and agreeably flavoured.

He also saw among the scattered pine near the top of the mountain, a blue bird about the size of a robin, but in action and form something like a jay; it is constantly in motion, hopping from spray to spray, and its note, which is loud and frequent, is, as far as letters can represent it, char ah! char ah! char ah!

After breakfast we proceeded on: at the distance of two and a quarter miles the river enters a high mountain, which forms rugged cliffs of nearly perpendicular rocks. These are of a black granite at the lower part, and the upper consists of a light coloured freestone; they continue from the point of rocks close to the river for nine miles, which we passed before breakfast, during which the current is very strong. At nine and a quarter miles we passed an island, and a rapid with a fall of six feet, and reached the entrance of a large creek on the left side. In passing this place the towline of one of the canoes broke just at the shoot of the rapids; it swung on the rocks and had nearly upset. To the creek as well as the rapid we gave the name of Frazier, after Robert Frazier, one of the party: here the country opens into a beautiful valley from six to eight miles in width: the river then becomes crooked and crowded with islands; its low grounds

wide and fertile, but though covered with fine grass
from nine inches to two feet high, possesses but a
small proportion of timber, and that consists almost
entirely of a few narrow-leafed cotton-wood distributed along the verge of the river. The soil of
the plain is tolerably fertile, and consists of a black
or dark yellow loam. It gradually ascends on each
side to the bases of two ranges of high mountains
which lie parallel to the river; the tops of them
are yet in part covered with snow, and while in the
valley we are nearly suffocated with heat during the
day, and at night the air is so cold that two blankets are not more than sufficient covering. In passing through the hills we observed some large
cedar trees, and some juniper also. From Frazier's
creek we went three and three quarter miles, and
encamped on the left side, having come thirteen
miles. Directly opposite our camp is a large creek
which we call Fields' creek, from Reuben Fields,
one of our men. Soon after we halted two of the
hunters went out and returned with five deer, which
with one big-horn, we killed in coming through the
mountain, on which we dined; and the elk left by
Captain Lewis. We were again well supplied with
fresh meat. In the course of the day we saw a
brown bear, but were not able to shoot him.

Friday, August 2. Captain Lewis, who slept in
the valley a few miles above us, resumed his
journey early; and after making five miles, and
finding that the river still bore to the south, determined to cross it in hopes of shortening the

route : for the first time therefore he waded across
it, although there are probably many places above
the Falls where it might be attempted with equal
safety. The river was about ninety yards wide,
the current rapid, and about waist deep : the bottom formed of smooth pebble with a small mixture of coarse gravel. He then continued
along the left bank of the river till sunset and encamped, after travelling twenty-four miles. He
met no fresh tracks of Indians. Throughout are
scattered the bones and excrement of the buffaloe
of an old date, but there seems no hope of meeting
the animals themselves in the mountains : he saw
an abundance of deer and antelope, and many
tracks of elk and bear. Having killed two deer
they feasted sumptuously, with a desert of currants
of different colours; two species of red, others
yellow, deep purple, and black : to these were
added black gooseberries and deep purple service-
berries, somewhat larger than ours, from which it
differs also in colour, size, and the superior ex-
cellence of its flavour. In the low grounds of the
river were many beaver-dams formed of willow
brush, mud, and gravel, so closely interwoven
that they resist the water perfectly : some of
them were five feet high and overflowed several
acres of land.

In the meantime we proceeded on slowly, the
current being so strong as to require the utmost
exertions of the men to make any advance, even
with the aid of the cord and pole, the wind be-

ing from the north-west. The river is full of large and small islands, and the plain cut by great numbers of bayous or channels, in which are multitudes of beaver. In the course of the day we passed some villages of barking squirrels: we saw several rattlesnakes in the plain; young ducks, both of the duckinmallard and redheaded fishing-duck species; some geese; also the black woodpecker, and a large herd of elk. The channel, current, banks, and general appearance of the river, are like that of yesterday. At fourteen and three-quarter miles we reached a rapid creek or bayou, about thirty yards wide, to which we gave the name of Birth creek. After making seventeen miles we halted in a smooth plain in a bend towards the left.

Saturday, 3. Captain Lewis continued his course along the river through the valley, which continued much as it was yesterday, except that it now widens to nearly twelve miles: the plains too are more broken and have some scattered pine near the mountains, where they rise higher than hitherto. In the level parts of the plains, and the river bottoms, there is no timber except small cotton-wood near the margin, and an undergrowth of narrow-leafed willow, small honeysuckle, rosebushes, currants, serviceberry, and gooseberry, and a little of a small species of birch; it is a finely indented oval, of a small size and a deep green colour; the stem is simple, ascending and branching, and seldom rises higher than ten or twelve feet. The mountains continue high on each side of the valley, but their only covering is a small species of pitch-pine with a short leaf, growing on the lower and middle regions, while for some distance below the snowy tops, there is neither timber nor herbage of any kind. About eleven o'clock Drewyer killed a doe on which they breakfasted, and after resting two hours continued till night, when they reached the river near a low ground more extensive than usual. From the appearance of the timber Captain Lewis supposed that the river forked above him, and therefore encamped with an intention of examining it more particularly in the morning. He had now made twenty-three miles, the latter part of which was for eight miles through a high plain, covered with prickly pears and bearded grass, which rendered the walking very inconvenient; but even this was better than the river bottoms we crossed in the evening, which, though apparently level, were formed into deep holes, as if they had been rooted up by hogs, and the holes were so covered with thick grass, that they were in danger of falling at every step. Some parts of these low grounds, however, contain turf or peat of an excellent quality for many feet deep apparently, as well as the mineral salts, which we have already mentioned on the Missouri. They saw many deer, antelopes, ducks, geese, some beaver, and great traces of their work, and the small birds and curlews as usual. The only fish which they observed in this part of the river is the trout, and a species of white fish, with a remarkably long small mouth, which one of our men recognises as the fish called in the eastern states the bottlenose.

On setting out with the canoes we found the river as usual much crowded with islands, the current more rapid as well as shallower, so that in many places they were obliged to man the canoes double, and drag them over the stone and gravel of the channel. Soon after we set off Captain Clarke, who was walking on shore, observed a fresh track, which he knew to be that of an Indian from the large toes being turned inwards, and following it found that it led to the point of a hill, from which our camp of last night could be seen. This circumstance strengthened the belief that some Indian had strayed thither, and had run off alarmed at the sight of us. At two and a quarter miles, is a small creek in a bend towards the right, which runs down from the mountains at a little distance; we called it Panther creek, from an animal of that kind killed by Reuben Fields at its mouth. It is precisely the same animal common to the western parts of the United States, and measured seven and a half feet from the nose to the extremity of the tail. Six and three-quarter miles beyond this stream is another on the left, formed by the drains which convey the melted snows from a mountain near it, under which the river passes, leaving the low grounds on the right side, and making several bends in its course. On this stream are many large beaver dams. One mile above it is a small run on the left, and after leaving which begins a very bad rapid, where the bed of the river is formed of solid rock : this we passed in the course of a mile, and encamped on the lower point of an island. Our journey had been only thirteen miles, but the badness of the river made it very laborious, as the men were compelled to be in the water during the greater part of the day. We saw only deer, antelopes, and the common birds of the country.

Saturday, 4. This morning Captain Lewis proceeded early, and after going south-east by east for four miles, reached a bold running creek, twelve yards wide, with clear cold water, furnished apparently by four drains from the snowy mountains on the left : after passing this creek he changed his direction to south-east, and leaving the valley in which he had travelled for the two last days, entered another which bore east. At the distance of three miles on this course he passed a handsome little river, about thirty yards wide, which winds through the valley : the current is not rapid nor the water very clear, but it affords a considerable quantity of water, and appears as if it might be navigable for some miles. The banks are low, and the bed formed of stone and gravel. He now changed his route to south-west, and passing a high plain which separates the vallies, returned to the more southern, or that which he had left : in passing this he found a river about forty-five yards wide, the water of which has a

whitish blue tinge, with a gentle current, and a
gravelly bottom. This he waded and found it
waist deep. He then continued down it, till, at
the distance of three-quarters of a mile, he saw the
entrance of the small river he had just passed ; as
he went on two miles lower down, he found the
mouth of the creek he had seen in the morning.
Proceeding further on three miles, he arrived at
the junction of this river with another which rises
from the south-west, runs through the south valley
about twelve miles before it forms its junction,
where it is fifty yards wide : we now found that
our camp of last night was about a mile and a half
above the entrance of this large river, on the right
side. This is a bold, rapid, clear stream, but its
bed is so much obstructed by gravelly bars, and
subdivided by islands, that the navigation must be
very insecure, if not impracticable. The other, or
middle stream, has about two-thirds its quantity of
water, and is more gentle, and may be safely
navigated. As far as it could be observed, its
course was about south-west, but the opening of
the valley induced him to believe that farther
above it turned more towards the west. Its water
is more turbid and warmer than that of the other
branch, whence it may be presumed to have its
sources at a greater distance in the mountains, and
to pass through a more open country. Under this
impression he left a note recommending to Captain
Clarke the middle fork, and then continued his
course along the right side of the other, or more

rapid branch. After travelling twenty-three miles he arrived near a place where the river leaves the valley and enters the mountains. Here he encamped for the night. The country he passed is like that of the rest of this valley, though there is more timber in this part on the rapid fork than there has been on the river in the same extent since we entered it; for on some parts of the valley the Indians seem to have destroyed a great proportion of the little timber there was, by setting fire to the bottoms. He saw some antelopes, deer, cranes, geese, and ducks of the two species common to this country, though the summer duck has ceased to appear, nor does it seem to be an inhabitant of this part of the river.

We proceeded soon after sun-rise: the first five miles we passed four bends on the left, and several bayous on both sides. At eight o'clock we stopped to breakfast, and found the note Captain Lewis had written on the 2d instant. During the next four miles we passed three small bends of the river to the right, two small islands and two bayous on the same side. Here we reached a bluff on the left; our next course was six miles to our encampment. In this course we met six circular bends on the right, and several small bayous, and halted for the night in a low ground of cotton-wood on the right. Our day's journey, though only fifteen miles in length, was very fatiguing. The river is still rapid, and the water, though clear, is very much obstructed by shoals or ripples at every two or three hundred yards: at all these places we are obliged to drag the canoes over the stones, as there is not a sufficient depth of water to float them, and in the other parts the current obliges us to have recourse to the cord. But as the brushwood on the banks will not permit us to walk on shore, we are under the necessity of wading through the river as we drag the boats. This soon makes our feet tender, and sometimes occasions severe falls over the slippery stones; and the men, by being constantly wet, are becoming more feeble. In the course of the day, the hunters killed two deer, some geese and ducks, and the party saw antelopes, cranes, beaver, and otter.

Monday, 5. This morning Chaboneau complained of being unable to march far to-day, and Captain Lewis therefore ordered him and sergeant Gass to pass the rapid river, and proceed through the level low ground, to a point of high timber on the middle fork, seven miles distant, and wait his return. He then went along the north side of the rapid river about four miles, where he waded it, and found it so rapid and shallow that it would be impossible to navigate it. He continued along the left side for a mile and a half, when the mountains came close on the river, and rose to a considerable height, with a partial covering of snow. From this place the course of the river was to the east of north. After ascending with some difficulty a high point of the mountain, he had a pleasing view of the valley he had passed, and which continued for about twenty miles further on each side of the middle fork, which then seemed to enter the mountains, and was lost to the view. In that direction, however, the hills which terminate the valley, are much lower than those along either of the other forks, particularly the rapid one, where they continue rising in ranges above each other as far as the eye could reach. The general course too of the middle fork, as well as that of the gap which it forms on entering the mountains, is considerably to the south of west; circumstances which gave a decided preference to this branch as our future route. Captain Lewis now descended the mountain, and crossed over to the middle fork, about five miles distant, and found it still perfectly navigable. There is a very large and plain Indian road leading up it, but it has at present no tracks, except those of horses which seem to have used it last spring. The river here made a great bend to the south-east, and he therefore directed his course, as well as he could, to the spot where he had ordered Chaboneau and Gass to repair, and struck the river about three miles above their camp. It was now dark, and he, therefore, was obliged to make his way through the thick brush of the pulpy-leafed thorn and the prickly pear, for two hours before he reached their camp. Here he was fortunate enough to find the remains of some meat, which was his only food during the march of twenty-five miles to-day. He had seen no game of any sort, except a few antelopes, who

were very shy. The soil of the plains is a meagre
clay, of a light yellow colour, intermixed with a
large proportion of gravel, and producing nothing
but twisted or bearded grass, sedge, and prickly
pears. The drier parts of the low grounds are also
more indifferent in point of soil than those farther
down the river, and although they have but little
grass, are covered with southern wood, pulpy-
leafed thorn, and prickly pears, while the moist
parts are fertile, and supplied with fine grass and
sandrushes.

We passed within the first four and a quarter
miles three small islands, and the same number of
bad rapids. At the distance of three quarters of
a mile is another rapid of difficult passage : three
miles and three quarters beyond this are the forks
of the river, in reaching which we had two islands
and several bayous on different sides to pass. Here
we had come nine miles and a quarter. The river
was straighter and more rapid than yesterday, the
labour of the navigation proportionally increased,
and we therefore proceeded very slowly, as the feet
of several of the men were swollen, and all were
languid with fatigue. We arrived at the forks
about four o'clock, but unluckily Captain Lewis's
note had been left on a green pole which the
beaver had cut down and carried off with the note,
an accident which deprived us of all information as
to the character of the two branches of the river.
Observing therefore that the north-west fork was
most in our direction, and contained as much water

as the other, we ascended it : we found it extremely rapid, and its waters were scattered in such a manner, that for a quarter of a mile we were forced to cut a passage through the willow brush that leaned over the little channels, and united at the top. After going up it for a mile we encamped on an island which had been overflowed, and was still so wet that we were compelled to make beds of brush to keep ourselves out of the mud. Our provision consisted of two deer which had been killed in the morning.

Tuesday, 6. We proceeded up the north-west fork, which we found still very rapid, and divided by several islands, while the plains near it were intersected by bayous. After passing with much difficulty over stones and rapids, we reached a bluff on the right, at the distance of nine miles, our general course south 30° west, and halted for breakfast. Here we were joined by Drewyer, who informed us of the state of the two rivers, and of Captain Lewis's note, and we immediately began to descend the river in order to take the other branch. On going down one of the canoes upset, and two others filled with water, by which all the baggage was wetted, and several articles irrecoverably lost. As one of them swung round in a rapid current, Whitehouse was thrown out of her, and whilst down the canoe passed over him, and had the water been two inches shallower would have crushed him to pieces; but he escaped with a severe bruise of his leg. In order to repair these misfortunes, we hastened to the forks, where we were joined by Captain Lewis, and then passed over to the left side opposite to the entrance of the rapid fork, and encamped on a large gravelly bar, near which there was plenty of wood. Here we opened and exposed to dry all the articles which had suffered from the water; none of them were completely spoiled except a small keg of powder; the rest of the powder, which was distributed in the different canoes was quite safe, although it had been under the water upwards of an hour. The air is indeed so pure and dry that any wood-work immediately shrinks unless it is kept filled with water; but we had placed our powder in small canisters of lead, each containing powder enough for the canister when melted into bullets, and secured with cork and wax, which answered our purpose perfectly.

Captain Lewis had risen very early, and having nothing to eat, sent out Drewyer to the wood-land on the left in search of a deer, and directed Serjeant Gass to keep along the middle branch to meet us if we were ascending it. He then set off with Chaboneau towards the forks, but five miles above them, hearing us on the left, struck the river as we were descending, and came on board at the forks.

In the evening we killed three deer and four elk, which furnished us once more with a plentiful supply of meat. Shannon, the same man who was lost before for fifteen days, was sent out this morning to hunt, up the north-west fork: when we decided on returning, Drewyer was directed to go in quest of him, but he returned with information that he had gone several miles up the river without being able to find Shannon. We now had the trumpet sounded, and fired several guns, but he did not return, and we fear he is again lost.

Wednesday, 7. We remained here this morning for the purpose of making some celestial observations, and also in order to refresh the men, and complete the drying of the baggage. We obtained a meridian altitude, which gave the latitude of our camp as north 45° 2' 43" 8'''. We were now completely satisfied that the middle branch was the most navigable, and the true continuation of the Jefferson. The north-west fork seems to be the drain of the melting snows of the mountains, its course cannot be so long as the other branch, and although it contains now as great a quantity of water, yet the water has obviously overflowed the old bed, and spread into channels which leave the low grounds covered with young grass, resembling that of the adjoining lands, which are not inundated : whence we readily infer that the supply is more precarious than that of the other branch, the waters of which, though more gentle, are more constant. This north-west fork we called Wisdom river.

As soon as the baggage was dried, it was reloaded on board the boats, but we now found it so much diminished, that we would be able to proceed with one canoe less. We therefore hauled up the superfluous one into a thicket of brush, where we secured her against being swept away by the high tide. At one o'clock, all set out, except Captain Lewis, who remained till the evening in order to complete the observation of equal altitudes : we passed several bends of the river both to the right and left, as well as a number of bayous on both sides, and made seven miles by water, though the distance by land is only three. We then encamped on a creek which rises in a high mountain to the north-east, and after passing through an open plain for several miles, discharges itself on the left, where it is a bold running stream twelve yards wide. We called it Turf creek, from the number of bogs and the quantity of turf on its waters. In the course of the afternoon there fell a shower of rain attended with thunder and lightning, which lasted about forty minutes, and the weather remained so cloudy all night that we were unable to take any lunar observations. Uneasy about Shannon, we sent R. Fields in search of him this morning, but we have as yet no intelligence of either of them. Our only game to-day was one deer.

Thursday, 8. There was a heavy dew this morning. Having left one of the canoes, there are now more men to spare for the chace : and four were sent out at an early hour, after which we proceeded. We made five miles by water along two islands and several bayous, but as the river formed seven different bends towards the left, the distance

by land was only two miles south of our encampment. At the end of that course we reached the
upper principal entrance of a stream which we
called Philanthropy river. This river empties itself
into the Jefferson on the south-east side, by two
channels a short distance from each other : from
its size and its south-eastern course, we presume
that it rises in the Rocky mountains near the
sources of the Madison. It is thirty yards wide at
its entrance, has a very gentle current, and is navigable for some distance. One mile above this
river we passed an island, a second at the distance
of six miles further, during which the river makes
a considerable bend to the east. Reuben Fields
returned about noon with information that he had
gone up Wisdom river till its entrance into the
mountains, but could find nothing of Shannon.
We made seven miles beyond the last island, and
after passing some small bayous, encamped under a
few high trees on the left, at the distance of fourteen miles above Philanthropy river by water,
though only six by land. The river has in fact
become so very crooked, that although by means
of the pole, which we now use constantly, we make
a considerable distance, yet being obliged to follow
its windings, at the end of the day, we find ourselves very little advanced on our general course.
It forms itself into small circular bends, which are
so numerous that within the last fourteen miles we
passed thirty-five of them, all inclining towards the
right : it is however much more gentle and deep

than below Wisdom river, and its general width is from thirty-five to forty-five yards. The general appearance of the surrounding country is that of a valley five or six miles wide, enclosed between two high mountains. The bottom is rich, with some small timber on the islands and along the river, which consists rather of underbrush, and a few cotton-wood, birch, and willow-trees. The high grounds have some scattered pine, which just relieve the general nakedness of the hills and the plain, where there is nothing except grass. Along the bottoms we saw to-day a considerable quantity of the buffaloe clover, the sun-flower, flax, green sward, thistle, and several species of rye grass, some of which rise to the height of three or four feet. There is also a grass with a soft smooth leaf, which rises about three feet high, and bears its seed very much like the timothy, but it does not grow luxuriantly, nor would it apparently answer so well in our meadows as that plant. We preserved some of its seed, which are now ripe, in order to make the experiment. Our game consisted of deer and antelope, and we saw a number of geese and ducks just beginning to fly, and some cranes. Among the inferior animals we have an abundance of the large biting or hare-fly, of which there are two species, one black, the other smaller and brown, except the head, which is green. The green or blowing flies unite with them in swarms to attack us, and seem to have relieved the eye-gnats, who have now disappeared. The musqui-

toes too are in large quantities, but not so troublesome as they were below. Through the valley are
scattered bogs, and some very good turf; the earth
of which the mud is composed is of a white or
blueish-white colour, and seems to be argillaceous.
On all the three rivers, but particularly on the
Philanthropy, are immense quantities of beaver,
otter, and musk-rat. At our camp there was an
abundance of rose-bushes and briars, but so little
timber that we were obliged to use willow-brush
for fuel. The night was again cloudy, which prevented the lunar observations.

On our right is the point of a high plain, which
our Indian woman recognizes as the place called
the Beaver's-head, from a supposed resemblance to
that object. This, she says, is not far from the
summer retreat of her countrymen, which is on a
river beyond the mountains, and running to the
west. She is therefore certain that we shall meet
them either on this river, or on that immediately
west of its source, which, judging from its present
size, cannot be far distant. Persuaded of the ab-
solute necessity of procuring horses to cross the
mountains, it was determined that one of us should
proceed in the morning to the head of the river,
and penetrate the mountains till he found the Shoshonees or some other nation who could assist us in
transporting our baggage, the greater part of which
we shall be compelled to leave, without the aid of
horses.

Friday, 9. The morning was fair and fine. We

set off early, and proceeded on very well, though there were more rapids in the river than yesterday. At eight o'clock we halted for breakfast, part of which consisted of two fine geese, killed before we stopped. Here we were joined by Shannon, for whose safety we had been so uneasy. The day on which he left us on his way up Wisdom river, after hunting for some time, and not seeing the party arrive, he returned to the place where he had left us. Not finding us there, he supposed we had passed him, and he therefore marched up the river during all the next day, when he was convinced that we had not gone on, as the river was no longer navigable. He now followed the course of the river down to the forks, and then took the branch which we are pursuing. During the three days of his absence, he had been much wearied with his march, but had lived plentifully, and brought the skins of three deer. As far as he had ascended Wisdom river, it kept its course obliquely down towards the Jefferson. Immediately after breakfast, Captain Lewis took Drewyer, Shields, and M'Neal, and slinging their knapsacks, they set out with a resolution to meet some nation of Indians before they returned, however long they might be separated from the party. He directed his course across the low ground to the plain on the right, leaving the Beaver's-head about two miles to the left. After walking eight miles to the river, which they waded, they went on to a commanding point, from which he saw the place at which it enters the mountain, but as the distance would not permit his reaching it this evening, he descended towards the river, and after travelling eight miles further, encamped for the evening some miles below the mountain. They passed, before reaching their camp, a handsome little stream formed by some large springs which rise in the wide bottom on the left side of the river. In their way they killed two antelopes, and took with them enough of the meat for their supper, and breakfast the next morning.

In the meantime we proceeded, and in the course of eleven miles from our last encampment, passed two small islands, sixteen short round bends in the river, and halted in a bend towards the right, where we dined. The river increases in rapidity as we advance, and is so crooked that the eleven miles, which have cost us so much labour, only bring us four miles in a direct line. The weather became overcast towards evening, and we experienced a slight shower, attended with thunder and lightning. The three hunters who were sent out, killed only two antelopes ; game of every kind being scarce.

Saturday, 10. Captain Lewis continued his route at an early hour, through the wide bottom, along the left bank of the river. At about five miles he passed a large creek, and then fell into an Indian road leading towards the point where the river entered the mountain. This he followed till he reached a high perpendicular cliff of rocks, where the river makes its passage through the hills, and which he called the Rattlesnake cliff, from the number of that animal which he saw there : here he kindled a fire, and waited the return of Drewyer, who had been sent out on the way to kill a deer: he came back about noon with the skins of three deer, and the flesh of one of the best of them. After a hasty dinner, they returned to the Indian road, which they had left for a short distance to see the cliff. It led them sometimes over the hills, sometimes in the narrow bottoms of the river, till at the distance of fifteen miles from the Rattlesnake cliffs, they reached a handsome open, and level valley, where the river divided into two nearly equal branches. The mountains over which they passed were not very high, but are rugged, and continue close to the river side. The river, which before it enters the mountain, was rapid, rocky, very crooked, much divided by islands, and shallow, now becomes more direct in its course, as it is hemmed in by the hills, and has not so many bends nor islands, but becomes more rapid and rocky, and continues as shallow. On examining the two branches of the river, it was evident that neither of them was navigable further. The road forked with the river; and Captain Lewis, therefore, sent a man up each of them for a short distance, in order that by comparing their respective information, he might be able to take that which seemed to have been most used this spring. From their account he resolved to choose

that which led along the south-west branch of the
river, which was rather the smaller of the two : he
accordingly wrote a note to Captain Clarke, informing him of the route, and recommending his
staying with the party at the forks till he should
return : this he fixed on a dry willow pole at the
forks of the river, and then proceeded up the
south-west branch; but after going a mile and a
half, the road became scarcely distinguishable, and
the tracks of the horses which he had followed
along the Jefferson, were no longer seen. Captain
Lewis therefore returned to examine the other
road himself, and found that the horses had in fact
passed along the western, or right fork, which
had the additional recommendation of being
larger than the other.

This road he concluded to take, and therefore
sent back Drewyer to the forks with a second
letter to Captain Clarke, apprising him of the
change, and then proceeded on. The valley of
the west fork, through which he now passed,
bears a little to the north of west, and is confined within the space of about a mile in width,
by rough mountains and steep cliffs of rock. At
the distance of four and a half miles, it opens into
a beautiful and extensive plain, about ten miles
long, and five or six in width : this is surrounded
on all sides by higher rolling or waving country,
intersected by several little rivulets from the mountains, each bordered by its wide meadows. The
whole prospect is bounded by these mountains,

which nearly surround it, so as to form a beautiful cove, about sixteen or eighteen miles in diameter. On entering this cove, the river bends to the north-west, and bathes the foot of the hills to the right. At this place they halted for the night, on the right side of the river, and having lighted a fire of dry willow brush, the only fuel which the country affords, supped on a deer. They had travelled to-day thirty miles by estimate; that is, ten to the Rattlesnake cliff, fifteen to the forks of Jefferson river, and five to their encampment. In this cove some parts of the low grounds are tolerably fertile, but much the greater proportion is covered with prickly pear, sedge, twisted grass, the pulpy-leafed thorn, southern-wood, and wild sage, and like the uplands have a very inferior soil. These last have little more than the prickly pear and the twisted or bearded grass, nor are there in the whole cove more than three or four cotton-wood trees, and those are small. At the apparent extremity of the bottom above, and about ten miles to the westward, are two perpendicular cliffs rising to a considerable height on each side of the river, and at this distance seem like a gate.

In the meantime we proceeded at sun-rise, and found the river not so rapid as yesterday, though more narrow and still very crooked, and so shallow that we were obliged to drag the canoes over many ripples in the course of the day. At six and a half miles we had passed eight bends on the north, and two small bayous on the left, and came to what the Indians call the Beaver's-head, a steep rocky cliff, about one hundred and fifty feet high, near the right side of the river. Opposite to this, at three hundred yards from the water, is a low cliff about fifty feet in height, which forms the extremity of a spur of the mountain, about four miles distant on the left. At four o'clock we were overtaken by a heavy shower of rain, attended with thunder, lightning, and hail. The party were defended from the hail, by covering themselves with willow bushes, but they got completely wet, and in this situation, as soon as the rain ceased, continued till we encamped. This we did at a low bluff on the left, after passing, in the course of six and a half miles, four islands and eighteen bends on the right, and a low bluff and several bayous on the same side. We had now come thirteen miles, yet were only four on our route towards the mountains. The game seems to be declining, for our hunters procured only a single deer, though we found another, that had been killed three days before, by one of the hunters during an excursion, and left for us on the river.

CHAPTER XIV.

SUNDAY, August 11. Captain Lewis again proceeded on early, but had the mortification to find that the track which he followed yesterday soon disappeared. He determined therefore to go on to the narrow gate or pass of the river which he had seen from the camp, in hopes of being able to recover the Indian path. For this purpose he waded across the river, which was now about twelve yards wide, and barred in several places by the dams of the beaver, and then went straight forward to the pass, sending one man along the river to his left, and another on the right, with orders to search for the road, and if they found it to let him know by raising a hat on the muzzle of their guns. In this order they went along for about five miles, when Captain Lewis perceived with the greatest delight a man on horseback at the distance of two miles coming down the plain towards them. On examining him with the glass, Captain Lewis saw that he was of a different nation from any Indians we had hitherto met: he was armed with a bow and a quiver of arrows; mounted on an elegant horse without a saddle, and a small string attached to the under jaw answered as a bridle. Convinced that he was a Shoshonee, and knowing how much of our success depended on the friendly offices of that nation, Captain Lewis was full of anxiety to approach without alarming him, and endeavour to convince him that he was a white man. He therefore proceeded on towards the Indian at his usual pace; when they were within a mile of each other the Indian suddenly stopt, Captain Lewis immediately followed his example, took his blanket from his knapsack, and holding it with both hands at the two corners, threw it above his head and unfolded it as he brought it to the ground, as if in the act of spreading it. This signal, which originates in the practice of spreading a robe or a skin, as a seat for guests to whom they wish to show a distinguished kindness, is the universal sign of friendship among the Indians on the Missouri and the Rocky mountains. As usual, Captain Lewis repeated this signal three times : still the Indian kept his position, and looked with an air of suspicion on Drewyer and Shields, who were now advancing on each side. Captain Lewis was afraid to make any signal for them to halt, lest he should increase the suspicions of the Indian, who began to be uneasy, and they were too distant to hear his voice. He, therefore, took from his pack some beads, a looking-glass, and a few trinkets, which he had brought for the purpose, and leaving his gun advanced unarmed towards the Indian. He remained in the same position till Captain Lewis came within two hundred yards of him, when he turned his horse, and began to move off slowly ; Captain Lewis then called out to him, in as loud a voice as he could, repeating the word, tabba bone ! which in the Shoshonee language means white man ; but looking over his shoulder the Indian kept his eyes on Drewyer and Shields, who were still advancing, without recollecting the impropriety of doing so at such a moment, till Captain Lewis made a signal to them to halt : this Drewyer obeyed, but Shields did not observe it, and still went forward : seeing Drewyer halt the Indian turned his horse about as if to wait for Captain Lewis, who now reached within one hundred and fifty paces, repeating the word tabba bone, and holding up the trinkets in his hand, at the same time stripping up the sleeve of his shirt to show the colour of his skin. The Indian suffered him to advance within one hundred paces, then suddenly turned his horse, and giving him the whip, leaped across the creek, and disappeared in an instant among the willow bushes: with him vanished all the hopes which the sight of him had inspired of a friendly introduction to his countrymen. Though sadly disappointed by the imprudence of his two men, Captain Lewis determined to make the incident of some use, and therefore calling the men to him they all set off after the track of the horse, which they hoped might lead them to the camp of the Indian who had fled, or if he had given the alarm to any small party, their track might conduct them to the body of the nation. They now fixed a small flag of the United States on a pole, which was carried by one of the men as a signal of their friendly intentions, should the Indians observe them as they were advancing. The route lay across an island formed by a nearly equal division of the creek in the bottom: after reaching the open grounds on the right side of the creek, the track turned towards some high hills about three miles distant. Presuming that the Indian camp might be among these hills, and that by advancing hastily he might be seen and alarm them, Captain Lewis sought an elevated situation near the creek, had a fire made of willow brush, and took breakfast. At the same time he prepared a small assortment of beads, trinkets, awls, some paint and a looking-glass, and placed them on a pole near the fire, in order that if the Indians returned they might discover that the party were white men and friends. Whilst making these preparations a very heavy shower of rain and hail came on, and wet them to the skin: in about twenty minutes it was over, and Captain Lewis then renewed his pursuit, but as the rain had made the grass which the horse had trodden down rise again, his track could with difficulty be distinguished. As they went along they passed several places where the Indians seemed to have been digging roots to-day, and saw the fresh track of eight or ten horses, but they had been wandering about in so confused a manner that he could not discern any particular path, and at last, after pursuing it about four miles along the valley to the left under the foot of the hills, he lost the track of the fugitive Indian. Near the head of the valley they had passed a large bog covered with moss and tall grass, among which were several springs of pure cold water: they now turned a little to the left along the foot of the high hills, and reached a small creek where they encamped for the night, having made about twenty miles, though not more than ten in a direct line from their camp of last evening.

The morning being rainy and wet we did not set out with the canoes till after an early breakfast.

During the first three miles we passed three small islands, six bayous on different sides of the river, and the same number of bends towards the right. Here we reached the lower point of a large island, which we called Three-thousand-mile island, on account of its being at that distance from the mouth of the Missouri. It is three miles and a half in length, and as we coasted along it we passed several small bends of the river towards the left, and two bayous on the same side. After leaving the upper point of Three-thousand-mile island, we followed the main channel on the left side, which led us by three small islands and several small bayous, and fifteen bends towards the right. Then at the distance of seven miles and a half we encamped on the upper end of a large island near the right. The river was shallow and rapid, so that we were obliged to be in the water during a great part of the day, dragging the canoes over the shoals and ripples. Its course too was so crooked, that notwithstanding we had made fourteen miles by water, we were only five miles from our encampment of last night. The country consists of a low ground on the river about five miles wide, and succeeded on both sides by plains of the same extent which reach to the base of the mountains. These low grounds are very much intersected by bayous, and in those on the left side is a large proportion of bog covered with tall grass, which would yield a fine turf. There are very few trees, and those small narrow-leafed cotton-wood: the principal growth being the narrow-leafed willow, and currant-bushes, among which were some bunches of privy near the river. We saw a number of geese, ducks, beaver, otter, deer, and antelopes, of all which one beaver was killed with a pole from the boat, three otters with a tomahawk, and the hunters brought in three deer and an antelope.

Monday, 12. This morning, as soon as it was light, Captain Lewis sent Drewyer to reconnoitre, if possible, the route of the Indians: in about an hour and a half he returned, after following the tracks of the horse which we had lost yesterday to the mountains, where they ascended, and were no longer visible. Captain Lewis now decided on making the circuit along the foot of the mountains which formed the cove, expecting by that means to find a road across them, and accordingly sent Drewyer on one side, and Shields on the other. In this way they crossed four small rivulets near each other, on which were some bowers or conical lodges of willow brush, which seemed to have been made recently. From the manner in which the ground in the neighbourhood was torn up the Indians appeared to have been gathering roots; but Captain Lewis could not discover what particular plant they were searching for, nor could he find any fresh track, till at the distance of four miles from his camp he met a large plain Indian road, which came into the cove from the north-east, and wound along the foot of the mountains to the south-west, approaching obliquely the main stream he had left yesterday. Down this road he now went towards the south-west: at the distance of five miles it crossed a large run or creek, which is a principal branch of the main stream into which it falls, just above the high cliffs or gates observed yesterday, and which they now saw below them: here they halted and breakfasted on the last of the deer, keeping a small piece of pork in reserve against accident: they then continued through the low bottom along the main stream near the foot of the mountains on their right. For the first five miles the valley continues towards the south-west from two to three miles in width; then the main stream, which had received two small branches from the left to the valley, turns abruptly to the west through a narrow bottom between the mountains. The road was still plain, and as it led them directly on towards the mountain, the stream gradually became smaller, till after going two miles it had so greatly diminished in width that one of the men in a fit of enthusiasm, with one foot on each side of the river, thanked God that he had lived to bestride the Missouri. As they went along, their hopes of soon seeing the waters of the Columbia, arose almost to painful anxiety, when after four miles from the last abrupt turn of the river, they reached a small gap formed by the high mountains which recede on each side, leaving room for the Indian road. From the foot of one of the lowest of these mountains, which rises with a gentle ascent of about half a mile, issues the remotest water of the Missouri. They had now reached the hidden sources of that river, which had never yet been seen by civilized man ; and as they quenched their thirst at the chaste and icy fountain — as they sat down by the brink of that little rivulet, which yielded its distant and modest tribute to the parent ocean, they felt themselves rewarded for all their labours and all their difficulties. They left reluctantly this interesting spot, and pursuing the Indian road through the interval of the hills, arrived at the top of a ridge, from which they saw high mountains, partially covered with snow, still to the west of them. The ridge on which they stood formed the dividing line between the waters of the Atlantic and Pacific oceans. They followed a descent much steeper than that on the eastern side, and at the distance of three quarters of a mile, reached a handsome bold creek of cold clear water running to the westward. They stopped to taste for the first time the waters of the Columbia ; and after a few minutes, followed the road across steep hills and low hollows, till they reached a spring on the side of a mountain : here they found a sufficient quantity of dry willow brush for fuel, and therefore halted for the night ; and having killed nothing in the course of the day, supped on their last piece of pork, and trusted to fortune for some other food to mix with a little flour and parched meal, which was all that now remained of their provisions. Before reaching the fountain of the Missouri, they saw several large hawks nearly

black, and some of the heath-cocks : these last
have a long pointed tail, and are of a uniform
dark brown colour, much larger than the common
dunghill-fowl, and similar in habits and the mode
of flying to the grouse or prairie hen. Drewyer
also wounded, at the distance of one hundred and
thirty yards, an animal which we had not yet seen,
but which, after falling, recovered itself and escaped. It seemed to be of the fox kind, rather
larger than the small wolf of the plains, and with
a skin in which black, reddish-brown, and yellow
were curiously intermixed. On the creek of the
Columbia they found a species of currant which
does not grow as high as that of the Missouri,
though it is more branching, and its leaf, the under
disk of which is covered with a hairy pubescence,
is twice as large. The fruit is of the ordinary size
and shape of the currant, and supported in the usual
manner, but is of a deep purple colour, acid, and
of a very inferior flavour.

We proceeded on in the boats, but as the river
was very shallow and rapid, the navigation is extremely difficult ; and the men, who are almost
constantly in the water, are getting feeble and sore,
and so much worn down by fatigue, that they are
very anxious to commence travelling by land. We
went along the main channel, which is on the right
side, and after passing nine bends in that direction,
three islands, and a number of bayous, reached, at
the distance of five and a half miles, the upper
point of a large island. At noon there was a storm

of thunder, which continued about half an hour; after which we proceeded, but as it was necessary to drag the canoes over the shoals and rapids, made but little progress. On leaving the island we passed a number of short bends, several bayous, and one run of water on the right side, and having gone by four small and two large islands, encamped on a smooth plain to the left, near a few cotton-wood trees : our journey by water was just twelve miles, and four in a direct line. The hunters supplied us with three deer and a fawn.

Tuesday, 13. Very early in the morning Captain Lewis resumed the Indian road, which led him, in a western direction, through an open broken country ; on the left was a deep valley at the foot of a high range of mountains running from south-east to north-west, with their sides better clad with timber than the hills to which we had been for some time accustomed, and their tops covered in part with snow. At five miles distance, after following the long descent of another valley, he reached a creek about ten yards wide, and on rising the hill beyond it had a view of a handsome little valley on the left, about a mile in width, through which they judged, from the appearance of the timber, that some stream of water most probably passed. On the creek they had just left were some bushes of the white maple, the sumach of the small species with the winged rib, and a species of honeysuckle, resembling in its general appearance and the shape of its leaf the small honeysuckle of the Missouri, except that it is rather larger, and bears a globular berry, about the size of a garden pea, of a white colour, and formed of a soft white mucilaginous substance, in which are several small brown seeds irregularly scattered without any cell, and enveloped in a smooth thin pellicle.

They proceeded along a waving plain parallel to this valley for about four miles, when they discovered two women, a man, and some dogs, on an eminence at the distance of a mile before them. The strangers first viewed them apparently with much attention for a few minutes, and then two of them sat down as if to await Captain Lewis's arrival. He went on till he reached within about half a mile, then ordered his party to stop, put down his knapsack and rifle, and unfurling the flag advanced alone towards the Indians. The females soon retreated behind the hill, but the man remained till Captain Lewis came within a hundred yards of him, when he too went off, though Captain Lewis called out tabba bone! loud enough to be heard distinctly. He hastened to the top of the hill, but they had all disappeared. The dogs however were less shy, and came close to him; he therefore thought of tying a handkerchief with some beads round their necks, and then let them loose to convince the fugitives of his friendly disposition, but they would not suffer him to take hold of them, and soon left him. He now made a signal to the men, who joined him, and then all followed the

track of the Indians, which led along a continuation
of the same road they had been already travelling.
It was dusty, and seemed to have been much used
lately both by foot passengers and horsemen. They
had not gone along it more than a mile, when on a sudden they saw three female Indians, from whom they
had been concealed by the deep ravines which intersected the road, till they were now within thirty
paces of each other; one of them, a young woman,
immediately took to flight; the other two, an elderly
woman and a little girl, seeing we were too near
for them to escape, sat on the ground, and holding
down their heads, seemed as if reconciled to the
death which they supposed awaited them. The
same habit of holding down the head and inviting
the enemy to strike, when all chance of escape is
gone, is preserved in Egypt to this day. Captain
Lewis instantly put down his rifle, and advancing
towards them, took the woman by the hand, raised
her up, and repeated the words tabba bone! at the
same time stripping up his shirt sleeve to prove
that he was a white man, for his hands and face
had become, by constant exposure, quite as dark
as their own. She appeared immediately relieved
from her alarm, and Drewyer and Shields now
coming up, Captain Lewis gave them some beads,
a few awls, pewter mirrors, and a little paint, and
told Drewyer to request the woman to recall her
companion who had escaped to some distance, and
by alarming the Indians might cause them to attack
him without any time for explanation. She did as

she was desired, and the young woman returned almost out of breath : Captain Lewis gave her an equal portion of trinkets, and painted the tawny cheeks of all three of them with vermilion, a ceremony which among the Shoshonees is emblematic of peace. After they had become composed, he informed them by signs of his wish to go to their camp in order to see their chiefs and warriors ; they readily obeyed, and conducted the party along the same road down the river. In this way they marched two miles, when they met a troop of nearly sixty warriors, mounted on excellent horses, riding at full speed towards them. As they advanced, Captain Lewis put down his gun, and went with the flag about fifty paces in advance. The chief, who, with two men, was riding in front of the main body, spoke to the women, who now explained that the party was composed of white men, and showed exultingly the presents they had received. The three men immediately leaped from their horses, came up to Captain Lewis, and embraced him with great cordiality, putting their left arm over his right shoulder and clasping his back, applying at the same time their left cheek to his, and frequently vociferating ah hi e! ah hi e! " I am much pleased, I am much rejoiced." The whole body of warriors now came forward, and our men received the caresses, and no small share of the grease and paint of their new friends. After this fraternal embrace, of which the motive was much more agreeable than the manner, Captain Lewis lighted a pipe and offered it to the Indians, who had now seated themselves in a circle around the party. But before they would receive this mark of friendship, they pulled off their moccasins, a custom, as we afterwards learnt, which indicates the sacred sincerity of their professions when they smoke with a stranger, and which imprecates on themselves the misery of going barefoot for ever if they are faithless to their words, a penalty by no means light to those who rove over the thorny plains of their country. It is not unworthy to remark the analogy which some of the customs of those wild children of the wilderness bear to those recorded in holy writ. Moses is admonished to pull off his shoes, for the place on which he stood was holy ground. Why this was enjoined as an act of peculiar reverence; whether it was from the circumstance that in the arid region, in which the patriarch then resided, it was deemed a test of the sincerity of devotion to walk upon the burning sands barefooted, in some measure analogous to the pains inflicted by the prickly pear, does not appear. After smoking a few pipes, some trifling presents were distributed amongst them, with which they seemed very much pleased, particularly with the blue beads and the vermilion. Captain Lewis then informed the chief that the object of his visit was friendly, and should be explained as soon as he reached their camp; but that, in the meantime, as the sun was oppressive, and no water near, he wished to go there as soon as possible.

They now put on their moccasins, and their chief, whose name was Cameahwait, made a short speech to the warriors. Captain Lewis then gave him the flag, which he informed him was among white men the emblem of peace, and now that he had received it was to be in future the bond of union between them. The chief then moved on, our party followed him, and the rest of the warriors in a squadron, brought up the rear. After marching a mile they were halted by the chief, who made a second harangue, on which six or eight young men rode forward to their camp, and no further regularity was observed in the order of march. At the distance of four miles from where they had first met, they reached the Indian camp, which was in a handsome level meadow on the bank of the river. Here they were introduced into an old leathern lodge, which the young men who had been sent from the party had fitted up for their reception. After being seated on green boughs and antelope skins, one of the warriors pulled up the grass in the centre of the lodge so as to form a vacant circle of two feet diameter, in which he kindled a fire. The chief then produced his pipe and tobacco, the warriors all pulled off their moccasins, and our party was requested to take off their own. This being done, the chief lighted his pipe at the fire within the magic circle, and then retreating from it began a speech several minutes long, at the end of which he pointed the stem towards the four cardinal points of the heavens, beginning with the east

and concluding with the north. After this ceremony he presented the stem in the same way to
Captain Lewis, who supposing it an invitation to
smoke, put out his hand to receive the pipe, but
the chief drew it back, and continued to repeat the
same offer three times, after which he pointed the
stem first to the heavens, then to the centre of the
little circle, took three whiffs himself, and presented
it again to Captain Lewis. Finding that this last
offer was in good earnest, he smoked a little; the
pipe was then held to each of the white men, and
after they had taken a few whiffs was given to the
warriors. This pipe was made of a dense transparent green stone, very highly polished, about two
and an half inches long, and of an oval figure, the
bowl being in the same situation with the stem. A
small piece of burnt clay is placed in the bottom
of the bowl to separate the tobacco from the end
of the stem, and is of an irregularly round figure,
not fitting the tube perfectly close, in order that
the smoke may pass with facility. The tobacco is
of the same kind with that used by the Minnetarees, Mandans, and Ricaras of the Missouri.
The Shoshonees do not cultivate this plant, but
obtain it from the Rocky mountain Indians, and
some of the bands of their own nation who live
further south. The ceremony of smoking being
concluded, Captain Lewis explained to the chief
the purposes of his visit, and as by this time all
the women and children of the camp had gathered
around the lodge to indulge in a view of the first

white men they had ever seen, he distributed among them the remainder of the small articles he had brought with him. It was now late in the afternoon, and our party had tasted no food since the night before. On apprising the chief of this circumstance, he said that he had nothing but berries to eat, and presented some cakes made of service-berry and choke-cherries which had been dried in the sun. On these Captain Lewis made a hearty meal, and then walked down towards the river : he found it a rapid clear stream, forty yards wide and three feet deep : the banks were low and abrupt, like those of the upper part of the Missouri, and the bed formed of loose stones and gravel. Its course, as far as he could observe it, was a little to the north of west, and was bounded on each side by a range of high mountains, of which those on the east are the lowest and most distant from the river.

The chief informed him that this stream discharged itself, at the distance of half a day's march, into another of twice its size, coming from the south-west ; but added, on further enquiry, that there was scarcely more timber below the junction of those rivers than in this neighbourhood, and that the river was rocky, rapid, and so closely confined between high mountains, that it was impossible to pass down it, either by land or water, to the great lake, where, as he had understood, the white men lived. This information was far from being satisfactory ; for there was no timber here that would

answer the purpose of building canoes, indeed not
more than just sufficient for fuel, and even that
consisted of the narrow-leafed cotton-wood, the red
and the narrow-leafed willow, the choke-cherry, service-berry, and a few currant bushes, such as are
common on the Missouri. The prospect of going
on by land is more pleasant ; for there are great
numbers of horses feeding in every direction round
the camp, which will enable us to transport our
stores if necessary over the mountains. Captain
Lewis returned from the river to his lodge, and
on his way an Indian invited him into his bower
and gave him a small morsel of boiled antelope
and a piece of fresh salmon roasted. This was
the first salmon he had seen, and perfectly satisfied
him that he was now on the waters of the Pacific.
On reaching this lodge, he resumed his conversation
with the chief, after which he was entertained with
a dance by the Indians. It now proved, as our
party had feared, that the men whom they had
first met this morning had returned to the camp
and spread the alarm that their enemies, the
Minnetarees of fort de Prairie, whom they call
Pahkees, were advancing on them. The warriors
instantly armed themselves and were coming down
in expectation of an attack, when they were agreeably surprised by meeting our party. The greater
part of them were armed with bows and arrows,
and shields, but a few had small fusils, such as are
furnished by the North-west Company traders, and
which they had obtained from the Indians on the

Yellowstone, with whom they are now at peace. They had reason to dread the approach of the Pahkees, who had attacked them in the course of this spring and totally defeated them. On this occasion twenty of their warriors were either killed or made prisoners, and they lost their whole camp, except the leathern lodge which they had fitted up for us, and were now obliged to live in huts of a conical figure made with willow brush. The music and dancing, which were in no respect different from those of the Missouri Indians, continued nearly all night; but Captain Lewis retired to rest about twelve o'clock, when the fatigues of the day enabled him to sleep, though he was awaked several times by the yells of the dancers.

Whilst all these things were occurring to Captain Lewis, we were slowly and laboriously ascending the river. For the first two and a half miles we went along the island opposite to which we encamped last evening, and soon reached a second island, behind which comes in a small creek on the left side of the river. It rises in the mountains to the east, and forms a handsome valley for some miles from its mouth, where it is a bold running stream, about seven yards wide: we called it M'Neal's creek, after Hugh M'Neal, one of our party. Just above this stream, and at the distance of four miles from our camp, is a point of limestone rock on the right, about seventy feet high, forming a cliff over the river. From the top of it the Beaver's-head bore north 24° east, twelve miles distant; the course of

Wisdom river, that is, the direction of its valley through the mountains, is north 25° west, while the gap, through which the Jefferson enters the mountains, is ten miles above us, on a course south 18° west. From this limestone rock we proceeded along several islands, on both sides, and after making twelve miles, arrived at a cliff of high rocks on the right, opposite to which we encamped in a smooth level prairie, near a few cotton-wood trees; but were obliged to use the dry willow brush for fuel. The river is still very crooked, the bends short and abrupt, and obstructed by so many shoals, over which the canoes were to be dragged, that the men were in the water three-fourths of the day. They saw numbers of otter, some beaver, antelopes, ducks, geese, and cranes, but they killed nothing except a single deer. They, however, caught some very fine trout, as they have done for several days past. The weather had been cloudy and cool during the forepart of the day, and at eight o'clock a shower of rain fell.

Wednesday, 14. In order to give time for the boats to reach the forks of the Jefferson river, Captain Lewis determined to remain here, and obtain all the information he could collect with regard to the country. Having nothing to eat but a little flour and parched meal, with the berries of the Indians, he sent out Drewyer and Shields, who borrowed horses from the natives, to hunt for a few hours. About the same time the young warriors set out for the same purpose. There are but few elk or black-tailed deer in this neighbourhood, and as the common red-deer secrete themselves in the bushes when alarmed, they are soon safe from the arrows, which are but feeble weapons against any animals which the huntsmen cannot previously run down with their horses. The chief game of the Shoshonees, therefore, is the antelope, which, when pursued, retreats to the open plains, where the horses have full room for the chace. But such is its extraordinary fleetness and wind, that a single horse has no chance of outrunning it, or tiring it down; and the hunters are therefore obliged to resort to stratagem. About twenty Indians, mounted on fine horses, and armed with bows and arrows, left the camp; in a short time they descried a herd of antelopes: they immediately separated into little squads of two or three, and formed a scattered circle round the herd for five or six miles, keeping at a wary distance, so as not to alarm them till they were perfectly enclosed, and usually selecting some commanding eminence as a stand. Having gained their positions, a small party rode towards the herd, and with wonderful dexterity the huntsman preserved his seat, and the horse his footing, as he ran at full speed over the hills, and down the steep ravines, and along the borders of the precipices. They were soon outstripped by the antelopes, which, on gaining the other extremity of the circle, were driven back and pursued by the fresh hunters. They turned and flew, rather than ran, in another direction; but there, too, they found new enemies. In this way they were alternately pursued backwards and forwards, till at length, notwithstanding the skill of the hunters, they all escaped; and the party, after running for two hours, returned without having caught any thing, and their horses foaming with sweat. This chase, the greater part of which was seen from the camp, formed a beautiful scene; but to the hunters is exceedingly laborious, and so unproductive, even when they are able to worry the animal down, and shoot him, that forty or fifty hunters will sometimes be engaged for half a day, without obtaining more than two or three antelopes. Soon after they returned, our two huntsmen came in with no better success. Captain Lewis therefore made a little paste with the flour, and with the addition of some berries, formed a very palatable repast. Having now secured the good-will of Cameahwait, Captain Lewis informed him of his wish that he would speak to the warriors, and endeavour to engage them to accompany him to the forks of Jefferson river, where by this time another chief, with a large party of white men, was waiting his return: that it would be necessary to take about thirty horses to transport the merchandize; that they should be well rewarded for their trouble; and that when all the party should have reached the Shoshonee camp, they would remain some time among them, and trade for horses as well as concert plans for furnishing them, in future, with regular supplies of merchandize. He readily consented to do so, and after collecting the tribe together, he made a long harangue, and in about an hour and a half returned, and told Captain Lewis that he would be ready to accompany him in the morning.

As the early part of the day was cold, and the men stiff and sore from the fatigues of yesterday, we did not set out till seven o'clock. At the distance of a mile we passed a bold stream on the right, which comes from a snowy mountain to the north, and its entrance is four yards wide, and three feet in depth : we called it Track creek : at six miles further we reached another stream, which heads in some springs at the foot of the mountains on the left. After passing a number of bayous and small islands on each side, we encamped about half a mile by land below the Rattlesnake cliffs. The river was cold, shallow, and as it approached the mountains, formed one continued rapid, over which we were obliged to drag the boats with great labour and difficulty. By using constant exertions we succeeded in making fourteen miles, but this distance did not carry us more than six and a half in a straight line : several of the men have received wounds, and lamed themselves in hauling the boats over the stones. The hunters supplied them with five deer and an antelope.

Thursday, 15. Captain Lewis rose early, and having eaten nothing yesterday, except his scanty meal of flour and berries, felt the inconveniences of extreme hunger. On enquiry he found that his whole stock of provisions consisted of two pounds of flour. This he ordered to be divided into two equal parts, and one half of it boiled with the berries into a sort of pudding; and after presenting a large share to the chief, he and his three men breakfasted on the remainder. Cameahwait was delighted at this new dish, he took a little of the flour in his hand, tasted and examined it very narrowly, asking if it was made of roots; Captain Lewis explained the process of preparing it, and he said it was the best thing he had eaten for a long time.

This being finished, Captain Lewis now endeavoured to hasten the departure of the Indians, who still hesitated, and seemed reluctant to move, although the chief addressed them twice for the purpose of urging them: on enquiring the reason, Cameahwait told him that some foolish person had suggested that he was in league with their enemies the Pahkees, and had come only to draw them into ambuscade, but that he himself did not believe it: Captain Lewis felt uneasy at this insinuation: he knew the suspicious temper of the Indians, accustomed from their infancy to regard every stranger as an enemy, and saw that if this suggestion were not instantly checked, it might hazard the total failure of the enterprise. Assuming therefore a serious air, he told the chief that he was sorry to find they placed so little confidence in him, but that he pardoned their suspicions, because they were ignorant of the character of white men, among whom it was disgraceful to lie and entrap even an

enemy by falsehood; that if they continued to
think thus meanly of us, they might be assured no
white men would ever come to supply them with
arms and merchandize; that there was at this moment a party of white men waiting to trade with
them at the forks of the river, and that if the greater
part of the tribe entertained any suspicion, he
hoped there were still among them some who were
men, who would go and see with their own eyes
the truth of what he said, and who, even if there
was any danger, were not afraid to die. To
doubt the courage of an Indian is to touch the
tenderest string of his mind, and the surest way to
rouse him to any dangerous achievement. Cameahwait instantly replied, that he was not afraid to die,
and mounting his horse, for the third time harangued the warriors: he told them that he was resolved to go if he went alone, or if he were sure of
perishing: that he hoped there were among those
who heard him some who were not afraid to die, and
who would prove it by mounting their horses and
following him. This harangue produced an effect
on six or eight only of the warriors, who now
joined their chief. With these Captain Lewis
smoked a pipe, and then, fearful of some change
in their capricious temper, set out immediately.
It was about twelve o'clock when his small party
left the camp, attended by Cameahwait and the
eight warriors: their departure seemed to spread
a gloom over the village; those who would not
venture to go were sullen and melancholy, and the

women were crying and imploring the Great Spirit
to protect their warriors, as if they were going to
certain destruction : yet such is the wavering in-
constancy of these savages, that Captain Lewis's
party had not gone far when they were joined by
ten or twelve more warriors, and before reaching
the creek which they had passed on the morning of
the 13th, all the men of the nation, and a number
of women had overtaken them, and had changed
from the surly ill temper in which they were two
hours ago, to the greatest cheerfulness and gaiety.
When they arrived at the spring, on the side of the
mountain, where the party had encamped on the
12th, the chief insisted on halting to let the horses
graze; to which Captain Lewis assented and
smoked with them. They are excessively fond of
the pipe, in which, however, they are not able to
indulge much, as they do not cultivate tobacco
themselves, and their rugged country affords them
but few articles to exchange for it. Here they remained for about an hour, and on setting out, by
engaging to pay four of the party, Captain Lewis
obtained permission for himself and each of his
men to ride behind an Indian; but he soon found
riding without stirrups more tiresome than walking,
and therefore dismounted, making the Indian carry
his pack. About sunset they reached the upper
part of the level valley, in the cove through which
he had passed, and which they now called Shoshonee cove. The grass being burnt on the north
side of the river, they crossed over to the south,

and encamped about four miles above the narrow pass between the hills, noticed as they traversed the cove before. The river was here about six yards wide, and frequently dammed up by the beaver. Drewyer had been sent forward to hunt, but he returned in the evening unsuccessful, and their only supper therefore was the remaining pound of flour stirred in a little water, and then divided between the four white men and two of the Indians.

In order not to exhaust the strength of the men, Captain Clarke did not leave his camp till after breakfast. Although he was scarcely half a mile below the Rattlesnake cliffs, he was obliged to make a circuit of two miles by water before he reached them. The river now passed between low and rugged mountains, and cliffs formed of a mixture of limestone and a hard black rock, with no covering except a few scattered pines. At the distance of four miles is a bold little stream, which throws itself from the mountains down a steep precipice of rocks on the left. One mile further is a second point of rocks, and an island, about a mile beyond which is a creek on the right, ten yards wide, and three feet three inches in depth, with a strong current: we called it Willard's creek, after one of our men, Alexander Willard. Three miles beyond this creek, after passing a high cliff on the right, opposite to a steep hill, we reached a small meadow on the left bank of the river. During its passage through these hills to Willard's creek, the river had been less tortuous than usual, so that in the first six miles to Willard's creek, we had advanced four miles on our route. We continued on for two miles, till we reached in the evening a small bottom covered with clover, and a few cottonwood trees: here we passed the night near the remains of some old Indian lodges of brush. The river is, as it has been for some days, shallow and rapid; and our men, who are for hours together in the river, suffer not only from fatigue, but from the extreme coldness of the water, the temperature of which is as low as that of the freshest springs in our country. In walking along the side of the river, Captain Clarke was very near being bitten twice by rattlesnakes, and the Indian woman narrowly escaped the same misfortune. We caught a number of fine trout; but the only game procured to-day was a buck, which had a peculiarly bitter taste, proceeding probably from its favourite food, the willow.

Friday, 16. As neither our party nor the Indians had any thing to eat, Captain Lewis sent two of his hunters a-head this morning, to procure some provision: at the same time he requested Cameahwait to prevent his young men from going out, lest by their noise they might alarm the game; but this measure immediately revived their suspicions. It now began to be believed that these men were sent forward in order to apprize the enemy of their coming; and as Captain Lewis was fearful of exciting any further uneasiness, he made

no objection on seeing a small party of Indians go
on each side of the valley, under pretence of hunting, but in reality to watch the movements of our
two men : even this precaution, however, did not
quiet the alarms of the Indians, a considerable
part of whom returned home, leaving only twenty-
eight men and three women. After the hunters
had been gone about an hour, Captain Lewis again
mounted with one of the Indians behind him, and
the whole party set out ; but just as they passed
through the narrows, they saw one of the spies
coming back at full speed across the plain : the
chief stopped and seemed uneasy, the whole band
were moved with fresh suspicions, and Captain
Lewis himself was much disconcerted, lest by some
unfortunate accident some of their enemies might
have, perhaps, straggled that way. The young
Indian had scarcely breath to say a few words as
he came up, when the whole troop dashed forward
as fast as their horses could carry them : and Captain Lewis astonished at this movement, was borne
along for nearly a mile before he learnt, with great
satisfaction, that it was all caused by the spy's having come to announce that one of the white men
had killed a deer. Relieved from his anxiety, he
now found the jolting very uncomfortable ; for the
Indian behind him, being afraid of not getting his
share of the feast, had lashed the horse at every
step since they set off; he therefore reined him in,
and ordered the Indian to stop beating him. The
fellow had no idea of losing time in disputing the

point, and jumping off the horse, ran for a mile at
full speed. Captain Lewis slackened his pace, and
followed at a sufficient distance to observe them.
When they reached the place where Drewyer
had thrown out the intestines, they all dismounted
in confusion, and ran tumbling over each other
like famished dogs : each tore away whatever part
he could, and instantly began to eat it : some
had the liver, some the kidneys, in short, no part
on which we are accustomed to look with disgust,
escaped them : one of them who had seized about
nine feet of the entrails, was chewing it at one
end, while with his hand he was diligently clearing
his way by discharging the contents at the other.
It was indeed impossible to see these wretches ra-
venously feeding on the filth of animals, and the
blood streaming from their mouths, without deplor-
ing how nearly the condition of savages approaches
that of the brute creation : yet, though suffering
with hunger, they did not attempt, as they might
have done, to take by force the whole deer, but
contented themselves with what had been thrown
away by the hunter. Captain Lewis now had the
deer skinned, and after reserving a quarter of it,
gave the rest of the animal to the chief to be divided among the Indians, who immediately devoured nearly the whole of it without cooking. They
now went forward towards the creek, where there
was some brushwood to make a fire, and found
Drewyer, who had killed a second deer : the same
struggle for the entrails was renewed here ; and on

giving nearly the whole deer to the Indians, they devoured it even to the soft part of the hoofs. A fire being made, Captain Lewis had his breakfast, during which Drewyer brought in a third deer: this too, after reserving one quarter, was given to the Indians, who now seemed completely satisfied, and in a good humour. At this place they remained about two hours, to let the horses graze, and then continued their journey; and towards evening reached the lower part of the cove, having on the way shot an antelope, the greater part of which was given to the Indians. As they were now approaching the place where they had been told by Captain Lewis they would see the white men, the chief insisted on halting: they, therefore, all dismounted, and Cameahwait, with great ceremony, and as if for ornament, put tippets or skins round the necks of our party, similar to those worn by themselves. As this was obviously intended to disguise the white men, Captain Lewis, in order to inspire them with more confidence, put his cocked hat and feather on the head of the chief, and as his own over-shirt was in the Indian form, and his skin browned by the sun, he could not have been distinguished from an Indian: the men followed his example, and the change seemed to be very agreeable to the Indians.

In order to guard, however, against any disappointment, Captain Lewis again explained the possibility of our not having reached the forks, in consequence of the difficulty of the navigation, so

that if they should not find us at that spot they
might be assured of our not being far below. They
again all mounted their horses and rode on rapidly,
making one of the Indians carry their flag, so that
we might recognise them as they approached us;
but to the mortification and disappointment of both
parties, on coming within two miles of the forks,
no canoes were to be seen. Uneasy lest at this
moment he should be abandoned, and all his hopes
of obtaining aid from the Indians be destroyed,
Captain Lewis gave the chief his gun, telling him
that if the enemies of his nation were in the bushes
he might defend himself with it; that for his own
part he was not afraid to die, and that the chief
might shoot him as soon as they discovered themselves betrayed. The other three men at the same
time gave their guns to the Indians, who now
seemed more easy, but still wavered in their re-
solutions. As they went on towards the point,
Captain Lewis perceiving how critical his situation
had become, resolved to attempt a stratagem which
his present difficulty seemed completely to justify.
Recollecting the notes he had left at the point for
us, he sent Drewyer for them with an Indian who
witnessed his taking them from the pole. When
they were brought, Captain Lewis told Cameahwait
that on leaving his brother chief at the place where
the river issues from the mountains, it was agreed
that the boats should not be brought higher than
the next forks we should meet; but that if the
rapid water prevented the boats from coming on

as fast as they expected, his brother chief was to
send a note to the first forks above him, to let him
know where the boats were ; that this note had
been left this morning at the forks, and mentioned
that the canoes were just below the mountains, and
coming slowly up in consequence of the current.
Captain Lewis added, that he would stay at the
forks for his brother chief, but would send a man
down the river, and that if Cameahwait doubted
what he said, one of their young men would go
with him whilst he and the other two remained at
the forks. This story satisfied the chief and the
greater part of the Indians, but a few did not
conceal their suspicions, observing that we told
different stories, and complaining that the chief
exposed them to danger by a mistaken confidence.
Captain Lewis now wrote by the light of some willow brush a note to Captain Clarke, which he gave
to Drewyer, with an order to use all possible expedition in descending the river, and engaged an Indian to accompany him by a promise of a knife
and some beads. At bed-time, the chief and five
others slept round the fire of Captain Lewis, and
the rest hid themselves in different parts of the
willow brush to avoid the enemy, who they feared
would attack them in the night. Captain Lewis
endeavoured to assume a cheerfulness he did not
feel, to prevent the desponde cy of the savages :
after conversing gayly with them, he retired to
his musquito bier, by the side of which the chief
now placed himself : he lay down, yet slept but

little, being in fact scarcely less uneasy than his Indian companions. He was apprehensive that, finding the ascent of the river impracticable, Captain Clarke might have stopped below the Rattlesnake bluff, and the messenger would not meet him. The consequence of disappointing the Indians at this moment would most probably be, that they would retire and secrete themselves in the mountains, so as to prevent our having an opportunity of recovering their confidence : they would also spread a panic through all the neighbouring Indians, and cut us off from the supply of horses so useful and almost so essential to our success : he was at the same time consoled by remembering that his hopes of assistance rested on better foundations than their generosity — their avarice, and their curiosity. He had promised liberal exchanges for their horses : but what was still more seductive, he had told them that one of their country-women who had been taken with the Minnetarees accompanied the party below ; and one of the men had spread the report of our having with us a man perfectly black, whose hair was short and curled. This last account had excited a great degree of curiosity, and they seemed more desirous of seeing this monster than of obtaining the most favourable barter for their horses.

In the meantime we had set out after breakfast, and although we proceeded with more ease than we did yesterday, the river was still so rapid and shallow as to oblige us to drag the large canoes during the greater part of the day. For the first seven miles the river formed a bend to the right, so as to make our advance only three miles in a straight line ; the stream is crooked, narrow, small, and shallow, with high lands occasionally on the banks, and strewed with islands, four of which are opposite to each other. Near this place we left the valley, to which we gave the name of Service-berry valley, from the abundance of that fruit, now ripe, which is found in it. In the course of the four following miles we passed several more islands and bayous on each side of the river, and reached a high cliff on the right. Two and a half miles beyond this the cliffs approach on both sides and form a very considerable rapid near the entrance of a bold running stream on the left. The water was now excessively cold, and the rapids had been frequent and troublesome. On ascending an eminence, Captain Clarke saw the forks of the river and sent the hunters up. They must have left it only a short time before Captain Lewis's arrival, but fortunately had not seen the note, which enabled him to induce the Indians to stay with him. From the top of this eminence he could discover only three trees through the whole country, nor was there, along the sides of the cliffs they had passed in the course of the day, any timber except a few small pines : the low grounds were supplied with willow, currant-bushes, and service-berries. After advancing half a mile further we came to the lower point of an island near the middle of the river,

and about the centre of the valley : here we halted
for the night, only four miles by land, though ten
by water, below the point where Captain Lewis
lay. Although we had made only fourteen miles,
the labours of the men had fatigued and exhausted them very much : we therefore collected
some small willow-brush for a fire, and lay down to
sleep.

CHAPTER XV.

AFFECTING INTERVIEW BETWEEN THE WIFE OF CHABONEAU
AND THE CHIEF OF THE SHOSHONEES — COUNCIL HELD
WITH THAT NATION, AND FAVOURABLE RESULT — THE
EXTREME NAVIGABLE POINT OF THE MISSOURI MEN-
TIONED — GENERAL CHARACTER OF THE RIVER AND OF
THE COUNTRY THROUGH WHICH IT PASSES — CAPTAIN
CLARKE IN EXPLORING THE SOURCE OF THE COLUMBIA
FALLS IN COMPANY WITH ANOTHER PARTY OF SHOSHO-
NEES — THE GEOGRAPHICAL INFORMATION ACQUIRED
FROM ONE OF THAT PARTY — THEIR MANNER OF CATCH-
ING FISH — THE PARTY REACH LEWIS RIVER — THE
DIFFICULTIES WHICH CAPTAIN CLARKE HAD TO ENCOUN-
TER IN HIS ROUTE — FRIENDSHIP AND HOSPITALITY OF
THE SHOSHONEES — THE PARTY WITH CAPTAIN LEWIS
EMPLOYED IN MAKING SADDLES, AND PREPARING FOR
THE JOURNEY.

SATURDAY, August 17. Captain Lewis rose
very early, and dispatched Drewyer and the
Indian down the river in quest of the boats. Shields
was sent out at the same time to hunt, while
M'Neal prepared a breakfast out of the remainder
of the meat. Drewyer had been gone about two
hours, and the Indians were all anxiously waiting
for some news, when an Indian who had straggled
a short distance down the river, returned with a

report that he had seen the white men, who were
only a short distance below, and were coming on.
The Indians were all transported with joy, and the
chief in the warmth of his satisfaction renewed his
embrace to Captain Lewis, who was quite as much
delighted as the Indians themselves, the report
proved most agreeably true. On setting out at
seven o'clock, Captain Clarke with Chaboneau and
his wife walked on shore, but they had not gone
more than a mile before Captain Clarke saw Sacajawea, who was with her husband one hundred
yards ahead, began to dance, and show every mark
of the most extravagant joy, turning round to him
and pointing to several Indians, whom he now saw
advancing on horseback, sucking her fingers
at the same time, to indicate that they were of
her native tribe. As they advanced Captain Clarke
discovered among them Drewyer dressed like an
Indian, from whom he learnt the situation of the
party. While the boats were performing the circuit, he went towards the forks with the Indians,
who as they went along, sang aloud with the
greatest appearance of delight. We soon drew
near to the camp, and just as we approached it a
woman made her way through the crowd towards
Sacajawea, and recognising each other, they embraced with the most tender affection. The meeting of these two young women had in it something
peculiarly touching, not only in the ardent manner
in which their feelings were expressed, but from the
real interest of their situation. They had been

companions in childhood, in the war with the Minnetarees they had both been taken prisoners in the
same battle, they had shared and softened the rigours of their captivity, till one of them had escaped from the Minnetarees, with scarce a hope of
ever seeing her friend relieved from the hands of
her enemies. While Sacajawea was renewing
among the women the friendships of former days,
Captain Clarke went on, and was received by Captain Lewis and the chief, who after the first embraces and salutations were over, conducted him
to a sort of circular tent or shade of willows.
Here he was seated on a white robe ; and the
chief immediately tied in his hair six small shells
resembling pearls, an ornament highly valued by
these people, who procured them in the course of
trade from the sea-coast. The moccasins of the
whole party were then taken off, and after much
ceremony the smoking began. After this the conference was to be opened, and glad of an opportunity of being able to converse more intelligibly,
Sacajawea was sent for ; she came into the tent,
sat down, and was beginning to interpret, when
in the person of Cameahwait she recognised her
brother : she instantly jumped up, and ran and
embraced him, throwing over him a blanket and
weeping profusely : the chief was himself moved,
though not in the same degree. After some conversation between them, she resumed her seat, and
attempted to interpret for us, but her new situation
seemed to overpower her, and she was frequently

interrupted by her tears. After the council was finished, the unfortunate woman learnt that all her family were dead except two brothers, one of whom was absent, and a son of her eldest sister, a small boy who was immediately adopted by her. The canoes arriving soon after, we formed a camp in a meadow on the left side, a little below the forks ; took out our baggage, and by means of our sails and willow poles formed a canopy for our Indian visitors. About four o'clock the chiefs and warriors were collected, and after the customary ceremony of taking off the moccasins and smoking a pipe, we explained to them in a long harangue the purposes of our visit, making themselves one conspicuous object of the good wishes of our government, on whose strength as well as its friendly disposition we expatiated. We told them of their dependence on the will of our government for all future supplies of whatever was necessary either for their comfort or defence ; that as we were sent to discover the best route by which merchandize could be conveyed to them, and no trade would be begun before our return, it was mutually advantageous that we should proceed with as little delay as possible ; that we were under the necessity of requesting them to furnish us with horses to transport our baggage across the mountains, and a guide to shew us the route, but that they should be amply remunerated for their horses, as well as for every other service they should render us. In the meantime our first wish was, that they should immediately collect as many horses as were necessary to transport our baggage to their village, where, at our leisure, we would trade with them for as many horses as they could spare.

The speech made a favourable impression : the chief in reply thanked us for our expressions of friendship towards himself and his nation, and declared their willingness to render us every service. He lamented that it would be so long before they should be supplied with fire-arms, but that till then they could subsist as they had heretofore done. He concluded by saying that there were not horses here sufficient to transport our goods, but that he would return to the village to-morrow, and bring all his own horses, and encourage his people to come over with theirs. The conference being ended to our satisfaction, we now inquired of Cameahwait what chiefs were among the party, and he pointed out two of them. We then distributed our presents : to Cameahwait we gave a medal of the small size, with the likeness of President Jefferson, and on the reverse a figure of hands clasped with a pipe and a tomahawk : to this was added an uniform coat, a shirt, a pair of scarlet leggings, a carrot of tobacco, and some small articles. Each of the other chiefs received a small medal struck during the presidency of General Washington, a shirt, handkerchief, leggings, a knife, and some tobacco. Medals of the same sort were also presented to two young warriors, who, though not chiefs, were promising youths, and very much respected in the tribe. These honorary gifts were followed by presents of paint, moccasins, awls, knives, beads, and looking-glasses. We also gave them all a plentiful meal of Indian corn, of which the hull is taken off by being boiled in lye; and as this was the first they had ever tasted, they were very much pleased with it. They had indeed abundant sources of surprise in all they saw : the appearance of the men, their arms, their clothing, the canoes, the strange looks of the negro, and the sagacity of our dog, all in turn shared their admiration, which was raised to astonishment by a shot from the air-gun : this operation was instantly considered as *a great medicine*, by which they, as well as the other Indians, mean something emanating directly from the Great Spirit, or produced by his invisible and incomprehensible agency. The display of all these riches had been intermixed with inquiries into the geographical situation of their country; for we had learnt by experience, that to keep the savages in good temper their attention should not be wearied with too much business; but that the serious affairs should be enlivened by a mixture of what is new and entertaining. Our hunters brought in very seasonably four deer and an antelope, the last of which we gave to the Indians, who in a very short time devoured it. After the council was over, we consulted as to our future operations. The game does not promise to last here for a number of days, and this circum-

stance combined with many others to induce our
going on as soon as possible. Our Indian information as to the state of the Columbia is of a very
alarming kind, and our first object is of course to
ascertain the practicability of descending it, of
which the Indians discourage our expectations. It
was therefore agreed that Captain Clarke should set
off in the morning with eleven men, furnished, besides their arms, with tools for making canoes : that
he should take Chaboneau and his wife to the camp
of the Shoshonees, where he was to leave them, in
order to hasten the collection of horses; that he
was then to lead his men down to the Columbia,
and if he found it navigable, and the timber in
sufficient quantity, begin to build canoes. As soon
as he had decided as to the propriety of proceeding down the Columbia or across the mountains,
he was to send back one of the men with information of it to Captain Lewis, who by that time would
have brought up the whole party, and the rest of
the baggage as far as the Shoshonee village.

Preparations were accordingly made this evening
for such an arrangement. The sun is excessively
hot in the day time, but the nights very cold, and
rendered still more unpleasant from the want of any
fuel except willow brush. The appearances too of
game, for many days' subsistence, are not very favourable.

Sunday, 18. In order to relieve the men of
Captain Clarke's party from the heavy weight of
their arms, provisions, and tools, we exposed a few

articles to barter for horses, and soon obtained three
very good ones, in exchange for which we gave a
uniform coat, a pair of leggings, a few handkerchiefs, three knives, and some other small articles,
the whole of which did not in the United States
cost more than twenty dollars: a fourth was purchased by the men for an old checkered shirt, a
pair of old leggings, and a knife. The Indians
seemed to be quite as well pleased as ourselves at
the bargains they had made. We now found that
the two inferior chiefs were somewhat displeased
at not having received a present equal to that given
to the great chief, who appeared in a dress so much
finer than their own. To allay their discontent, we
bestowed on them two old coats, and promised
them that if they were active in assisting us across
the mountains they should have an additional present. This treatment completely reconciled them,
and the whole Indian party, except two men and
two women, set out in perfect good humour to
return home with Captain Clarke. After going
fifteen miles through a wide level valley with no
wood but willows and shrubs, he encamped in the
Shoshonee cove, near a narrow pass where the highlands approach within two hundred yards of each
other, and the river is only ten yards wide. The
Indians went on further, except the three chiefs
and two young men, who assisted in eating two
deer brought in by the hunters. After their departure every thing was prepared for the trans-
portation of the baggage, which was now exposed

to the air and dried. Our game was one deer and a beaver, and we saw an abundance of trout in the river, for which we fixed a net in the evening.

We have now reached the extreme navigable point of the Missouri, which our observation places in latitude 43° 30′ 43″ north. It is difficult to comprise in any general description the characteristics of a river so extensive, and fed by so many streams which have their sources in a great variety of soils and climates. But the Missouri is still sufficiently powerful to give to all its waters something of a common character, which is of course decided by the nature of the country through which it passes. The bed of the river is chiefly composed of a blue mud, from which the water itself derives a deep tinge. From its junction here to the place near which it leaves the mountains, its course is embarrassed by rapids and rocks which the hills on each side have thrown into its channel. From that place, its current, with the exception of the Falls, is not difficult of navigation, nor is there much variation in its appearance till the mouth of the Platte. That powerful river throws out vast quantities of coarse sand, which contribute to give a new face to the Missouri, which is now much more impeded by islands. The sand, as it is drifted down, adheres in time to some of the projecting points from the shore, and forms a barrier to the mud, which at length fills to the same height with the sandbar itself: as soon as it has acquired a consistency, the willow grows there the first year, and by its roots assists the solidity of the whole : as the mud and sand accumulate the cotton-wood tree next appears ; till the gradual excretion of soils raises the surface of the point above the highest freshets. Thus stopped in its course the water seeks a passage elsewhere, and as the soil on each side is light and yielding, what was only a peninsula, becomes gradually an island, and the river indemnifies itself for the usurpation by encroaching on the adjacent shore. In this way the Missouri, like the Mississippi, is constantly cutting off the projections of the shore, and leaving its ancient channel, which is then marked by the mud it has deposited, and a few stagnant ponds.

The general appearance of the country as it presents itself on ascending may be thus described. From its mouth to the two Charletons, a ridge of highlands borders the river at a small distance, leaving between them fine rich meadows. From the mouth of the two Charletons the hills recede from the river, giving greater extent to the low grounds, but they again approach the river for a short distance near Grand river, and again at Snake creek. From that point they retire, nor do they come again to the neighbourhood of the river till above the Sauk prairie, where they are comparatively low and small. Thence they diverge and reappear at the Charaton Searty, after which they are scarcely, if at all discernible, till they advance to the Missouri, nearly opposite to the Kanzas.

The same ridge of hills extends on the south side, in almost one unbroken chain, from the

mouth of the Missouri to the Kanzas, though de-
creasing in height beyond the Osage. As they are
nearer the river than the hills on the opposite sides,
the intermediate low grounds are of course narrower, but the general character of the soil is common to both sides.

In the meadows and along the shore, the tree
most common is the cotton-wood, which with the
willow forms almost the exclusive growth of the
Missouri. The hills, or rather high grounds, for
they do not rise higher than from one hundred and
fifty to two hundred feet, are composed of a good
rich black soil, which is perfectly susceptible of
cultivation, though it becomes richer on the hills
beyond the Platte, and are in general thinly covered with timber. Beyond these hills the country
extends into high open plains, which are on both
sides sufficiently fertile, but the south has the advantage of better streams of water, and may therefore
be considered as preferable for settlements. The
lands, however, become much better, and the timber more abundant between the Osage and the
Kanzas. From the Kanzas to the Nadawa the
hills continue at nearly an equal distance, varying
from four to eight miles from each other, except
that from the little Platte to nearly opposite the
ancient Kanzas village, the hills are more remote,
and the meadows of course wider on the north side
of the river. From the Nadawa the northern hills
disappear, except at occasional intervals, where
they are seen at a distance, till they return
about twenty-seven miles above the Platte, near

the ancient village of the Ayoways. On the
south the hills continue close to the river from
the ancient village of the Kanzas up to Council bluff, fifty miles beyond the Platte; forming
high prairie lands. On both sides the lands are
good, and perhaps this distance from the Osage to
the Platte may be recommended as among the
best districts on the Missouri for the purposes
of settlers.

From the Ayoway village the northern hills
again retire from the river, to which they do not
return till three hundred and twenty miles above,
at Floyd's river. The hills on the south also leave
the river at Council bluffs, and re-appear at the
Mahar village, two hundred miles up the Missouri.
The country thus abandoned by the hills is more
open, and the timber in smaller quantities than below the Platte, so that although the plain is rich,
and covered with high grass, the want of wood
renders it less calculated for cultivation than below
that river.

The northern hills, after remaining near the
Missouri for a few miles at Floyd's river, recede
from it at the Sioux river, the course of which
they follow : and though they again visit the Missouri at Whitestone river, where they are low, yet
they do not return to it till beyond James river.
The highlands on the south, after continuing near
the river at the Mahar villages, again disappear,
and do not approach it till the Cobalt bluffs, about
forty-four miles from the villages, and then from

those bluffs to the Yellowstone river, a distance of about one thousand miles, they follow the banks of the river with scarcely any deviation.

From the James river, the lower grounds are confined within a narrow space by the hills on both sides, which now continue near each other up to the mountains. The space between them however varies from one to three miles as high as the Muscle-shell river, from which the hills approach so high as to leave scarcely any low grounds on the river, and near the Falls reach the water's edge. Beyond the Falls the hills are scattered and low to the first range of mountains.

The soil, during the whole length of the Mis-souri below the Platte, is, generally speaking, very fine, and although the timber is scarce, there is still sufficient for the purposes of settlers. But beyond that river, although the soil is still rich, yet the almost total absence of timber, and particularly the want of good water, of which there is but a small quantity in the creeks, and even that brackish, oppose powerful obstacles to its settlement. The difficulty becomes still greater between the Muscle-shell river and the Falls, where, besides the greater scarcity of timber, the country itself is less fertile.

The elevation of these highlands varies as they pass through this extensive tract of country. From Wood river they are about one hundred and fifty feet above the water, and continue at that height till they rise near the Osage, from which place to the ancient fortification, they again diminish in size. Thence they continue higher till the Mandan village, after which they are rather lower till the neighbourhood of Muscle-shell river, where they are met by the Northern hills, which have advanced at a more uniform height, varying from one hundred and fifty to two hundred or three hundred feet. From this place to the mountains the height of both is nearly the same, from three hundred to five hundred feet, and the low grounds so narrow that the traveller seems passing through a range of high country. From Maria's river to the Falls, the hills descend to the height of about two or three hundred feet.

Monday, 19. This morning was cold, and the grass perfectly whitened by the frost. We were engaged in preparing packs and saddles to load the horses as soon as they should arrive. A beaver was caught in a trap, but we were disappointed in trying to catch trout in our net ; we therefore made a seine of willow brush, and by hauling it procured a number of fine trout, and a species of mullet which we had not seen before : it is about sixteen inches long, the scales small ; the nose long, obtusely pointed, and exceeding the under jaw ; the mouth opens with folds at the sides ; it has no teeth, and the tongue and palate are smooth. The colour of its back and sides is a blueish-brown, while the belly is white : it has the faggot bones, whence we concluded it to be of the mullet species. It is by no means so well flavoured a fish as the trout, which are the same as those we first saw at the Falls, larger than the speckled trout of the mountains in the Atlantic states, and equally well flavoured. In the evening the hunters returned with two deer.

Captain Clarke, in the meantime, proceeded through a wide level valley, in which the chief pointed out a spot where many of his tribe were killed in battle a year ago. The Indians accompanied him during the day, and as they had nothing to eat, he was obliged to feed them from his own stores, the hunters not being able to kill any thing. Just as he was entering the mountains, he met an Indian with two mules and a Spanish saddle, who was so polite as to offer one of them to him to ride over the hills. Being on foot, Captain Clarke accepted his offer, and gave him a waistcoat as a reward for his civility. He encamped for the night on a small stream, and the next morning,

Tuesday, August 20, he set out at six o'clock. In passing through a continuation of the hilly broken country, he met several parties of Indians. On coming near the camp, which had been removed since we left them two miles higher up the river, Cameahwait request that the party should halt. This was complied with : a number of Indians came out from the camp, and with great ceremony several pipes were smoked. This being over, Captain Clarke was conducted to a large leathern lodge prepared for his party in the middle of the encampment, the Indians having only shelters of willow bushes. A few dried berries, and one sal-

mon, the only food the whole village could contribute, were then presented to him ; after which
he proceeded to repeat in council, what had been
already told them, the purposes of his visit : urged
them to take their horses over and assist in transporting our baggage, and expressed a wish to obtain a guide to examine the river. This was explained and enforced to the whole village by Cameahwait, and an old man was pointed out who was
said to know more of their geography to the north
than any other person, and whom Captain Clarke
engaged to accompany him. After explaining his
views he distributed a few presents, the council
was ended, and nearly half the village set out to
hunt the antelope, but returned without success.

Captain Clarke in the meantime made particular
inquiries as to the situation of the country, and
the possibility of soon reaching a navigable water.
The chief began by drawing on the ground a delineation of the rivers, from which it appeared that
his information was very limited. The river on
which the camp is he divided into two branches
just above us, which, as he indicated by the opening of the mountains, were in view : he next made
it discharge itself into a large river ten miles below, coming from the south-west : the joint-stream
continued one day's march to the north-west, and
then inclined to the westward for two days march
farther. At that place he placed several heaps of
sand on each side, which, as he explained them,
represented vast mountains of rock always covered

with snow, in passing through which the river was
so completely hemmed in by the high rocks, that
there was no possibility of travelling along the
shore ; that the bed of the river was obstructed by
sharp-pointed rocks, and such its rapidity, that as
far as the eye could reach it presented a perfect
column of foam. The mountains, he said, were
equally inaccessible, as neither man nor horse could
cross them ; that such being the state of the country neither he nor any of his nation had ever attempted to go beyond the mountains. Cameahwait
said also that he had been informed by the Chopunnish, or Pierced-nose Indians, who reside on
this river west of the mountains, that it ran a great
way towards the setting sun, and at length lost
itself in a great lake of water which was ill tasted,
and where the white men lived. An Indian belonging to a band of Shoshonees who lived to the
south-west, and who happened to be at camp, was
then brought in, and inquiries made of him as to
the situation of the country in that direction :
this he described in terms scarcely less terrible
than those in which Cameahwait had represented the west. He said that his relations lived
at the distance of twenty days march from this
place, on a course a little to the west of south
and not far from the whites, with whom they
traded for horses, mules, cloth, metal, beads,
and the shells here worn as ornaments, and which
are those of a species of pearl oyster. In order to
reach his country we should be obliged during the

first seven days to climb over steep rocky mountains where there was no game, and we should find nothing but roots for subsistence. Even for these, however, we should be obliged to contend with a fierce warlike people, whom he called the Broken-moccasin, or moccasin with holes, who lived like bears in holes, and fed on roots and the flesh of such horses as they could steal or plunder from those who passed through the mountains. So rough, indeed, was the passage, that the feet of the horses would be wounded in such a manner that many of them would be unable to proceed. The next part of the route was for ten days, through a dry parched desert of sand, inhabited by no animal which would supply us with subsistence, and as the sun had now scorched up the grass and dried up the small pools of water which are sometimes scattered through this desert in the spring, both ourselves and our horses would perish for want of food and water. About the middle of this plain, a large river passes from south-east to north-west, which, though navigable, afforded neither timber nor salmon. Three or four days march beyond this plain, his relations lived, in a country tolerably fertile and partially covered with timber, on another large river running in the same direction as the former; that this last discharges itself into a third large river, on which resided many numerous nations, with whom his own were at war, but whether this last emptied itself into the great or stinking lake, as they called the ocean, he did not know;

that from his country to the stinking lake was a great distance, and that the route to it, taken by such of his relations as had visited it, was up the river on which they lived, and over to that on which the white people lived, and which they knew discharged itself into the ocean. This route he advised us to take, but added, that we had better defer the journey till spring, when he would himself conduct us. This account persuaded us that the streams of which he spoke were southern branches of the Columbia, heading with the Rio des Apostolos, and Rio Colorado, and that the route which he mentioned was to the gulf of California : Captain Clarke therefore told him, that this road was too much towards the south for our purpose, and then requested to know if there was no route on the left of the river where we now are, by which we might intercept it below the mountains ; but he knew of none except that through the barren plains, which he said joined the mountains on that side, and through which it was impossible to pass at this season, even if we were fortunate enough to escape the Broken-moccasin Indians. Captain Clarke recompensed the Indian by a present of a knife, with which he seemed much gratified, and now inquired of Cameahwait by what route the Pierced-nose Indians, who, he said, lived west of the mountains, crossed over to the Missouri : this, he said, was towards the north, but that the road was a very bad one ; that during the passage, he had been told, they suffered excessively from hunger, being obliged to subsist for many days on berries alone, there being no game in that part of the mountains, which were broken and rocky, and so thickly covered with timber that they could scarcely pass. Surrounded by difficulties, as all the other routes are, this seems to be the most practicable of all the passages by land, since, if the Indians can pass the mountains with their women and children, no difficulties which they could encounter could be formidable to us ; and if the Indians below the mountains are so numerous as they are represented to be, they must have some means of subsistence equally within our power. They tell us, indeed, that the nations to the westward subsist principally on fish and roots, and that their only game were a few elk, deer, and antelope, there being no buffaloe west of the mountain. The first inquiry, however, was to ascertain the truth of their information relative to the difficulty of descending the river : for this purpose Captain Clarke set out at three o'clock in the afternoon, accompanied by the guide and all his men, except one, whom he left with orders to purchase a horse and join him as soon as possible. At the distance of four miles, he crossed the river, and eight miles from the camp, halted for the night at a small stream. The road which he followed was a beaten path through a wide rich meadow, in which were several old lodges. On the route, he met a number of men, women, and children, as well as horses; and one of the men, who appeared to possess some consideration, turned back with him, and observing a woman with three salmon, obtained them from her, and presented them to the party. Captain Clarke shot a mountain cock, or cock of the plains, a dark brown bird larger than the dunghill fowl, with a long and pointed tail, and a fleshy protuberance about the base of the upper chop, something like that of the turkey, though without the snout. In the morning,

Wednesday 21, he resumed his march early, and at the distance of five miles reached an Indian lodge of brush, inhabited by seven families of Shoshonees. They behaved with great civility, gave the whole party as much boiled salmon as they could eat, and added as a present several dried salmon and a considerable quantity of choke-cherries. After smoking with them all, he visited the fish weir, which was about two hundred yards distant; the river was here divided by three small islands, which occasioned the water to pass along four channels. Of these, three were narrow, and stopped by means of trees, which were stretched across, and supported by willow stakes, sufficiently near each other to prevent the passage of the fish. About the centre of each was placed a basket formed of willows, eighteen or twenty feet in length, of a cylindrical form, and terminating in a conic shape at its lower extremity; this was situated with its mouth upwards, opposite to an aperture in the weir. The main channel of the water was then conducted to this weir, and as the fish entered it they were so entangled with each other that they could not move, and were taken out by untying the small end of the willow basket. The weir in the main channel was formed in a manner somewhat different; there were in fact two distinct weirs formed of poles and willow sticks quite across the river, approaching each other obliquely with an aperture in each side near the angle. This is made by tying a number of poles together at the top, in parcels of three, which were then set up in a triangular form at the base, two of the poles being in the range desired for the weir, and the third down the stream. To these poles two ranges of other poles are next lashed horizontally, with willow bark and withes, and willow sticks joined in with these crosswise, so as to form a kind of wicker-work from the bottom of the river to the height of three or four feet above the surface of the water. This is so thick as to prevent the fish from passing, and even in some parts, with the help of a little gravel and some stone, enables them to give any direction which they wish to the water. These two weirs being placed near to each other, one for the purpose of catching the fish as they ascend, the other as they go down the river, are provided with two baskets made in the form already described, and which are placed at the apertures of the weir.

After examining these curious objects, he returned to the lodges, and soon passed the river to the left, where an Indian brought him a tomahawk, which he said he had found in the grass, near the lodge where Captain Lewis had staid on his first visit to the village. This was a tomahawk which had been missed at the time, and supposed to be stolen; it was, however, the only article which had been lost in our intercourse with the nation, and as even that was returned, the inference is highly honourable to the integrity of the Shoshonees. On leaving the lodges, Captain Clarke crossed to the left side of the river, and dispatched five men to the forks of it in search of the man left behind yesterday, who procured a horse, and passed by another road, as they learnt, to the forks. At the distance of fourteen miles, they killed a very large salmon, two and a half feet long, in a creek six miles below the forks: and after travelling about twenty miles through the valley, following the course of the river, which runs nearly northwest, halted in a small meadow on the right side, under a cliff of rocks. Here they were joined by the five men who had gone in quest of Crusatte. They had been to the forks of the river, where the natives resort in great numbers for the purpose of gigging fish, of which they made our men a present of five fresh salmon. In addition to this food, one deer was killed to-day. The western branch of this river is much larger than the eastern, and after we passed the junction, we found the river about one hundred yards in width, rapid and and shoally, but containing only a small quantity of timber. As Captain Lewis was the first white man who visited its waters, Captain Clarke gave it the

name of Lewis's river. The low grounds through
which he had passed to-day were rich and wide,
but at his camp this evening the hills begin to assume a formidable aspect. The cliff under which
he lay is of a reddish-brown colour; the rocks
which have fallen from it, are a dark brown
flint-stone. Near the place are gullies of white
sand-stone, and quantities of a fine sand, of a snowy
whiteness: the mountains on each side are high
and rugged, with some pine trees scattered over
them.

Thursday, 22. He soon began to perceive that
the Indian accounts had not exaggerated: at the
distance of a mile he passed a small creek, and the
points of four mountains, which were rocky, and
so high that it seemed almost impossible to cross
them with horses. The road lay over the sharp
fragments of rocks which had fallen from the
mountains, and were strewed in heaps for miles
together; yet the horses, altogether unshod, travelled across them as fast as the men, and without
detaining them a moment. They passed two bold
running streams, and reached the entrance of a
small river, where a few Indian families resided.
They had not been previously acquainted with the
arrival of the whites, the guide was behind, and
the wood so thick, that we came upon them unobserved, till at a very short distance. As soon as
they saw us, the women and children fled in great
consternation: the men offered us every thing they
had, the fish on the scaffolds, the dried berries and

the collars of elks' tushes worn by the children.
We took only a small quantity of the food, and
gave them in return some small articles, which con-
duced very much to pacify them. The guide now
coming up, explained to them who we were, and
the object of our visit, which seemed to relieve
their fears, but still a number of the women and
children did not recover from their fright, but
cried during our stay, which lasted about an hour.
The guide, whom we found a very intelligent
friendly old man, informed us, that up this river
there was a road which led over the mountains to
the Missouri. On resuming his route, Captain
Clarke went along the steep side of a mountain
about three miles, and then reached the river near
a small island, at the lower part of which he encamped; he here attempted to gig some fish, but
could only obtain one small salmon. The river is
here shoal and rapid, with many rocks scattered in
various directions through its bed. On the sides
of the mountains are some scattered pines, and of
those on the left the tops are covered with them;
there are, however, but few in the low grounds
through which they passed; indeed they have seen
only a single tree fit to make a canoe, and even
that was small. The country has an abundant
growth of berries, and we met several women and
children gathering them, who bestowed them upon
us with great liberality. Among the woods Captain Clarke observed a species of woodpecker, the
beak and tail of which were white, the wings black,

and every other part of the body of a dark brown ; its size was that of the robin, and it fed on the seeds of the pine.

Friday 23. Captain Clarke set off very early, but as his route lay along the steep side of a mountain, over irregular and broken masses of rocks, which wounded the horses' feet, he was obliged to proceed slowly. At the distance of four miles he reached the river, but the rocks here became so steep, and projected so far into the river, that there was no mode of passing, except through the water. This he did for some distance, though the river was very rapid, and so deep that they were forced to swim their horses. After following the edge of the water for about a mile under this steep cliff, he reached a small meadow, below which the whole current of the river beat against the right shore on which he was, and which was formed of a solid rock perfectly inaccessible to horses. Here, too, the little track which he had been pursuing terminated. He therefore resolved to leave the horses, and the greater part of the men, at this place, and examine the river still further, in order to determine if there were any possibility of descending it in canoes. Having killed nothing except a single goose to-day, and the whole of our provision being consumed last evening, it was by no means adviseable to remain any length of time where they were. He now directed the men to fish and hunt at this place till his return, and then with his guide and three men he proceeded, clambering over immense rocks, and along the sides of lofty precipices which bordered the river, when at about twelve miles distance he reached a small meadow, the first he had seen on the river since he left his party. A little below this meadow, a large creek twelve yards wide, and of some depth, discharges itself from the north. Here were some recent signs of an Indian encampment, and the tracks of a number of horses, who must have come along a plain Indian path, which he now saw following the course of the creek. This stream his guide said led towards a large river running to the north, and was frequented by another nation for the purpose of catching fish. He remained here two hours, and having taken some small fish, made a dinner on them, with the addition of a few berries. From the place where he had left the party, to the mouth of this creek, the river presents one continued rapid, in which are five shoals, neither of which could be passed with loaded canoes ; and the baggage must therefore be transported for a considerable distance over the steep mountains, where it would be impossible to employ horses for the relief of the men. Even the empty canoes must be let down the rapids by means of cords, and not even in that way without great risk both to the canoes as well as to the men. At one of these shoals, indeed, the rocks rise so perpendicularly from the water as to leave no hope of a passage or even a portage without great labour in removing rocks, and in some instances cutting away the earth. To surmount

these difficulties would exhaust the strength of the
party, and, what is equally discouraging, would
waste our time and consume our provisions, of
neither of which we have much to spare. The
season is now far advanced, and the Indians tell us
we shall shortly have snow : the salmon too have
so far declined that the natives themselves are
hastening from the country, and not an animal of
any kind larger than a pheasant or a squirrel, and
of even these a few only, will then be seen in this
part of the mountains; after which we shall be
obliged to rely on our own stock of provisions,
which will not support us more than ten days.
These circumstances combine to render a passage
by water impracticable in our present situation.
To descend the course of the river on horseback is
the other alternative, and scarcely a more inviting
one. The river is so deep that there are only a few
places where it can be forded, and the rocks approach so near the water as to render it impossible
to make a route along the water's edge. In crossing the mountains themselves we should have to
encounter, besides their steepness, one barren surface of broken masses of rock, down which in certain seasons the torrents sweep vast quantities of
stone into the river. These rocks are of a whitish-
brown, and towards the base of a grey colour, and
so hard, that on striking them with steel, they yield
a fire like flint. This sombre appearance is in some
places scarcely relieved by a single tree, though
near the river and on the creeks there is more

timber, among which are some tall pine: several
of these might be made into canoes, and by lashing
two of them together, one of a tolerable size might
be formed.

After dinner he continued his route, and at the
distance of half a mile passed another creek about
five yards wide. Here his guide informed him that
by ascending the creek for some distance he would
have a better road, and cut off a considerable bend
of the river towards the south. He therefore pursued a well-beaten Indian track up this creek for
about six miles, when leaving the creek to the
right he passed over a ridge, and after walking a
mile, again met the river, where it flows through a
meadow of about sixty acres in extent. This they
passed, and then ascended a high and steep point
of a mountain, from which the guide now pointed
out where the river broke through the mountains,
about twenty miles distant. Near the base of the
mountains a small river falls in from the south:
this view was terminated by one of the loftiest
mountains Captain Clarke had ever seen, which was
perfectly covered with snow. Towards this formidable barrier the river went directly on, and
there it was, as the guide observed, that the difficulties and dangers of which he and Cameahwait
had spoken, commenced. After reaching the
mountain, he said, the river continues its course
towards the north for many miles, between high
perpendicular rocks, which were scattered through
its bed: it then penetrated the mountain through

a narrow gap, on each side of which arose perpendicularly, a rock as high as the top of the mountain
before them; that the river then made a bend
which concealed its future course from view; and
as it was alike impossible to descend the river, or
clamber over that vast mountain, eternally covered
with snow, neither he nor any of his nation had
ever been lower than a place whence they could
see the gap made by the river on entering the
mountain. To that place he said he would conduct Captain Clarke, if he desired it, by the next
evening. But he was in need of no further evi-
dence to convince him of the utter impracticability
of the route before him. He had already witnessed the difficulties of part of the road, yet after
all these dangers, his guide, whose intelligence
and fidelity he could not doubt, now assured him
that the difficulties were only commencing, and
what he saw before him too clearly convinced him
of the ndian's veracity. He therefore determined
to abandon this route, and returned to the upper
part of the last creek he had passed, and reaching
it an hour after dark, encamped for the night: on
this creek he had seen, in the morning, an Indian
road coming in from the north. Disappointed in
finding a route by water, Captain Clarke now ques-
tioned his guide more particularly as to the direction of this road, which he seemed to understand
perfectly. He drew a map on the sand, and represented this road, as well as that we passed
yesterday on Berry creek, as both leading towards

two forks of the same great river, where resided a nation called Tushepaws, who having no salmon on their river, came by these roads to the fish weirs on Lewis's river. He had himself been among these Tushepaws, and having once accompanied them on a fishing party to another river, he had there seen Indians who had come across the Rocky mountains. After a great deal of conversation, or rather signs, and a second and more particular map from his guide, Captain Clarke felt persuaded that his guide knew of a road from the Shoshonee village they had left, to the great river to the north, without coming so low down as this, on a route impracticable for horses. He was desirous of hastening his return, and therefore set out early,

Saturday 24, and after descending the creek to the river, stopped to breakfast on berries, in the meadow above the second creek. He then went on, but unfortunately fell from a rock and injured his leg very much; he however walked on as rapidly as he could, and at four in the afternoon rejoined his men. During his absence they had killed one of the mountain cocks, a few pheasants, and some small fish, on which, with haws and service-berries, they had subsisted. Captain Clarke immediately sent forward a man on horseback, with a note to Captain Lewis, apprising him of the result of his inquiries, and late in the afternoon set out with the rest of the party, and encamped at the distance of two miles. The men were much disheartened at the bad prospect of escaping from the mountains, and having nothing to eat but a few berries, which have made several of them sick, they all passed a disagreeable night, which was rendered more uncomfortable by a heavy dew.

Sunday, 25. The want of provisions urged Captain Clarke to return as soon as possible ; he therefore set out early, and halted an hour in passing the Indian camp, near the fish weirs. These people treated them with great kindness, and though poor and dirty, they willingly give what little they possess ; they gave the whole party boiled salmon and dried berries, which were not however in sufficient quantities to appease their hunger. They soon resumed their old road, but as the abstinence, or strange diet, had given one of the men a very severe illness, they were detained very much on his account, and it was not till late in the day they reached the cliff, under which they had encamped on the twenty-first. They immediately began to fish and hunt, in order to procure a meal. We caught several small fish, and by means of our guide, obtained two salmon from a small party of women and children, who, with one man, were going below to gather berries. This supplied us with about half a meal, but after dark we were regaled with a beaver, which one of the hunters brought in. The other game seen in the course of the day, were one deer, and a party of elk among the pines on the sides of the mountains.

Monday, 26. The morning was fine, and three men were dispatched a-head to hunt while the

rest were detained until nine o'clock, in order to
retake some horses which had strayed away during
the night. They then proceeded along the route
by the forks of the river, till they reached the
lower Indian camp, where they first were when we
met them. The whole camp immediately flocked
around him with great appearance of cordiality,
but all the spare food of the village did not
amount to more than two salmon, which they gave
to Captain Clarke, who distributed them among
his men. The hunters had not been able to kill
any thing, nor had Captain Clarke, or the greater
part of the men, any food during the twenty-four
hours, till towards evening one of them shot a salmon in the river, and a few small fish were caught,
which furnished them with a scanty meal. The
only animals they had seen were a few pigeons,
some very wild hares, a great number of the
large black grasshopper, and a quantity of ground
lizards.

Tuesday, 27. The men who were engaged last
night in mending their moccasins, all, except one,
went out hunting, but no game was procured. One
of the men, however, killed a small salmon, and
the Indians made him a present of another, on which
the whole party made a very slight breakfast.
These Indians, to whom this life is familiar, seem
contented, although they depend for subsistence
on the scanty productions of the fishery. But our
men, who are used to hardships, but have been
accustomed to have the first wants of nature re-

gularly supplied, feel very sensibly their wretched situation; their strength is wasting away; they begin to express their apprehensions of being without food, in a country perfectly destitute of any means of supporting life, except a few fish. In the course of the day an Indian brought into the camp five salmon, two of which Captain Clarke bought, and made a supper for the party.

Wednesday, 28. There was a frost again this morning. The Indians gave the party two salmon, out of several which they caught in their traps, and having purchased two more, the party was enabled to subsist on them during the day. A camp of about forty Indians from the west fork passed us to-day, on their route to the eastward. Our prospect of provisions is getting worse every day: the hunters who had ranged through the country in every direction where game might be reasonably expected, have seen nothing. The fishery is scarcely more productive, for an Indian who was out all day with his gig, killed only one salmon. Besides the four fish procured from the Indians, Captain Clarke obtained some fish-roe in exchange for three small fish-hooks, the use of which he taught them, and which they very readily comprehended. All the men who are not engaged in hunting, are occupied in making pack-saddles for the horses, which Captain Lewis informed us he had bought.

August 29. Two hunters were dispatched early in the morning, but they returned without killing any thing, and the only game we procured was a beaver, who was caught last night in a trap; which he carried off two miles before he was found. The fur of this animal is as good as any we have ever seen, nor does it in fact appear to be ever out of season on the upper branches of the Missouri. This beaver, with several dozen of fine trout, gave us a plentiful subsistence for the day. The party were occupied chiefly in making pack-saddles, in the manufacture of which, we supply the place of nails and boards, by substituting for the first thongs of raw hide, which answer very well; and for boards we use the handles of our oars, and the plank of some boxes, the contents of which we empty into sacks of raw hides made for the purpose. The Indians who visit us behave with the greatest decorum, and the women are busily engaged in making and mending the moccasins of the party. As we had still some superfluous baggage which would be too heavy to carry across the mountains, it became necessary to make a cache or deposit. For this purpose we selected a spot on the bank of the river, three-quarters of a mile below the camp, and three men were set to dig it, with a sentinel in the neighbourhood, who was ordered if the natives were to straggle that way, to fire a signal for the workmen to desist and separate. Towards evening the cache was completed, without being perceived by the Indians, and the packages prepared for deposit.

CHAPTER XVI.

WEDNESDAY, August 21. The weather was very cold; the water which stood in the vessels exposed to the air being covered with ice a quarter of an inch thick: the ink freezes in the pen, and the low grounds are perfectly whitened with frost: after this the day proved excessively warm. The party were engaged in their usual occupations, and completed twenty saddles with the necessary harness, who all prepared to set off as soon as the Indians should arrive. Our two hunters, who were dispatched early in the morning, have not returned, so that we were obliged to encroach on our pork and corn, which we consider as the last resource, when our casual supplies of game fail. After dark we carried our baggage to the cache, and deposited what we thought too cumbrous to carry with us: a small assortment of medicines, and all the specimens of plants, seeds, and minerals, collected since leaving the Falls of Missouri. Late at night Drewyer, one of the hunters, returned with a fawn and a considerable quantity of Indian plunder, which he had taken by way of reprisal. While hunting this morning in the Shoshonee cove, he came suddenly upon an Indian camp, at which were an old man, a young one, three women, and a boy: they showed no surprise at the sight of him, and he therefore rode up to them, and after turning his horse loose to graze, sat down and began to converse with them by signs. They had just finished a repast on some roots, and in about twenty minutes one of the women spoke to the rest of the party, who immediately went out, collected their horses, and began to saddle them. Having rested himself, Drewyer thought that he would continue his hunt, and rising, went to catch his horse, who was at a short distance, forgetting at the moment to take up his rifle. He had scarcely gone more than fifty paces when the Indians mounted their horses, the young man snatched up the rifle, and leaving all their baggage, whipt their horses, and set off at full speed towards tbe passes of the mountains: Drewyer instantly jumped on his horse

and pursued them. After running about ten miles
the horses of the women nearly gave out, and the
women, finding Drewyer gain on them, raised
dreadful cries, which induced the young man to
slacken his pace, and being mounted on a very
fleet horse rode round them at a short distance. Drewyer now came up with the women,
and by signs persuaded them that he did not mean
to hurt them : they then stopped, and as the
young man came towards them Drewyer asked
him for his rifle, but the only part of the answer
which he understood was Pahkee, the name by
which they call their enemies, the Minnetarees of
Fort de Prairie. While they were thus engaged
in talking, Drewyer watched his opportunity, and
seeing the Indian off his guard, galloped up to him
and seized his rifle : the Indian struggled for some
time, but finding Drewyer getting too strong for
him, had the presence of mind to open the pan
and let the priming fall out : he then let go his
hold, and giving his horse the whip, escaped at
full speed, leaving the women to the mercy of the
conqueror. Drewyer then returned to where he
had first seen them, where he found that their baggage had been left behind, and brought it to camp
with him.

Thursday, 22. This morning early two men
were sent to complete the covering of the cache,
which could not be so perfectly done during the
night as to elude the search of the Indians. On
examining the spoils which Drewyer had obtained,

they were found to consist of several dressed and
undressed skins; two bags woven with the bark
of the silk-grass, each containing a bushel of
dried serviceberries, and about the same quantity
of roots : an instrument made of bone for ma-
nufacturing the flints into heads for arrows;
and a number of flints themselves : these were
much of the same colour, and nearly as transparent as common black glass, and, when cut,
detached itself into flakes, leaving a very sharp
edge.

The roots were of three kinds, and folded separate from each other in hides of buffaloe made into
parchment. The first is a fusiform root six inches
long, and about the size of a man's finger at the
largest end, with radicles larger than is usual in
roots of the fusiform sort : the rind is white and
thin ; the body is also white, mealy, and easily re-
ducible, by pounding, to a substance resembling
flour, like which it thickens by boiling, and is of
an agreeable flavour : it is eaten frequently in its
raw state either green or dried. The second
species was much mutilated, but appeared to be
fibrous ; it is of a cylindrical form, about the size
of a small quill, hard and brittle. A part of the
rind which had not been detached in the preparation was hard and black, but the rest of the root
was perfectly white : this the Indians informed us
was always boiled before eating ; and on making
the experiment we found that it became perfectly
soft, but had a bitter taste, which was nauseous to

our taste, but which the Indians seemed to relish ; for on giving the roots to them they were very heartily swallowed.

The third species was a small nut about the size of a nutmeg, of an irregularly rounded form, something like the smallest of the Jerusalem artichokes, which, on boiling, we found them to resemble also in flavour, and is certainly the best root we have seen in use among the Indians. On inquiring of the Indians from what plant those roots were procured, they informed us that none of them grew near this place.

The men were chiefly employed in dressing the skins belonging to the party who accompanied Captain Clarke. About eleven o'clock Chaboneau and his wife returned with Cameahwait, accompanied by about fifty men with their women and children. After they had encamped near us and turned loose their horses, we called a council of all the chiefs and warriors, and addressed them in a speech : additional presents were then distributed, particularly to the two second chiefs, who had, agreeably to their promises exerted themselves in our favour. The council was then adjourned, and all the Indians were treated with an abundant meal of boiled Indian corn and beans. The poor wretches, who had no animal food, and scarcely any thing but a few fish, had been almost starved, and received this new luxury with great thankfulness. Out of compliment to the chief we gave him a few dried squashes which we had brought from the Mandans, and he declared it was the best food he had ever tasted except sugar, a small lump of which he had received from his sister, : he now declared how happy they should all be to live in a country which produced so many good things, and we told him that it would not be long before the white men would put it in their power to live below the mountains, where they might themselves cultivate all these kinds of food instead of wandering in the mountains. He appeared to be much pleased with this information, and the whole party being now in excellent temper after their repast, we began our purchase of horses. We soon obtained five very good ones on very reasonable terms : that is, by giving for each merchandize which cost us originally about six dollars. We have again to admire the perfect decency and propriety of their conduct; for although so numerous, they do not attempt to crowd round our camp, or take any thing which they see lying about, and whenever they borrow knives or kettles, or any other article from the men, they return them with great fidelity.

Towards evening we formed a drag of bushes, and in about two hours caught five hundred and twenty-eight very good fish, most of them large trout. Among them we observed, for the first time ten or twelve trout of a white or silvery colour, except on the back and head, where they are of a blueish cast: in appearance and shape they resemble exactly the speckled trout, except that they are not quite so large, though the scales are much larger, and the flavour equally good. The greater part of the fish was distributed among the Indians.

Friday, 23. Our visitors seem to depend wholly on us for food, and as the state of our provisions obliges us to be careful of our remaining stock of corn and flour, this was an additional reason for urging our departure; but Cameahwait requested us to wait till the arrival of another party of his nation who were expected to-day. Knowing that it would be in vain to oppose his wish, we consented, and two hunters were sent out with orders to go further up the south-east fork than they had hitherto been. At the same time the chief was informed of the low state of our provisions, and advised to send out his young men to hunt. This he recommended them to do, and most of them set out: we then sunk our canoes by means of stones to the bottom of the river, a situation which better than any other secured them against the effects of the high waters, and the frequent fires of the plains; the Indians having promised not to disturb them during our absence, a promise we believe the more readily, as they are almost too lazy to take the trouble of raising them for fire-wood. We were desirous of purchasing some more horses, but they declined selling any until we reached their camp in the mountains. Soon after starting the Indian hunters discovered a mule buck, and twelve of their horsemen pursued it, for four miles. We saw the chase, which was very enter-

L 4

taining, and at length they rode it down and killed it. This mule buck was the largest deer of any kind we have seen, being nearly as large as a doe elk. Besides this they brought in another deer and three goats ; but instead of a general distribution of the meat, and such as we have hitherto seen among all tribes of Indians, we observed that some families had a large share, while others received none. On inquiring of Cameahwait the reason of this custom, he said that meat among them was scarce, that each hunter reserved what he killed for the use of himself and his own family, none of the rest having any claim on what he chose to keep. Our hunters returned soon after with two mule deer and three common deer, three of which we distributed among the families who had received none of the game of their own hunters. About three o'clock the expected party consisting of fifty men, women, and children arrived. We now learnt that most of the Indians were on their way down the valley towards the buffaloe country, and some anxiety to accompany them appeared to prevail among those who had promised to assist us in crossing the mountains. We ourselves were not without some apprehension that they might leave us, but as they continued to say that they would return with us, nothing was said upon the subject. We were, however, resolved to move early in the morning, and therefore dispatched two men to hunt in the cove and leave the game on the route we should pass to-morrow.

Saturday, 24. As the Indians who arrived yesterday, had a number of spare horses, we thought it probable they might be willing to dispose of them, and desired the chief to speak to them for that purpose. They declined giving any positive answer, but requested to see the goods which we proposed to exchange. We then produced some battle-axes which we had made at fort Mandan, and a quantity of knives; with both of which they appeared very much pleased; and we were soon able to purchase three horses, by giving for each an axe, a knife, a handkerchief, and a little paint. For a mule we were obliged to add a second knife, a shirt, a handkerchief, and a pair of leggings; and such is the estimation in which those animals are held, that even at this price, which was double that given for a horse, the fellow who sold him took upon himself great merit in having given away a mule to us. They now said that they had no more horses for sale, and as we had now nine of our own, two hired horses, and a mule, we began loading them as heavily as was prudent, and placing the rest on the shoulders of the Indian women, left our camp at twelve o'clock. We were all on foot, except Sacajawea, for whom her husband had purchased a horse with some articles which we gave him for that purpose; an Indian, however, had the politeness to offer Captain Lewis one of his horses to ride, which he accepted, in order better to direct the march of the party. We crossed the river below the forks, directed our course towards the cove by the route already passed, and had just reached the lower part of the cove, when an Indian rode up to Captain Lewis to inform him that one of his men was very sick, and unable to come on. The party was immediately halted at a run which falls into the creek on the left, and Captain Lewis rode back two miles, and found Wiser severely afflicted with the colic: by giving him some of the essence of peppermint and laudanum, he recovered sufficiently to ride the horse of Captain Lewis, who then rejoined the party on foot. When he arrived, he found that the Indians, who had been impatiently expecting his return, at last unloaded their horses, and turned them loose, and had now made their camp for the night. It would have been fruitless to remonstrate, and not prudent to excite any irritation, and, therefore, although the sun was still high, and we had made only six miles, we thought it best to remain with them: after we had encamped, there fell a slight shower of rain. One of the men caught several fine trout; but Drewyer had been sent out to hunt without having killed any thing. We, therefore, gave a little corn to those of the Indians who were actually engaged in carrying our baggage, and who had absolutely nothing to eat. We also advised Cameahwait, as we could not supply all his people with provisions, to recommend to all who were not assisting us, to go on before us to their camp. This he did: but in the morning,

Sunday, 25, a few only followed his advice, the rest accompanying us at some distance on each side.

We set out at sun-rise, and after going seventeen miles, halted for dinner, within two miles of the narrow pass in the mountains. The Indians who were on the sides of our party had started some antelopes, but were obliged, after a pursuit of seve- ral hours, to abandon the chase: our hunters had, in the meantime brought in three deer, the greater part of which was distributed among the Indians. Whilst at dinner, we learnt, by means of Sacaja- wea, that the young men who left us this morning, carried a request from the chief, that the village would break up its encampment, and meet this party to-morrow, when they would all go down the Missouri into the buffaloe country. Alarmed at this new caprice of the Indians, which, if not counteracted, threatened to leave ourselves and our baggage on the mountains, or even if we reached the waters of the Columbia, prevent our obtaining horses to go on further, Captain Lewis immediately called the three chiefs together. Af- ter smoking a pipe, he asked them if they were men of their words, and if we can rely on their promises. They readily answered in the affirma- tive. He then asked, if they had not agreed to assist us in carrying our baggage over the moun- tains. To this they also answered yes; and why then, said he, have you requested your people to meet us to-morrow, where it will be impossible for us to trade for horses, as you promised we should. If, he continued, you had not promised to help us in transporting our goods over the mountains, we should not have attempted it, but have returned down the river, after which no white men would ever have come into your country. If you wish the whites to be your friends, and to bring you arms, and protect you from your enemies, you should never promise what you do not mean to perform: when I first met you, you doubted what I said, yet you afterwards saw that I told you the truth. How, therefore, can you doubt what I now tell you; you see that I have divided amongst you the meat which my hunters kill; and I promise to give all who assist us, a share of whatever we have to eat. If, therefore, you intend to keep your promise, send one of the young men immediately to order the people to remain at the village till we arrive.

The two inferior chiefs then said, that they had wished to keep their words and to assist us; that they had not sent for the people, but, on the contrary, had disapproved of the measure, which was done wholly by the first chief. Cameahwait remained silent for some time: at last he said that he knew he had done wrong, but that seeing his people all in want of provisions, he had wished to hasten their departure for the country where their wants might be supplied. He, however, now declared, that having passed his word he would never violate it, and counter-orders were immediately sent to the village by a young man, to whom we gave a handkerchief in order to ensure dispatch and fidelity.

This difficulty being now adjusted, our march was resumed with an unusual degree of alacrity on the part of the Indians. We passed a spot, where six years ago the Shoshonees suffered a very severe defeat from the Minnetarees; and, late in the evening, we reached the upper part of the cove where the creek enters the mountains. The part of the cove on the north-east side of the creek has lately been burnt, most probably as a signal on some occasion. Here we were joined by our hunters with a single deer, which Captain Lewis gave, as a proof of his sincerity, to the women and children, and remained supperless himself. As we came along we observed several large hares, some ducks, and many of the cock of the plains: in the low grounds of the cove were also considerable quantities of wild onions.

Monday, 26. The morning was excessively cold, and the ice in our vessels was nearly a quarter of an inch in thickness: we set out at sunrise, and soon reached the fountain of the Missouri, where we halted for a few minutes, and then crossing the dividing ridge, reached the fine spring where Captain Lewis had slept on the 12th in his first excursion to the Shoshonee camp. The grass on the hill sides is perfectly dry and parched by the sun, but near the spring was a fine green grass: we therefore halted for dinner, and turned our horses to graze. To each of the Indians, who were engaged in carrying our baggage, was distributed a pint of corn, which they parched, then pounded, and made a sort of soup. One of the women who had been leading two of our pack-horses halted at a rivulet about a mile behind, and sent on the two horses by a female friend : on enquiring of Came-ahwait the cause of her detention, he answered with great appearance of unconcern, that she had just stopped to lie in, but would soon overtake us. In fact, we were astonished to see her in about an hour's time come on with her newborn infant and pass us on her way to the camp, apparently in perfect health.

This wonderful facility with which the Indian women bring forth their children, seems rather some benevolent gift of nature, in exempting them from pains which their savage state would render doubly grievous, than any result of habit. If, as has been imagined, a pure dry air or a cold and elevated country are obstacles to easy delivery, every difficult incident to that operation might be expected in this part of the continent : nor can another reason, the habit of carrying heavy bur-dens during pregnancy, be at all applicable to the Shoshonee women, who rarely carry any burdens, since their nation possesses an abundance of horses. We have, indeed, been several times informed by those conversant with Indian manners, and who asserted their knowledge of the fact, that Indian women pregnant by white men experience more difficulty in child-birth than when the father is an Indian. If this account be true, it may contribute to strengthen the belief, that the easy delivery of the Indian women is wholly constitutional.

The tops of the high irregular mountains to the westward are still entirely covered with snow; and the coolness which the air acquires in passing them, is a very agreeable relief from the heat, which has dried up the herbage on the sides of the hills. While we stopped, the women were busily employed in collecting the root of a plant with which they feed their children, who, like their mothers, are nearly half starved, and in a wretched condition. It is a species of fennel which grows in the moist grounds; the radix is of the knob kind, of a long ovate form, terminating in a single radicle, the whole being three or four inches long, and the thickest part about the size of a man's little finger: when fresh, it is white, firm, and crisp; and when dried and pounded makes a fine white meal. Its flavour is not unlike that of aniseed, though less pungent. From one to four of these knobbed roots are attached to a single stem, which rises to the height of three or four feet, and is jointed, smooth, cylindric, and has several small peduncles, one at each joint above the sheathing leaf. Its colour is a deep green, as is also that of the leaf, which is sheathing, sessile, and *polipartite*, the divisions being long and narrow. The flowers, which are now in bloom, are small and numerous, with white and umbelliferous petals: there are no root leaves. As soon as the seeds have matured, the roots of the present year, as well as the stem, decline, and are

I

renewed in the succeeding spring from the little knot which unites the roots. The sun-flower is also abundant here, and the seeds, which are now ripe, are gathered in considerable quantities, and after being pounded and rubbed between smooth stones, form a kind of meal, which is a favourite dish among the Indians.

After dinner, we continued our route, and were soon met by a party of young men on horseback, who turned with us and went to the village. As soon as we were within sight of it, Cameahwait requested that we would discharge our guns; the men were, therefore, drawn up in a single rank, and gave a running fire of two rounds, to the great satisfaction of the Indians. We then proceeded to the encampment, where we arrived about six o'clock, and were conducted to the leathern lodge in the centre of thirty-two others made of brush. The baggage was arranged near this tent, which Captain Lewis occupied, and surrounded by those of the men, so as to secure it from pillage. This camp was in a beautiful smooth meadow near the river, and about three miles above their camp when we first visited the Indians. We here found Colter, who had been sent by Captain Clarke with a note apprising us that there were no hopes of a passage by water, and that the most practicable route seemed to be that mentioned by his guide, towards the north. Whatever road we meant to take, it was now necessary to provide ourselves with horses; we therefore informed Cameahwait of our intention of going to the great river beyond the mountains, and that we would wish to purchase twenty more horses : he said the Minnetarees had stolen a great number of their horses this spring, but he still hoped they could spare us that number. In order not to lose the present favourable moment, and to keep the Indians as cheerful as possible, the violins were brought out and our men danced, to the great diversion of the Indians. This mirth was the more welcome, because our situation was not precisely that which would most dispose us for gaiety, for we have only a little parched corn to eat, and our means of subsistence, or of success, depend on the wavering temper of the natives, who may change their minds to-morrow.

The Shoshonees are a small tribe of the nation called Snake Indians, a vague denomination, which embraces at once the inhabitants of the southern parts of the rocky mountains and of the plains on each side. The Shoshonees, with whom we now are, amount to about one hundred warriors, and three times that number of women and children. Within their own recollection they formerly lived in the plains, but they have been driven into the mountains by the Pawkees, or the roving Indians of the Sascatchawain, and are now obliged to visit occasionally, and by stealth, the country of their ancestors. Their lives are indeed migratory. From the middle of May to the beginning of September, they reside on the waters of the Columbia, where they consider themselves perfectly secure from the

Pawkees, who have never yet found their way to that retreat. During this time they subsist chiefly on salmon, and as that fish disappears on the approach of autumn, they are obliged to seek subsistence elsewhere. They then cross the ridge to the waters of the Missouri, down which they proceed slowly and cautiously, till they are joined near the three forks by other bands, either of their own nation or of the Flatheads, with whom they associate against the common enemy. Being now strong in numbers, they venture to hunt buffaloe in the plains eastward of the mountains, near which they spend the winter, till the return of the salmon invites them to the Columbia. But such is their terror of the Pawkees, that as long as they can obtain the scantiest subsistence, they do not leave the interior of the mountains; and as soon as they collect a large stock of dried meat, they again retreat, and thus alternately obtaining their food at the hazard of their lives, and hiding themselves to consume it. In this loose and wandering existence they suffer the extremes of want: for two-thirds of the year they are forced to live in the mountains, passing whole weeks without meat, and with nothing to eat but a few fish and roots. Nor can any thing be imagined more wretched than their condition at the present time, when the salmon is fast retiring, when roots are becoming scarce, and they have not yet acquired strength to hazard an encounter with their enemies. So insensible are they however to these calamities, that the Shoshonees

are not only cheerful, but even gay ; and their
character, which is more interesting than that of
any Indians we have seen, has in it much of the
dignity of misfortune. In their intercourse with
strangers they are frank and communicative, in their
dealings perfectly fair, nor have we had during our
stay with them, any reason to suspect that the display of all our new and valuable wealth, has tempted them into a single act of dishonesty. While
they have generally shared with us the little they
possess, they have always abstained from begging
any thing from us. With their liveliness of temper
they are fond of gaudy dresses, and of all sorts of
amusements, particularly of games of hazard ; and
like most Indians, fond of boasting of their own
warlike exploits, whether real or fictitious. In their
conduct towards ourselves they were kind and
obliging, and though on one occasion they seemed
willing to neglect us, yet we scarcely knew how to
blame the treatment by which we suffered, when
we recollected how few civilized chiefs would have
hazarded the comforts or the subsistence of their
people for the sake of a few strangers. This
manliness of character may arise, or may be
formed by the nature of their government, which
is perfectly free from any restraint. Each indi·
vidual is his own master, and the only controul to
which his conduct is subjected, is the advice of a
chief, supported by his influence over the opinions
of the rest of the tribe. The chief himself is in
fact no more than the most confidential person

among the warriors, a rank neither distinguished
by any external honour, nor invested by any
ceremony, but gradually acquired from the good
wishes of his companions, and by superior merit.
Such an officer has therefore strictly no power; he
may recommend, or advise, or influence, but his
commands have no effect on those who incline to
disobey, and who may at any time withdraw from
their voluntary allegiance. His shadowy authority,
which cannot survive the confidence which sup-
ports it, often decays with the personal vigour of
the chief, or is transferred to some more fortunate
or favourite hero.

In their domestic economy, the man is equally
sovereign. The man is the sole proprietor of his
wives and daughters, and can barter them away,
or dispose of them in any manner he may think
proper. The children are seldom corrected; the
boys, particularly, soon become their own masters;
they are never whipped, for they say that it breaks
their spirit, and that after being flogged, they never
recover their independence of mind, even when
they grow to manhood. A plurality of wives is
very common; but these are not generally sisters,
as among the Minnetarees and Mandans; but are
purchased of different fathers. The infant daughters are often betrothed by their father to men who
are grown, either for themselves or for their sons,
for whom they are desirous of providing wives.
The compensation to the father is usually made in
horses or mules; and the girl remains with her

parents till the age of puberty, which is thirteen
or fourteen, when she is surrendered to her husband. At the same time the father often makes a
present to the husband equal to what he had formerly received as the price of his daughter, though
this return is optional with her parent. Sacajawea
had been contracted in this way before she was
taken prisoner, and when we brought her back,
her betrothed was still living. Although he was
double the age of Sacajawea, and had two other
wives, he claimed her, but on finding that she had
a child by her new husband, Chaboneau, he relinquished his pretensions, and said he did not want
her.

The chastity of the women does not appear to
be held in much estimation. The husband will for
a trifling present lend his wife for a night to a
stranger, and the loan may be protracted by increasing the value of the present. Yet strange as
it may seem, notwithstanding this facility, any connexion of this kind, not authorized by the husband,
is considered highly offensive, and quite as disgraceful to his character as the same licentiousness
in civilized societies. The Shoshonees are not so im-
portunate in volunteering the services of their wives
as we found the Sioux were ; and indeed we observed
among them some women who appeared to be held
in more respect than those of any nation we had
seen. But the mass of the females are condemned,
as among all savage nations, to the lowest and
most laborious drudgery. When the tribe is sta-

tionary, they collect the roots, and cook; they build the huts, dress the skins, and make clothing; collect the wood, and assist in taking care of the horses on the route; they load the horses, and have the charge of all the baggage. The only business of the man is to fight; he therefore takes on himself the care of his horse, the companion of his warfare; but he will descend to no other labour than to hunt and to fish. He would consider himself degraded by being compelled to walk any distance; and were he so poor as to possess only two horses, he would ride the best of them, and leave the other for his wives and children and their baggage; and if he has too many wives or too much baggage for the horse, the wives have no alternative but to follow him on foot; they are not however often reduced to those extremities, for their stock of horses is very ample. Notwithstanding their losses this spring, they still have at least seven hundred, among which are about forty colts, and half that number of mules. There are no horses here which can be considered as wild; we have seen two only on this side of the Muscleshell river, which were without owners, and even those, although shy, showed every mark of having been once in the possession of man. The original stock was procured from the Spaniards, but they now raise their own. The horses are generally very fine, of a good size, vigorous, and patient of fatigue as well as hunger. Each warrior has one or two tied to a stake near his hut both day and night, so as to be always prepared for action. The mules are obtained in the course of trade from the Spaniards, with whose brand several of them are marked, or stolen from them by the frontier Indians. They are the finest animals of that kind we have ever seen, and at this distance from the Spanish colonies are very highly valued. The worst are considered as worth the price of two horses, and a good mule cannot be obtained for less than three and sometimes four horses.

We also saw a bridle bit, stirrups, and several other articles, which, like the mules, came from the Spanish colonies. The Shoshonees say that they can reach those settlements in ten days' march by the route of the Yellow-stone river; but we readily perceive that the Spaniards are by no means favourites. They complain that the Spaniards refuse to let them have fire-arms, under pretence that these dangerous weapons will only induce them to kill each other. In the mean-time, say the Shoshonees, we are left to the mercy of the Minnetarees, who having arms, plunder them of their horses, and put them to death without mercy. " But this should not be," said Cameahwait fiercely, "if we had guns, instead of hiding ourselves in the mountains, and living like the bears on roots and berries, we would then go down and live in the buffaloe country in spite of our enemies, whom we never fear when we meet on equal terms."

As war is the chief occupation, bravery is the

first virtue among the Shoshonees. None can hope to be distinguished without having given proofs of it, nor can there be any preferment, or influence among the nation, without some warlike achievement. Those important events which give reputation to a warrior, and which entitle him to a new name, are killing a white bear, stealing individually the horses of the enemy, leading out a party who happen to be successful either in plundering horses or destroying the enemy, and lastly, scalping a warrior. These acts seem of nearly equal dignity, but the last, that of taking an enemy's scalp, is an honour quite independent of the act of vanquishing him. To kill your adversary is of no importance, unless the scalp is brought from the field of battle; and were a warrior to slay any number of his enemies in action, and others were to obtain the scalps, or first touch the dead, they would have all the honours, since they have borne off the trophy.

Although thus oppressed by the Minnetarees, the Shoshonees are still a very military people. Their cold and rugged country inures them to fatigue; their long abstinence makes them support the dangers of mountain warfare, and worn down as we saw them, by want of sustenance, have a look of fierce and adventurous courage. The Shoshonee warrior always fights on horseback; he possesses a few bad guns, which are reserved exclusively for war, but his common arms are the bow

and arrow, a shield, a lance, and a weapon called
by the Chippeways, by whom it was formerly used,
the poggamoggon. The bow is made of cedar or
pine, covered on the outer side with sinews and glue.
It is about two and a half feet long, and does not
differ in shape from those used by the Sioux, Mandans, and Minnetarees. Sometimes, however, the
bow is made of a single piece of the horn of an elk,
covered on the back like those of wood with sinews
and glue, and occasionally ornamented by a strand
wrought of porcupine quills and sinews, which is
wrapped round the horn near its two ends. The
bows made of the horns of the bighorn, are still
more prized, and are formed by cementing with
glue flat pieces of the horn together, covering the
back with sinews and glue, and loading the whole
with an unusual quantity of ornaments. The arrows resemble those of the other Indians, except
in being more slender than any we have seen. They
are contained, with the implements for striking
fire, in a narrow quiver formed of different kinds of
skin, though that of the otter seems to be preferred.
It is just long enough to protect the arrows from
the weather, and is worn on the back by means of
a strap passing over the right shoulder and under
the left arm. The shield is a circular piece of buffaloe hide about two feet four or five inches in diameter, ornamented with feathers, and a fringe
round it of dressed leather, and adorned or de-
formed with paintings of strange figures. The
buffaloe hide is perfectly proof against any arrow.

But in the minds of the Shoshonees, its power to
protect them is chiefly derived from the virtues
which are communicated to it by the old men and
jugglers. To make a shield is indeed one of their
most important ceremonies : it begins by a feast,
to which all the warriors, old men and jugglers are
invited. After the repast a hole is dug in the
ground about eighteen inches in depth, and of
the same diameter as the intended shield : into
this hole red-hot stones are thrown and water
poured over them, till they emit a very strong hot
steam. The buffaloe skin, which must be the entire hide of a male two years old, and never suffered to dry since it was taken from the animal, is
now laid across the hole, with the fleshy side to
the ground, and stretched in every direction by
as many as can take hold of it. As the skin becomes heated, the hair separates and is taken off
by the hand; till at last the skin is contracted into
the compass designed for the shield. It is then
taken off and placed on a hide prepared into
parchment, and then pounded during the rest of
the festival by the bare heels of those who are
invited to it. This operation sometimes continues
for several days, after which it is delivered to the
proprietor, and declared by the old men and
jugglers to be a security against arrows ; and provided the feast has been satisfactory, against even
the bullets of their enemies. Such is the delusion,
that many of the Indians implicitly believe that
this ceremony has given to the shield supernatural

powers, and that they have no longer to fear any weapons of their enemies.

The poggamoggon is an instrument, consisting of a handle twenty-two inches long, made of wood, covered with dressed leather about the size of a whip-handle: at one end is a thong of two inches in length, which is tied to a round stone weighing two pounds, and held in a cover of leather: at the other end is a loop of the same material, which is passed round the wrist so as to secure the hold of the instrument, with which they strike a very severe blow.

Besides these, they have a kind of armour something like a coat of mail, which is formed by a great many folds of dressed antelope skins, united by means of a mixture of glue and sand. With this they cover their own bodies and those of their horses, and find it impervious to the arrow.

The caparison of their horses is a halter and a saddle: the first is either a rope of six or seven strands of buffaloe hair platted or twisted together, about the size of a man's finger and of great strength: or merely a thong of raw hide, made pliant by pounding and rubbing; though the first kind is much preferred. The halter is very long, and is never taken from the neck of the horse when in constant use. One end of it is first tied round the neck in a knot, and then brought down to the under jaw, round which it is formed into a simple noose, passing through the mouth: it is then drawn up on the right side and held by the rider in his left hand, while the rest trails after him to some distance. At other times the knot is formed at a little distance from one of the ends, so as to let that end serve as a bridle, while the other trails on the ground. With these cords dangling along side of them, the horse is put to his full speed without fear of falling; and when he is turned to graze, the noose is merely taken from his mouth. The saddle is formed, like the pack-saddles used by the French and Spaniards, of two flat thin boards, which fit the sides of the horse, and are kept together by two cross pieces, one before and the other behind, which rise to a considerable height, ending sometimes in a flat point extending outwards, and always making the saddle deep and narrow. Under this a piece of buffaloe skin, with the hair on, is placed, so as to prevent the rubbing of the boards, and when they mount, they throw a piece of skin or robe over the saddle, which has no permanent cover. When stirrups are used, they consist of wood covered with leather; but stirrups and saddles are conveniences reserved for old men and women. The young warriors rarely use any thing except a small leather pad, stuffed with hair, and secured by a girth made of a leathern thong. In this way they ride with great expertness, and they have a particular dexterity in catching the horse when he is running at large. If he will not immediately submit when they wish to take him, they make a noose in the rope, and although the horse may be at a distance, or even running, rarely fail

to fix it on his neck; and such is the docility of
the animal, that however unruly he may seem, he
surrenders as soon as he feels the rope on him.
This cord is so useful in this way, that it is never
dispensed with, even when they use the Spanish
bridle, which they prefer, and always procure when
they have it in their power. The horse becomes
almost an object of attachment: a favourite is frequently painted, and his ears cut into various
shapes: the mane and tail, which are never drawn
nor trimmed, are decorated with feathers of birds,
and sometimes a warrior suspends at the breast of
his horse the finest ornaments he possesses.

Thus armed and mounted, the Shoshonee is a
formidable enemy, even with the feeble weapons
which he is still obliged to use. When they attack
at full speed, they bend forward, and cover their
bodies with the shield, while with the right hand
they shoot under the horse's neck.

The only articles of metal which the Shoshonees
possess, are a few bad knives, some brass kettles,
some bracelets or arm-bands of iron and brass, a few
buttons worn as ornaments in their hair, one or two
spears about a foot in length, and some heads for
arrows, made of iron and brass. All these they
had obtained in trading with the Crow or Rocky
mountain Indians, who live on the Yellowstone.
The few bridle-bits and stirrups they procured from
the Spanish colonies.

The instrument which supplies the place of a
knife among them, is a piece of flint, with no re-

gular form, and the sharp part of it not more than one or two inches long: the edge of this is renewed, and the flint itself is formed into heads for arrows, by means of the point of a deer or elk horn, an instrument which they use with great art and ingenuity. There are no axes or hatchets; all the wood being cut with flint or elk-horn, the latter of which is always used as a wedge in splitting wood. Their utensils consist, besides the brass kettles, of pots in the form of a jar, made either of earth, or of a stone found in the hills between Madison and Jefferson rivers, which, though soft and white in its natural state, becomes very hard and black after exposure to the fire. The horns of the buffaloe and the bighorn supply them with spoons.

The fire is always kindled by means of a blunt arrow, and a piece of well-seasoned wood, of a soft spongy kind, such as the willow or cotton-wood.

The Shoshonees are of a diminutive stature, with thick flat feet and ancles, crooked legs, and are, generally speaking, worse formed than any nation of Indians we have seen. Their complexion resembles that of the Sioux, and is darker than that of the Minnetarees, Mandans, or Shawnees. The hair of both sexes is suffered to fall loosely over the face and down the shoulders: some men, however, divide it by means of thongs of dressed leather, or otter skin, into two equal queues, which hang over the ears, and are drawn in front of the body; but at the present moment, when the nation is afflicted by the loss of so many relations killed in war, most of them have the hair cut quite short in the neck, and Cameahwait has the hair cut short all over his head, this being the customary mourning for a deceased kindred.

The dress of the men consists of a robe, a tippet, a shirt, long leggings, and moccasins. The robe is formed most commonly of the skins of antelope, bighorn, or deer, though, when it can be procured, the buffaloe hide is preferred. Sometimes too, they are made of beaver, moonax, and small wolves; and frequently, during the summer, of elk skin. These are dressed with the hair on, and reach about as low as the middle of the leg. They are worn loosely over the shoulders, the sides being, at pleasure, either left open, or drawn together by the hand, and in cold weather kept close by a girdle round the waist. This robe answers the purpose of a cloak during the day, and at night is their only covering.

The tippet is the most elegant article of Indian dress we have ever seen. The neck or collar of it is a strip about four or five inches wide, cut from the back of the otter skin, the nose and eyes forming one extremity, and the tail another. This being dressed with the fur on, they attach to one edge of it, from one hundred to two hundred and fifty little rolls of ermine skin, beginning at the ear, and proceeding towards the tail. These ermine skins are the same kind of narrow strips from the back of that animal, which are sewed round a

small cord of twisted silk-grass, thick enough to
make the skin taper towards the tail which hangs
from the end, and are generally about the size of
a large quill. These are tied at the head into little
bundles, of two, three, or more, according to the
caprice of the wearer, and then suspended from
the collar, and a broad fringe of ermine skin is
fixed, so as to cover the parts where they unite,
which might have a coarse appearance. Little
tassels of fringe of the same materials are also
fastened to the extremities of the tail, so as to
shew its black colour to greater advantage. The
centre of the collar is further ornamented with the
shells of the pearl-oyster. Thus adorned, the
collar is worn close round the neck, and the little
rolls fall down over the shoulders nearly to the
waist, so as to form a sort of short cloak, which
has a very handsome appearance. These tippets
are very highly esteemed, and are given or disposed of on important occasions only. The ermine
is the fur known to the north-west traders by the
name of the white weazel, but is the genuine
ermine; and by encouraging the Indians to take
them, might no doubt be rendered a valuable
branch of trade. These animals must be very
abundant, for the tippets are in great numbers,
and the construction of each requires at least one
hundred skins.

The shirt is a covering of dressed skin without
the hair, and formed of the hide of the antelope,
deer, bighorn, or elk, though the last is more

rarely used than any other for this purpose. It fits the body loosely, and reaches half way down the thigh. The aperture at the top is wide enough to admit the head, and has no collar, but is either left square, or most frequently terminates in the tail of the animal, which is left entire, so as to fold outwards, though sometimes the edges are cut into a fringe, and ornamented with quills of the porcupine. The seams of the shirt are on the sides, and are richly fringed and adorned with porcupine quills, till within five or six inches of the sleeve, where it is left open, as is also the under side of the sleeve from the shoulder to the elbow, where it fits closely round the arm as low as the wrist, and has no fringe like the sides, and the under part of the sleeve above the elbow. It is kept up by wide shoulder-straps, on which the manufacturer displays his taste by the variety of figures wrought with porcupine quills of different colours, and sometimes by beads when they can be obtained. The lower end of the shirt retains the natural shape of the fore-legs and neck of the skin, with the addition of a slight fringe; the hair too is left on the tail and near the hoofs, part of which last is retained and split into a fringe.

The leggings are generally made of antelope skins, dressed without the hair, and with the legs, tail, and neck, hanging to them. Each legging is formed of a skin nearly entire, and reaches from the angle to the upper part of the thigh, and the legs of the skin are tucked before and behind under a girdle round the waist. It fits closely to the leg, the tail being worn upwards, and the neck, highly ornamented with fringe and porcupine quills, drags on the ground behind the heels. As the legs of the animal are tied round the girdle, the wide part of the skin is drawn so high as to conceal the parts usually kept from view, in which respect their dress is much more decent than that of any nation of Indians on the Missouri. The seams of the leggings down the sides are also fringed and ornamented, and occasionally decorated with tufts of hair taken from enemies whom they have slain. In making all these dresses, their only thread is the sinew taken from the backs and lions of deer, elk, buffaloe, or any other animal.

The moccasin is of the deer, elk, or buffaloe skin, dressed without the hair, though in winter they use the buffaloe skin with the hairy side inward, as do most of the Indians who inhabit the buffaloe country. Like the Mandan moccasin, it is made with a single seam on the outer edge, and sewed up behind, a hole being left at the instep to admit the foot. It is variously ornamented with figures wrought with porcupine quills, and sometimes the young men most fond of dress, cover it with the skin of a pole-cat, and trail at their heels the tail of the animal.

The dress of the women consists of the same articles as that of their husbands. The robe, though smaller, is worn in the same way: the moccasins are precisely similar. The shirt or chemise reaches half way down the leg, is in the same form, except that there is no shoulder-strap, the seam coming quite up to the shoulder; though for women who give suck both sides are open, almost down to the waist. It is also ornamented in the same way with the addition of little patches of red cloth, edged round with beads at the skirts. The chief ornament is over the breast, where there are curious figures made with the usual luxury of porcupine quills. Like the men, they have a girdle round the waist, and when either sex wishes to disengage the arm, it is drawn up through the hole near the shoulder, and the lower part of the sleeve thrown behind the body.

Children alone wear beads round their necks; grown persons of both sexes prefer them suspended in little bunches from the ear, and sometimes intermixed with triangular pieces of the shell of the pearl-oyster. Sometimes the men tie them in the same way to the hair of the fore-part of the head, and increase the beauty of it by adding the wings and tails of birds, and particularly the feathers of the great eagle or calumet bird, of which they are extremely fond. The collars are formed either of sea-shells procured from their relations to the south-west, or of the sweet-scented grass, which grows in the neighbourhood, and which they twist or plait together, to the thickness of a man's finger, and then cover them with porcupine quills of various colours. The first of these is worn indiscriminately by both sexes,

the second principally confined to the men, while
a string of elks' tusks is a collar almost peculiar to
the women and children. Another collar worn by
the men is a string of round bones like the joints
of a fish's back, but the collar most preferred, because most honourable, is one of the claws of the
brown bear. To kill one of these animals is as
distinguished an achievement as to have put to
death an enemy, and in fact with their weapons is
a more dangerous trial of courage. These claws
are suspended on a thong of dressed leather, and
being ornamented with beads, are worn round the
neck by the warriors with great pride. The men
also frequently wear the skin of a fox, or a strip of
otter skin, round the head in the form of a ban-
deau.

In short, the dress of the Shoshonees is as convenient and decent as that of any Indians we have
seen.

They have many more children than might have
been expected, considering their precarious means
of support and their wandering life. This inconvenience is however balanced by the wonderful
facility with which their females undergo the operations of child-birth. In the most advanced state
of pregnancy they continue their usual occupations,
which are scarcely interrupted longer than the
mere time of bringing the child into the world.

The old men are few in number, and do not
appear to be treated with much tenderness or
respect.

The tobacco used by the Shoshonees is not cultivated among them, but obtained from the Indians of the Rocky mountains, and from some of the bands of their own nation who live to the south of them : it is the same plant which is in use among the Minnetarees, Mandans, and Ricaras.

Their chief intercourse with other nations seems to consist in their association with other Snake Indians, and with the Flatheads when they go eastward to hunt buffaloe, and in the occasional visits made by the Flatheads to the waters of the Columbia for the purpose of fishing. Their intercourse with the Spaniards is much more rare, and it furnishes them with a few articles, such as mules, and some bridles, and other ornaments for horses, which, as well as some of their kitchen utensils, are also furnished by the bands of Snake Indians from the Yellowstone. The pearl ornaments which they esteem so highly come from other bands, whom they represent as their friends and relations, living to the south-west, beyond the barren plains on the other side of the mountains : these relations they say inhabit a good country, abounding with elk, deer, bear, and antelope, where horses and mules are much more abundant than they are here, or, to use their own expression, as numerous as the grass of the plains.

The names of the Indians vary in the course of their life : originally given in childhood, from the mere necessity of distinguishing objects, or from some accidental resemblance to external objects, the young warrior is impatient to change it by some achievement of his own. Any important event, the stealing of horses, the scalping an enemy, or killing a brown bear, entitles him at once to a new name, which he then selects for himself, and it is confirmed by the nation. Sometimes the two names subsist together : thus, the chief Cameahwait, which means, " one who never walks," has the war-name of Tooettecone, or " black gun," which he acquired when he first signalized himself. As each new action gives a warrior a right to change his name, many of them have had several in the course of their lives. To give to a friend his own name is an act of high courtesy, and a pledge, like that of pulling off the moccasin, of sincerity and hospitality. The chief in this way gave his name to Captain Clarke when he first arrived, and he was afterwards known among the Shoshonees by the name of Cameahwait.

The diseases incident to this state of life may be supposed to be few, and chiefly the result of accidents. We were particularly anxious to ascertain whether they had any knowledge of the venereal disorder. After inquiring by means of the interpreter and his wife, we learnt that they sometimes suffered from it, and that they most usually die with it ; nor could we discover what was their remedy. It is possible that this disease may have reached them in their circuitous communications with the whites through the intermediate Indians ; but the situation of the Shoshonees is so insulated, that it is not probable that it could have reached them in that way, and the existence of such a disorder among the Rocky mountains seems rather a proof of its being aboriginal.

CHAPTER XVII.

THE PARTY, AFTER PROCURING HORSES FROM THE SHOSHO-
NEES, PROCEED ON THEIR JOURNEY THROUGH THE MOUN-
TAINS — THE DIFFICULTIES AND DANGERS OF THE ROUTE
— A COUNCIL HELD WITH ANOTHER BAND OF THE SHO-
SHONEES, OF WHOM SOME ACCOUNT IS GIVEN — THEY ARE
REDUCED TO THE NECESSITY OF KILLING THEIR HORSES
FOR FOOD — CAPTAIN CLARKE WITH A SMALL PARTY
PRECEDES THE MAIN BODY IN QUEST OF FOOD, AND IS
HOSPITABLY RECEIVED BY THE PIERCED-NOSE INDIANS —
ARRIVAL OF THE MAIN BODY AMONGST THIS TRIBE, WITH
WHOM A COUNCIL IS HELD — THEY RESOLVE TO PER-
FORM THE REMAINDER OF THEIR JOURNEY IN CANOES
— SICKNESS OF THE PARTY — THEY DESCEND THE KOOS-
KOOSKEE TO ITS JUNCTION WITH LEWIS RIVER, AFTER
PASSING SEVERAL DANGEROUS RAPIDS — SHORT DESCRIP-
TION OF THE MANNERS AND DRESS OF THE PIERCED-NOSE
INDIANS.

AUGUST 27. We were now occupied in determining our route, and procuring horses
from the Indians. The old guide, who had been
sent on by Captain Clarke, now confirmed, by
means of our interpreter, what he had already asserted, of a road up Berry creek which would lead
to Indian establishments on another branch of the
Columbia: his reports, however, were contradicted

by all the Shoshonees. This representation we ascribed to a wish, on their part, to keep us with them during the winter, as well for the protection we might afford against their enemies, as for the purpose of consuming our merchandise amongst them ; and as the old man promised to conduct us himself, that route seemed to be the most eligible. We were able to procure some horses, though not enough for all our purposes. This traffic, and our inquiries and councils with the Indians, consumed the remainder of the day.

August 2. The purchase of horses was resumed, and our stock raised to twenty-two. Having now crossed, more than once, the country which separates the head-waters of the Missouri from those of the Columbia, we can designate the easiest and most expeditious route for a portage : it is as follows :

From the forks of the river north 60° west, five miles to the point of a hill on the right : then south 80° west, ten miles to a spot where the creek is ten yards wide, and the highlands approach within two hundred yards ; south-west five miles to a narrow part of the bottom ; then turning south 70° west, two miles to a creek on the right : thence south 80° west, three miles to a rocky point opposite to a thicket of pines on the left : from that place west, three miles to the gap where is the fountain of the Missouri : on leaving this fountain south 80° west, six miles across the dividing ridge, to a run from the right passing several small streams north 80°

west, four miles over hilly ground to the east fork of Lewis's river, which is here forty yards wide.

Thursday, 29. Captain Clarke joined us this morning, and we continued our bargains for horses. The late misfortunes of the Shoshonees make the price higher than common, so that one horse cost a pistol, one hundred balls, some powder, and a knife; another was changed for a musket; and in this way we obtained twenty-nine. The horses themselves are young and vigorous, but they are very poor, and most of them have sore backs, in consequence of the roughness of the Shoshonee saddle. We are therefore afraid of loading them too heavily, and are anxious to obtain one at least for each man, to carry the baggage, or the man himself, or in the last resource to serve as food; but with all our exertions we could not provide all our men with horses. We have, however, been fortunate in obtaining, for the last three days, a sufficient supply of flesh, our hunters having killed two or three deer every day.

Friday, 30. The weather was fine, and having now made all our purchases, we loaded our horses and prepared to start. The greater part of the band who had delayed their journey on our account, were also ready to depart. We then took our leave of the Shoshonees, who set out on their visit to the Missouri, at the same time that we, accompanied by the old guide, his four sons, and another Indian, began the descent of the river, along the same road which Captain Clarke had previously pursued.

After riding twelve miles, we encamped on the south bank of the river, and as the hunters had brought in three deer early in the morning, we did not feel the want of provisions.

Saturday, 31. At sun-rise we resumed our journey, and halted for three hours on Salmon creek, to let the horses graze. We then proceeded to the stream called Berry creek, eighteen miles from the camp of last night : as we passed along, the vallies and prairies were on fire in several places, in order to collect the bands of the Shoshonees and the Flatheads, for their journey to the Missouri. The weather was warm and sultry, but the only inconvenience which we apprehend is a dearth of food, of which we had to-day an abundance, having procured a deer, a goose, one duck, and a prairie fowl. On reaching Tower creek we left the former track of Captain Clarke, and began to explore the new route, which is our last hope of getting out of the mountains. For four miles, the road, which is tolerably plain, led us along Berry creek to some old Indian lodges, where we encamped for the night; the next day,

Sunday, September 1, 1805, we followed the same road which here left the creek, and turned to the north-west across the hills. During all the day we were riding over these hills, from which are many drains and small streams running into the river to the left, and at the distance of eighteen miles came to a large creek, called Fish creek, emptying into the Columbia, which is about six

miles from us. It had rained in the course of the
day, and commenced raining again towards evening. We therefore determined not to leave the
low grounds to-night, and after going up Fish
creek four miles, formed our encampment. The
country over which we passed is well watered,
but poor and rugged or stony, except the bottoms
of Fish creek, and even these are narrow. Two
men were sent to purchase fish of the Indians at
the mouth of the creek; and with the dried fish
which they obtained, and a deer and a few salmon
killed by the party, we were still well supplied.
Two bears were also wounded, but we could procure neither of them.

Monday, 2. This morning all the Indians left
us, except the old guide, who now conducted us
up Fish creek: at one mile and a half we passed a
branch of the river, coming in through a low ground
covered with pine on the left, and two and a half
miles further, is a second branch from the right:
after continuing our route along the hills covered
with pine, and a low ground of the same growth,
we arrived, at the distance of three and a half miles,
at the forks of the creek. The road which we
were following, now turned up the east side of
these forks, and, as our guide informed us, led to
the Missouri. We were therefore left without any
track; but as no time was to be lost, we began to
cut our road up the west branch of the creek.
This we effected with much difficulty; the thickets
of trees and brush, through which we were obliged

to cut our way, required great labour; the road itself was over the steep and rocky sides of the hills, where the horses could not move without danger of slipping down, while their feet were bruised by the rocks and stumps of trees. Accustomed as these animals were to this kind of life, they suffered severely; several of them fell to some distance down the sides of the hills, some turned over with the baggage, one was crippled, and two gave out, exhausted with fatigue. After crossing the creek several times, we at last made five miles, with great fatigue and labour, and encamped on the left side of the creek, in a small stony low ground. It was not, however, till after dark that the whole party was collected; and then, as it rained, and we killed nothing, we passed an uncomfortable night. The party had been too busily occupied with the horses, to make any hunting excursion; and though, as we came along Fish creek, we saw many beaver dams, we saw none of the animals themselves. In the morning,

Tuesday, 3, the horses were very stiff and weary. We sent back two men for the load of the horse which had been crippled yesterday, and which we had been forced to leave two miles behind. On their return we set out at eight o'clock, and proceeded up the creek, making a passage through the brush and timber along its borders. The country is generally supplied with pine, and in the low ground is a great abundance of fir trees and under bushes. The mountains are high and rugged, and those to the east of us covered with snow. With all our precautions, the horses were very much injured in passing over the ridges and steep points of the hills, and to add to the difficulty, at the distance of eleven miles, the high mountains closed the creek, so that we were obliged to leave the creek to the right, and cross the mountain abruptly. The ascent was here so steep, that several of the horses slipped and hurt themselves, but at last we succeeded in crossing the mountain, and encamped on a small branch of Fish creek. We had now made fourteen miles, in a direction nearly north, from the river; but this distance, though short, was very fatiguing, and rendered still more disagreeable by the rain, which began at three o'clock. At dusk it commenced snowing, and continued till the ground was covered to the depth of two inches, when it changed into a sleet. We here met with a serious misfortune, the last of our thermometers being broken by accident. After making a scanty supper on a little corn, and a few pheasants killed in the course of the day, we laid down to sleep; and next morning,

Wednesday, 4, found every thing frozen, and the ground covered with snow. We were obliged to wait some time, in order to thaw the covers of the baggage, after which we began our journey at eight o'clock. We crossed a high mountain, which forms the dividing ridge between the waters of the creek we had been ascending, and those running to the north and west. We had not gone more than six miles over the snow, when we reached the head of a stream from the right, which directed its course more to the westward. We descended the steep sides of the hills along its border, and at the distance of three miles found a small branch coming in from the eastward. We saw several of the argalia, but they were too shy to be killed, and we therefore made a dinner from a deer shot by one of the hunters. Then we pursued the course of the stream for three miles, till it emptied itself into a river from the east. In the wide valley at their junction, we discovered a large encampment of Indians : when we had reached them, and alighted from our horses, we were received with great cordiality. A council was immediately assembled, white robes were thrown over our shoulders, and the pipe of peace introduced. After this ceremony, as it was too late to go any farther, we encamped, and continued smoking and conversing with the chiefs till a late hour. The next morning,

Thursday, 5, we assembled the chiefs and warriors, and informed them who we were, and the purpose for which we visited their country. All this was however conveyed to them through so many different languages, that it was not comprehended without difficulty. We therefore proceeded to the more intelligible language of presents, and made four chiefs, by giving a medal and a small quantity of tobacco to each. We received in turn from the principal chief, a present consisting of the skins of a braro, an otter, and two antelopes, and were treated by the women to some dried roots and berries. We then began to traffic for horses, and succeeded in exchanging seven, and purchasing eleven, for which we gave a few articles of merchandize.

This encampment consists of thirty-three tents, in which were about four hundred souls, among whom eighty were men. They are called Ootlashoots, and represent themselves as one band of a nation called Tushepaws, a numerous people of four hundred and fifty tents, residing on the heads of the Missouri and Columbia rivers, and some of them lower down the latter river. In person these Indians are stout, and their complexion lighter than that common among Indians. The hair of the men is worn in queues of otter skin, falling in front over the shoulders. A shirt of dressed skin covers the body to the knee, and on this is worn occasionally a robe. To these were added leggings and moccasins. The women suffer their hair to fall in disorder over their face and shoulders, and their chief article of covering is a long shirt of skin, reaching down to the ancles, and tied round the waist. In other respects, as also in the few ornaments which they possess, their appearance is similar to that of the Shoshonees; there is, however, a difference between the language of these people, which is still farther increased by the very extraordinary pronunciation of the Ootlashoots. Their words have all a remarkably guttural sound, and there is nothing which seems to represent the tone of their speaking more exactly than the clucking of a fowl, or the noise of a parrot. This peculiarity renders their voices scarcely audible, except at a short distance, and when many of them are talking, forms a strange confusion of sounds. The common conversation we overheard, consisted of low guttural sounds, occasionally broken by a loud word or two, after which it would relapse and scarcely be distinguished. They seem kind and friendly, and willingly shared with us berries and roots, which formed their only stock of provisions. Their only wealth is their horses, which are very fine, and so numerous that this party had with them at least five hundred.

Friday, 6. We continued this morning with the Ootlashoots, from whom we purchased two more horses, and procured a vocabulary of their language. The Ootlashoots set off about two o'clock to join the different bands who were collecting at the three forks of the Missouri. We ourselves proceeded at the same time, and taking a direction N. 30 W. crossed within the distance of one mile and a half, a small river from the right, and a creek coming in from the north. This river is the main stream, and when it reaches the end of the valley, where the mountains close in upon it, is joined by the river on which we encamped last evening, as well as by the creek just mentioned. To the river, thus formed, we gave the name of

Captain Clarke, he being the first white man who had ever visited its waters. At the end of five miles on this course we had crossed the valley, and reached the top of a mountain covered with pine; this we descended along the steep sides and ravines for a mile and a half, when we came to a spot on the river, where the Ootlashoots had encamped a few days before. We then followed the course of the river, which is from twenty-five to thirty yards wide, shallow, stony, and the low grounds on its borders narrow. Within the distance of three and a half miles, we crossed it several times, and after passing a run on each side, encamped on its right bank, after making ten miles during the afternoon. The horses were turned out to graze, but those we had lately bought were secured and watched, lest they should escape, or be stolen by their former owners. Our stock of flour was now exhausted, and we had but little corn, and as our hunters had killed nothing, except two pheasants, our supper consisted chiefly of berries.

Saturday, 7. The greater part of the day the weather was dark and rainy; we continued through the narrow low grounds along the river, till at the distance of six miles we came to a large creek from the left, after which the bottoms widen. Four miles lower is another creek on the same side, and the valley now extends from one to three miles, the mountains on the left being high and bald, with snow on the summits, while the country to the right is open and hilly. Four miles beyond this is a creek running from the snow-topped mountains, and several runs on both sides of the river. Two miles from this last is another creek on the left. The afternoon was now far advanced, but not being able to find a fit place to encamp, we continued six miles further till after dark, when we halted for the night. The river here is still shallow and stony, but is increased to the width of fifty yards. The valley through which we passed is of a poor soil, and its fertility injured by the quantity of stone scattered over it. We met two horses which had strayed from the Indians, and were now quite wild. No fish was to be seen in the river, but we obtained a very agreeable supply of two deer, two cranes, and two pheasants.

Sunday, 8. We set out early : the snow-top'd hills on the left approach the river near our camp, but we soon reached a valley four or five miles wide, through which we followed the course of the river in a direction due north. We passed three creeks on the right, and several runs emptying themselves into the opposite side of the river. At the distance of eleven miles the river turned more towards the west : we pursued it for twelve miles, and encamped near a large creek coming in from the right, which, from its being divided into four different channels, we called Scattering creek. The valley continues to be a poor stony land, with scarcely any timber, except some pine trees along the waters and partially scattered on the hills to the right, which, as well as those on the left, have snow on them. The plant which forces itself most on our attention is a species of prickly pear very common on this part of the river : it grows in clusters, in an oval form about the size of a pigeon's egg, and its thorns are so strong and bearded, that when it penetrates our feet it brings away the pear itself. We saw two mares and a colt, which, like the horses seen yesterday, seemed to have lost themselves and become wild. Our game to-day consisted of two deer, an elk, and a prairie fowl.

Monday, 9. We resumed our journey through the valley, and leaving the road on our right, crossed the Scattering creek, and halted at the distance of twelve miles on a small run from the east, where we breakfasted on the remains of yesterday's hunt : we here took a meridian altitude, which gave the latitude of 46° 41′ 38″ 9‴ : we then continued, and at the distance of four miles passed over to the left bank of the river, where we found a large road through the valley. At this place is a handsome stream of very clear water, a hundred yards wide, with low banks, and a bed formed entirely of gravel : it has every appearance of being navigable, but as it contains no salmon, we presume there must be some fall below which obstructs their passage. Our guide could not inform us where this river discharged its waters : he said that, as far as he knew its course, it ran along the mountains to the north, and that not far from our present position, it was joined by another stream nearly as large as itself, which rises in the mountains to the east, near the Missouri, and flows through an extensive valley or open prairie. Through this prairie is the great Indian road to the waters of the Missouri ; and so direct is the route, that in four days' journey from this place we might reach the Missouri about thirty miles above what we called the Gates of the Rocky mountains, or the spot where the valley of that river widens into an extensive plain on entering the chain of mountains. At ten miles from our camp is a small creek falling in from the eastward, five miles below which we halted at a large stream which empties itself on the west side of the river. It is a fine bold creek of clear water about twenty yards wide, and we called it Traveller's-rest creek ; for as our guide told us that we should here leave the river, we determined to remain for the purpose of making celestial observations and collecting some food, as the country through which we are to pass has no game for a great distance.

The valley of the river through which we have been passing is generally a prairie from five to six miles in width, and with a cold gravelly white soil. The timber which it possesses is almost exclusively pine, chiefly of the long-leafed kind, with some spruce, and a species of fir resembling the Scotch fir : near the water courses are also seen a few narrow-leafed cotton-wood trees, and the only underbrush is the red-wood, honeysuckle, and rose-bushes. Our game was four deer, three geese, four ducks, and three prairie fowls : one of the hunters brought in a red-headed woodpecker of the large kind, common in the United States, but the first of the kind we have seen since leaving the Illinois.

Tuesday, 10. The morning being fair all the hunters were sent out, and the rest of the party employed in repairing their clothes : two of them were sent to the junction of the river from the east, along which the Indians go to the Missouri : it is about seven miles below Traveller's-rest creek ; the country at the forks is seven or eight miles wide, level and open, but with little timber : its course is to the north, and we incline to believe that this is the river which the Minnetarees had described to us as running from south to north along the west side of the Rocky mountains, not far from the sources of Medicine river : there is, moreover, reason to suppose, that after going as far northward as the head-waters of that river, it turns to the westward and joins the Tacootchetessee. Towards evening one of the hunters returned with three Indians, whom he had met in his excursion up Traveller's-rest creek : as soon as they saw him they prepared to attack him with arrows, but he quieted them by laying down his gun and advancing towards them, and soon persuaded them to come to the camp. Our Shoshonee guide could not speak the language of these people, but by the universal language of signs and gesticulations, which is perfectly intelligible among the Indians,

he found that these were three Tushepaw Flatheads
in pursuit of two men, supposed to be Shoshonees,
who had stolen twenty-three of their horses: we
gave them some boiled venison and a few presents:
such as a fish-hook, a steel to strike fire, and a little
powder; but they seemed better pleased with a
piece of riband which we tied in the hair of each
of them. They were, however, in such haste, lest
their horses should be carried off, that two of them
set off after sunset in quest of the robbers: the
third, however, was persuaded to remain with us
and conduct us to his relations: these, he said,
were numerous, and resided on the Columbia in
the plain below the mountains. From that place,
he added, the river was navigable to the ocean;
that some of his relations had been there last fall,
and seen an old white man who resided there by
himself, and who gave them some handkerchiefs
like those we have. The distance from this place
is five sleeps or days' journey. When our hunters
had all joined us, we found our provisions consisted
of four deer, a beaver, and three grouse.

The observation of to-day gave 46° 48′ 28″ as the
latitude of Traveller's-rest creek.

Wednesday, 11. Two of our horses having strayed
away, we were detained all the morning before
they were caught. In the mean-time our Tushepaw
Indian became impatient of the delay, and set out
to return home alone. As usual we had dispatched
four of our best hunters a-head, and as we hoped,
with their aid, and our present stock of provisions

o 4

to subsist on the route, we proceeded at three
o'clock up the right side of the creek, and encamped under some old Indian huts at the distance of
seven miles. The road was plain and good : the
valley is however narrower than that which we
left, and bordered by high and rugged hills to the
right, while the mountains on the left were covered
with snow. The day was fair and warm, the wind
from the north-west.

Thursday, 12. There was a white frost this morning. We proceeded at seven o'clock, and soon passed
a stream falling in on the right, near which was an
old Indian camp with a bath or sweating-house covered with earth. At two miles distance we ascended a high hill, and thence continued through
a hilly and thickly timbered country for nine miles,
when we came to the forks of the creek, where the
road branches up each fork. We followed the
western route, and finding that the creek made a
considerable bend at the distance of four miles,
crossed a high mountain in order to avoid the circuit. The road had been very bad during the first
part of the day, but the passage of the mountain,
which was eight miles across, was very painful to
the horses, as we were obliged to go over steep
stony sides of hills, and along the hollows and
ravines, rendered more disagreeable by the fallen
timber, chiefly pine, spruce pine and fir. We at
length reached the creek, having made twenty-three
miles of a route, so difficult, that some of the party
did not join us before ten o'clock. We found the

account of the scantiness of game but too true, as we were not able to procure any thing during the whole of yesterday, and to day we killed only a single pheasant. Along the road we observed many of the pine trees peeled off, which is done by the Indians to procure the inner bark for food in the spring.

Friday, 13. Two of our horses strayed away during the night, and one of them being Captain Lewis's, he remained with four men to search for them, while we proceeded up the creek: at the distance of two miles we came to several springs issuing from large rocks of a coarse hard grit, and nearly boiling hot. These seem to be much frequented, as there are several paths made by elk, deer, and other animals, and near one of the springs a hole or Indian bath, and roads leading in different directions. These embarrassed our guide, who mistaking the road, took us three miles out of the proper course over an exceedingly bad route. We then fell into the right road, and proceeded on very well, when, having made five miles, we stopped to refresh the horses. Captain Lewis here joined us, but not having been able to find his horse, two men were sent back to continue the search. We then proceeded along the same kind of country which we passed yesterday, and after crossing a mountain, and leaving the sources of the Traveller's-rest creek on the left, reached, after five miles riding, a small creek, which also came in from the left hand, passing through open glades, some of which were half a mile wide. The road which had been as usual rugged and stony, became firm, plain and level, after quitting the head of Traveller's-rest. We followed the course of this new creek for two miles, and encamped at a spot where the mountains close on each side. Other mountains covered with snow are in view, to the south-east and south-west. We were somewhat more fortunate to-day, in killing a deer and several pheasants, which were of the common species, except that the tail was black.

Saturday, 14. The day was very cloudy, with rain and hail in the vallies, while on the top of the mountains some snow fell. We proceeded early, and continuing along the right side of Glade creek, crossed a high mountain, and at the distance of six miles, reached the place where it is joined by another branch of equal size from the right. Near the forks the Tushepaws have had an encampment which is but recently abandoned, for the grass is entirely destroyed by horses, and two fish weirs across the creek are still remaining; no fish were however, to be seen. We here passed over to the left side of the creek, and began the ascent of a very high and steep mountain nine miles across. On reaching the other side we found a large branch from the left, which seems to rise in the snowy mountains to the south and south-east. We continued along the creek two miles further, when night coming on, we encamped opposite a small island at the mouth of a branch on the right side of the river. The mountains which we crossed to-

day were much more difficult than those of yesterday : the last was particularly fatiguing, being steep
and stony, broken by fallen timber, and thickly over-
grown by pine, spruce, fir, hacmatack, and tamarac.
Although we had made only seventeen miles we
were all very weary. The whole stock of animal
food was now exhausted, and we therefore killed
a colt, on which we made a hearty supper. From
this incident we called the last creek we had passed
from the south Colt-killed creek. The river itself
is eighty yards wide, with a swift current, and a
stony channel. Its Indian name is Kooskooskee.

Sunday, 15. At an early hour we proceeded
along the right side of the Kooskooskee over
steep rocky points of land, till at the distance of
four miles we reached an old Indian fishing-place :
the road here turned to the right of the water, and
began to ascend a mountain : but the fire and wind
had prostrated or dried almost all the timber on
the south side, and the ascents were so steep that
we were forced to wind in every direction round
the high knobs which constantly impeded our progress. Several of the horses lost their foot-hold
and slipped : one of them, which was loaded with
a desk and small trunk, rolled over and over for
forty yards, till his fall was stopped by a tree. The
desk was broken ; but the poor animal escaped
without much injury. After clambering in this
way for four miles, we came to a high snowy part
of the mountain where was a spring of water, at
which we halted two hours to refresh our horses.

On leaving the spring the road continued as bad
as it was below, and the timber more abundant.
At four miles we reached the top of the mountain,
and foreseeing no chance of meeting with water,
we encamped on the northern side of the mountain, near an old bank of snow, three feet deep.
Some of this we melted, and supped on the remains
of the colt killed yesterday. Our only game to-
day was two pheasants, and the horses on which
we calculated as a last resource begin to fail us, for
two of them were so poor, and worn out with
fatigue, that we were obliged to leave them behind.
All around us are high rugged mountains, among
which is a lofty range from south-east to north-
west, whose tops are without timber, and in
some places covered with snow. The night was
cloudy and very cold, and three hours before day-
break,

Monday, 16, it began to snow, and continued all
day, so that by evening it was six or eight inches
deep. This covered the track so completely, that
we were obliged constantly to halt and examine,
lest we should lose the route. In many places we
had nothing to guide us except the branches of
the trees, which being low had been rubbed by the
burdens of the Indian horses. The road was, like
that of yesterday, along steep hill sides, obstructed
with fallen timber, and a growth of eight different
species of pine, so thickly strewed that the snow
falls from them as we pass, and keeps us continually wet to the skin, and so cold, that we are

anxious lest our feet should be frozen, as we have only thin moccasins to defend them.

At noon we halted to let the horses feed on some long grass on the south side of the mountains, and endeavoured, by making fires, to keep ourselves warm. As soon as the horses were refreshed, Captain Clarke went a-head with one man, and at the distance of six miles reached a stream from the right, and prepared fires by the time of our arrival at dusk. We here encamped in a piece of low ground, thickly timbered, but scarcely large enough to permit us to lie level. We had now made thirteen miles. We were all very wet, cold, and hungry : but although before setting out this morning, we had seen four deer, yet we could not procure any of them, and were obliged to kill a second colt for our supper.

Thursday, 17. Our horses became so much scattered during the night, that we were detained till one o'clock before they were all collected. We then continued our route over high rough knobs, and several drains and springs, and along a ridge of country separating the waters of two small rivers. The road was still difficult, and several of the horses fell and injured themselves very much, so that we were unable to advance more than ten miles to a small stream, on which we encamped.

We had killed a few pheasants, but these being insufficient for our subsistence, we killed another of the colts. This want of provisions, and the extreme fatigue to which we were subjected, and the dreary prospects before us, began to dispirit the men. It was therefore agreed that Captain Clarke should go on a-head with six hunters, and endeavour to kill something for the support of the party. He therefore set out,

Wednesday, 18, early in the morning, in hopes of finding a level country from which he might send back some game. His route lay S. 85° W. along the same high dividing ridge, and the road was still very bad ; but he moved on rapidly, and at the distance of twenty miles was rejoiced on discovering far off an extensive plain towards the west and south-west, bounded by a high mountain. He halted an hour to let the horses eat a little grass on the hill sides, and then went on twelve and a half miles, till he reached a bold creek, running to the left, on which he encamped. To this stream he gave the very appropriate name of Hungry creek ; for having procured no game, they had nothing to eat.

In the meantime we were detained till after eight o'clock by the loss of one of our horses which had strayed away and could not be found. We then proceeded, but having soon finished the remainder of the colt killed yesterday, felt the want of provisions, which was more sensible from our meeting with no water, till towards nightfall we found some in a ravine among the hills. By pushing on our horses, almost to their utmost strength, we made eighteen miles.

We then melted some snow, and supped on a

little portable soup, a few canisters of which, with about twenty weight of bears oil, are our only remaining means of subsistence. Our guns are scarcely of any service, for there is no living creature in these mountains, except a few small pheasants, a small species of grey squirrel, and a blue bird of the vulture kind, about the size of a turtle-dove or jay, and even these are difficult to shoot.

Thursday, 19. Captain Clarke proceeded up the creek, along which the road was more steep and stony than any he had yet passed. At six miles distance he reached a small plain, in which he fortunately found a horse, on which he breakfasted, and hung the rest on a tree for the party in the rear. Two miles beyond this he left the creek, and crossed three high mountains, rendered almost impassable from the steepness of the ascent and the quantity of fallen timber. After clambering over these ridges and mountains, and passing the heads of some branches of Hungry creek, he came to a large creek running westward. This he followed for four miles, and then turned to the right down the mountain, till he came to a small creek to the left. Here he halted, having made twenty-two miles on his course, south eighty degrees west, though the winding route over the mountains almost doubled the distance. On descending the last mountain, the heat became much more sensible after the extreme cold he had experienced for several days past. Besides the breakfast in the morning, two pheasants were their only food during the day, and the only kinds of birds they saw were the blue jay, a small white-headed hawk, a larger hawk, crows, and ravens.

We followed soon after sun-rise. At six miles the ridge terminated, and we had before us the cheering prospect of the large plain to the south-west. On leaving the ridge we again ascended and went down several mountains, and six miles further came to Hungry creek where it was fifteen yards wide, and received the waters of a branch from the north. We went up it on a course nearly due west, and at three miles crossed a second branch flowing from the same quarter. The country is thickly covered with pine timber, of which we have enumerated eight distinct species. Three miles beyond this last branch of Hungry creek we encamped, after a fatiguing route of eighteen miles. The road along the creek is a narrow rocky path, near the borders of very high precipices, from which a fall seems almost inevitable destruction. One of our horses slipped, and rolling over with his load down the hill side, which was nearly perpendicular, and strewed with large irregular rocks, nearly a hundred yards, and did not stop till he fell into the creek : we all expected he was killed, but, to our astonishment, on taking off his load, he rose, and seemed but little injured, and in twenty minutes proceded with his load. Having no other provision we took some portable soup, our only refreshment during the day. This abstinence, joined with fatigue, has a visible effect on our health. The men are growing weak and losing their flesh very fast: several are afflicted with the dysentery, and eruptions of the skin are very common.

Friday, 20. Captain Clarke went on through a country as rugged as usual, till on passing a low mountain he came, at the distance of four miles, to the forks of a large creek. Down this he kept on a course south 60° west for two miles, then turning to the right, continued over a dividing ridge, where were the heads of several little streams, and at twelve miles distance descended the last of the Rocky mountains, and reached the level country. A beautiful open plain, partially supplied with pine, now presented itself. He continued for five miles, when he discovered three Indian boys, who, on observing the party, ran off and hid themselves in the grass. Captain Clarke immediately alighted, and giving his horse and gun to one of the men, went after the boys. He soon relieved their apprehensions, and sent them forward to the village, about a mile off, with presents of small pieces of ribband. Soon after the boys had reached home, a man came out to meet the party, with great caution, but he conducted them to a large tent in the village, and all the inhabitants gathered round to view, with a mixture of fear and pleasure, these wonderful strangers. The conductor now informed Captain Clarke, by signs, that this spacious tent was the residence of the great

chief, who had set out three days ago, with all
the warriors, to attack some of their enemies towards the south-west; that he would not return
before fifteen or eighteen days, and that in the
mean time there were only a few men left to guard
the women and children. They now set before
them a small piece of buffaloe meat, some dried
salmon, berries, and several kinds of roots. Among
these last is one which is round and much like an
onion in appearance, and sweet to the taste : it is
called quamash, and is eaten either in its natural
state, or boiled into a kind of soup, or made into
a cake, which is then called pasheco. After the
long abstinence this was a sumptuous treat; we
returned the kindness of the people by a few small
presents, and then went on in company with one
of the chiefs to a second village in the same plain,
at the distance of two miles. Here the party was
treated with great kindness and passed the night.
The hunters were sent out, but though they saw
some tracks of deer were not able to procure any
thing.

We were detained till ten o'clock before we could
collect our scattered horses; we then proceeded
for two miles, when to our great joy we found the
horse which Captain Clarke had killed, and a note,
apprising us of his intention of going to the plains
towards the south-west and collect provisions by
the time we reached him. At one o'clock we halted
on a small stream, and made a hearty meal of horse
flesh. On examination it now appeared that one

of the horses was missing, and the man in whose charge he had been was directed to return and search for him. He came back in two hours without having been able to find the horse ; but as the load was too valuable to be lost, two of the best woodsmen were directed to continue the search while we proceeded. Our general course was south 25° west, through a thick forest of large pine, which has fallen in many places, and very much obstructs the road. After making about fifteen miles, we encamped on a ridge where we could find but little grass and no water. We succeeded, however, in procuring a little from a distance, and supped on the remainder of the horse.

On descending the heights of the mountains, the soil becomes gradually more fertile, and the land through which we passed this evening, is of an excellent quality. It has a dark grey soil, though very broken, and with large masses of grey free-stone, above the ground in many places. Among the vegetable productions we distinguished the alder, honey-suckle, and huckle-berry, common in the United States, and a species of honey-suckle, known only westward of the Rocky mountains, which rises to the height of about four feet, and bears a white berry. There is also a plant resembling the choke-cherry, which grows in thick clumps eight or ten feet high, and bears a black berry, with a single stone, of a sweetish taste. The arbor vitæ too is very common, and grows to a great size, being from two to six feet in diameter.

Saturday 21. The free use of food to which he had not been accustomed, made Captain Clarke very sick both yesterday evening and during the whole of to-day. He therefore sent out all the hunters and remained himself at the village, as well on account of his sickness as for the purpose of avoiding suspicion, and collecting information from the Indians as to the route.

The two villages consist of about thirty double tents, and the inhabitants call themselves Chopunnish, or Pierced-nose. The chief drew a chart of the river, and explained, that a greater chief than himself, who governed this village and was called the Twisted-hair, was now fishing at the distance of half a day's ride down the river : his chart made the Kooskooskee fork a little below his camp, a second fork below, still further on a large branch flowed in on each side, below which the river passed the mountains : here was a great fall of water, near which lived white people, from whom were procured the white beads and brass ornaments worn by the women.

A chief of another band made a visit this morning, and smoked with Captain Clarke. The hunters returned without having been able to kill any thing; Captain Clarke purchased as much dried salmon, roots, and berries, as he could, with the few articles he chanced to have in his pockets, and having sent them, by one of the men, and a hired Indian back to Captain Lewis, he went on towards the camp of the Twisted-hair. It was four o'clock before he set

out, and the night soon came on ; but having met
an Indian coming from the river, they engaged him,
by a present of a neck-cloth, to guide them to the
Twisted-hair's camp. For twelve miles they proceeded through the plain before they reached the
river-hills, which are very high and steep. The
whole valley from these hills to the Rocky mountain is a beautiful level country, with a rich soil
covered with grass: there is, however, but little
timber, and the ground is badly watered; the plain
is so much lower than the surrounding hills, or so
much sheltered by them, that the weather is quite
warm, while the cold of the mountains was extreme.
From the top of the river hills they proceeded
down for three miles, till they reached the water
side, between eleven and twelve o'clock at night :
here they found a small camp of five squaws and
three children, the chief himself being encamped,
with two others, on a small island in the river : the
guide called to him and he soon came over. Captain Clarke gave him a medal, and they smoked
together till one o'clock.

We could not set out till eleven o'clock, because
being obliged in the evening to loosen our horses,
to enable them to find subsistence, it is always difficult to collect them in the morning. At that hour
we continued along the ridge on which we had
slept, and at a mile and a half reached a large creek
running to our left, just above its junction with
one of its branches. We proceeded down the low
grounds of this creek, which are level, wide, and

heavily timbered, but turned to the right at the distance of two and a half miles, and began to pass the broken and hilly country : but the thick timber had fallen in so many places that we could scarcely make our way. After going five miles we passed the creek on which Captain Clarke had encamped during the night of the 19th, and continued five miles further over the same kind of road, till we came to the forks of a large creek. We crossed the northern branch of this stream, and proceeded down it on the west side for a mile : here we found a small plain where there was tolerable grass for the horses, and therefore remained during the night, having made fifteen miles on a course, S. 30° W.

The arbor vitæ increases in size and quantity as we advance : some of the trees which we passed to-day being capable of forming perioques, at least forty-five feet in length. We were so fortunate also as to kill a few pheasants and a prairie wolf, which, with the remainder of the horse, supplied us with one meal, the last of our provisions, our food for the morrow being wholly dependent on the chance of our guns.

Sunday, 22. Captain Clarke passed over to the island with the Twisted-hair, who seemed to be cheerful and sincere in his conduct. The river at this place is about one hundred and sixty yards wide, but interrupted by shoals; and the low grounds on its borders are narrow. The hunters brought in three deer; after which Captain Clarke left his party, and accompanied by the Twisted-hair and his son, rode back to the village, where he arrived about sun-set: they then walked up together to the second village, where we had just arrived. We had intended to set out early, but one of the men having neglected to hobble his horse, he strayed away, and we were obliged to wait till nearly twelve o'clock. We then proceeded on a western course for two and a half miles, when we met the hunters sent by Captain Clarke from the village, seven and a half miles distant, with provisions. This supply was most seasonable, as we had tasted nothing since last night; and the fish, and roots, and berries, in addition to a crow which we killed on the route, completely satisfied our hunger. After this refreshment we proceeded in much better spirits, and at a few miles were overtaken by the two men who had been sent back after a horse on the 20th. They were perfectly exhausted with the fatigue of walking and the want of food; but as we had two spare horses, they were mounted and brought on to the village.

They had set out about three o'clock in the afternoon of the 20th, with one horse between them: after crossing the mountain, they came to the place where we had eaten the horse. Here they encamped, and having no food, made a fire, and roasted the head of the horse, which even our appetites had spared, and supped on the ears, skin, lips, &c. of the animal. The next morning, 21st, they found the track of the horse, and pursuing it, recovered the saddle-bags, and, at length, about eleven o'clock, the horse himself. Being now both mounted, they set out to return, and slept at a small stream : during the day they had nothing at all, except two pheasants, which were so torn to pieces by the shot, that the head and legs were the only parts fit for food. In this situation they found the next morning, 22d, that during the night their horses had run away from them, or been stolen by the Indians. They searched for them until nine o'clock, when seeing that they could not re-cover them, and fearful of starving if they remain-ed where they were, they set out on foot to join us, carrying the saddle-bags alternately. They walked as fast as they could during the day, till they reached us in a deplorable state of weakness and inanition.

As we approached the village, most of the wo-men, though apprised of our being expected, fled with their children into the neighbouring woods. The men, however, received us without any ap-prehension, and gave us a plentiful supply of pro-visions. The plains were now crowded with In-dians, who came to see the persons of the whites, and the strange things they brought with them ; but as our guide was perfectly a stranger to their language, we could converse by signs only. Our inquiries were chiefly directed to the situation of the country, the courses of the rivers, and the Indian villages, of all which we received information from several of the Indians; and as their accounts varied but little from each other, we were induced to place confidence in them. Among others, the Twisted-hair drew a chart of the river on a white elk skin. According to this, the Kooskooskee forks a few miles from this place; two days towards the south is another and larger fork, on which the Shoshonee, or Snake Indians fish; five days' journey further, is a large river from the northwest, into which Clarke's river empties itself: from the mouth of that river to the falls, is five days journey further: on all the forks, as well as on the main river, great numbers of Indians reside, and at the falls are establishments of whites. This was the story of the Twisted-hair.

Monday, 23. The chiefs and warriors were all assembled this morning, and we explained to them where we came from, the objects of our visiting them, and our pacific intentions towards all the Indians. This being conveyed by signs, might not have been perfectly comprehended, but appeared to give perfect satisfaction. We now gave a medal to two of the chiefs, a shirt in addition to the medal already received by the Twisted-hair, and delivered a flag and a handkerchief for the grand chief on his return. To these were added a knife, a handkerchief, and a small piece of tobacco for each chief. The inhabitants did not give us any provisions gratuitously. We therefore purchased a quantity of fish, berries (chiefly red haws), and roots; and in the afternoon went on to the second village. The Twisted-hair introduced us into his own tent, which consisted, however, of nothing more than pine bushes and bark, and gave us some dried salmon boiled. We continued our purchases, and obtained as much provision as our horses could carry, in their present weak condition, as far as the river. The men exchanged a few old canisters for dressed elk skins, of which they made shirts : great crowds of the natives were round us all night, but we have not yet missed any thing except a knife, and a few other articles stolen yesterday from a shot pouch. At dark we had a hard wind from the south-west, accompanied with rain, which lasted half' an hour, but in the morning,

Tuesday, 24, the weather was fair. We sent back Colter in search of the horses lost in the mountains, and having collected the rest, set out at ten o'clock along the same route already passed by Captain Clarke towards the river. All round the village, the women are busily employed in gathering and dressing the pasheco root, of which large quantities are heaped up in piles over the plain. We now felt severely the consequence of eating heartily after our late privations : Captain Lewis and two of the men were taken very ill last evening, and to-day he could scarcely sit on his horse, while others were obliged to be put on horseback, and some, from extreme weakness and pain, were forced to lie down along side of the road for some time. At sun-set, we reached the island where the hunters had been left on the 22d. They had been unsuccessful, having killed only two deer since that time, and two of them are very sick. A little below this island is a larger one, on which we encamped, and administered Rush's pills to the sick.

Wednesday, 25. The weather was very hot, and oppressive to the party, most of whom are now complaining of sickness. Our situation, indeed, rendered it necessary to husband our remaining strength, and it was determined to proceed down the river in canoes. Captain Clarke therefore set out with the Twisted-hair, and two young men, in quest of timber for canoes. As he went down the river, he crossed, at the distance of a mile, a creek from the right, which, from the rocks which obstructed its passage, he called Rockdam river. The hills along the river are high and steep : the low grounds are narrow, and the navigation of the river embarrassed by two rapids. At the distance of three miles further he reached two nearly equal forks of the river, one of which flowed in from the north. Here he rested for an hour, and cooked a few salmon which one of the Indians caught with a gig. Here, too, he was joined by two canoes of Indians from below : they were long, steady, and loaded with the furniture and provisions of two families. He now crossed the south fork, and returned to the camp on the south side, through a narrow pine bottom the greater part of the way, in which was found much fine timber for canoes. One

of the Indian boats with two men, set out at the
same time, and such was their dexterity in managing the pole, that they reached the camp within
fifteen minutes after him, although they had to drag
the canoe over three rapids. He found Captain
Lewis, and several of the men still very sick ; and
distributed to such as were in need of it, salts and
tartar emetic.

Thursday, 26. Having resolved to go down to
some spot calculated for building canoes, we set
out early this morning and proceeded five miles,
and encamped on low ground on the south, opposite the forks of the river. But so weak were the
men, that several were taken sick in coming down ;
the weather being oppressively hot. Two chiefs
and their families followed us, and encamped with
a great number of horses near us : and soon after
our arrival we were joined by two Indians, who
came down the north fork on a raft. We purchased some fresh salmon, and having distributed
axes, and portioned off the labour of the party,
began,

Friday, 27, at an early hour, the preparations for
making five canoes. But few of the men, however,
were able to work, and of these several were soon
taken ill, as the day proved very hot. The hunters,
too, returned without any game, and seriously in-
disposed, so that nearly the whole party was now
ill. We procured some fresh salmon ; and Colter,
who now returned with one of the horses, brought

half a deer, which was very nourishing to the invalids : several Indians, from a camp below, came up to see us.

Saturday, 28. The men continue ill, though some of those first attacked are recovering. Their general complaint is a heaviness at the stomach, and a lax, which is rendered more painful by the heat of the weather, and the diet of fish and roots, to which they are confined, as no game is to be procured. A number of Indians collect about us in the course of the day, to gaze at the strange appearance of every thing belonging to us.

Sunday, 29. The morning was cool, the wind from the south-west ; but in the afternoon the heat returned. The men continue ill ; but all those who are able to work are occupied at the canoes. The spirits of the party were much recruited by three deer brought in by the hunters ; and the next day,

Monday, 30th, the sick began to recruit their strength, the morning being fair and pleasant. The Indians pass in great numbers up and down the river, and we observe large quantities of small duck going down this morning.

Tuesday, October 1, 1805. The morning was cool, the wind easterly, but the latter part of the day was warm. We were visited by several Indians from the tribes below, and others from the main south fork. To two of the most distinguished men we made presents of a ring and broach, and to five others a piece of ribband, a little tobacco, and the fifth part of a neckcloth. We now dried our clothes and other articles, and selected some articles, such as the Indians admire, in order to purchase some provisions, as we have nothing left except a little dried fish, which operates as a complete purgative.

Wednesday, 2. The day is very warm. Two men were sent to the village, with a quantity of these articles, to purchase food. We are now reduced to roots, which produce violent pains in the stomach. Our work continued as usual, and many of the party are convalescent. The hunters returned in the afternoon with nothing but a small prairie-wolf, so that our provisions being exhausted, we killed one of the horses to eat, and provide soup for the sick.

Thursday, 3. The fine cool morning and easterly wind had an agreeable effect upon the party, most of whom are now able to work. The Indians from below left us, and we were visited by others from different quarters.

Friday, 4. Again we had a cool east wind from the mountains. The men were now much better, and Captain Lewis himself so far recovered as to walk about a little. Three Indians arrived to-day from the Great river to the south. The two men also returned from the village with roots and fish, and as the flesh of the horse killed yesterday was exhausted, we were confined to that diet, although unwholesome as well as unpleasant. The afternoon was warm.

6

Saturday 5. The wind easterly and the water cool. The canoes being nearly finished, it became necessary to dispose of our horses. They were therefore collected to the number of thirty-eight, and being branded and marked, were delivered to three Indians, the two brothers, and the son of a chief, who promises to accompany us down the river. To each of these men we gave a knife and some small articles, and they agreed to take good care of the horses till our return, The hunters with all their diligence are unable to kill any thing, the hills being high and rugged, and the woods too dry to hunt deer, which is the only game in the country. We therefore continue to eat dried fish and roots, which are purchased from the squaws, by means of small presents, but chiefly white beads, of which they are extravagantly fond. Some of these roots seem to possess very active properties, for after supping on them this evening, we were swelled to such a degree, as to be scarcely able to breathe for several hours. Towards night we launched two canoes, which proved to be very good.

Sunday, 6. This morning is again cool, and the wind easterly. The general course of the winds seems to resemble that which we observed on the east side of the mountain. While on the head waters of the Missouri, we had every morning a cool wind from the west. At this place a cool breeze springs up during the latter part of the night or near day-break, and continues till seven or eight o'clock, when it subsides, and the latter part of the day is warm. Captain Lewis is not so well as he was, and Captain Clarke was also taken ill. We had all our saddles buried in a cache near the river, about half a mile below, and deposited at the same time a canister of powder, and a bag of balls. The time which could be spared from our labours on the canoes, was devoted to some astronomical observations. The latitude of our camp as deduced from the mean of two observations is 46° 34′ 56″ 3‴ north.

Monday 7. This morning all the canoes were put in the water and loaded, the oars fixed, and every preparation made for setting out, but when we were all ready, the two chiefs who had promised to accompany us, were not to be found, and at the same time we missed a pipe tomahawk. We therefore proceeded without them. Below the Forks this river is called the Kooskooskee, and is a clear rapid stream, with a number of shoals and difficult places. For some miles the hills are steep, the low grounds narrow, but then succeeds an open country, with a few trees scattered along the river. At the distance of nine miles is a small creek on the left. We passed in the course of the day ten rapids, in descending which, one of the canoes struck a rock, and sprung a leak : we however continued for nineteen miles, and encamped on the left side of the river, opposite to the mouth of a small run. Here the canoe was unloaded and repaired, and two lead canisters of powder deposited ;

several camps of Indians were on the sides of the
river, but we had little intercourse with any of
them.

Tuesday, 8. We set out at nine o'clock. At
eight and a half miles we passed an island : four
and a half miles lower a second island, opposite a
small creek on the left side of the river. Five miles
lower is another island on the left: a mile and a
half below which is a fourth. At a short distance
from this is a large creek from the right, to which
we gave the name of Colter's creek, from Colter,
one of the men. We had left this creek about a
mile and a half, and were passing the last of fifteen
rapids, which we had been fortunate enough to
escape, when one of the canoes struck, and a hole
being made in her side, she immediately filled and
sunk. The men, several of whom could not swim,
clung to the boat till one of our canoes could be
unloaded, and with the assistance of an Indian
boat, they were all brought to shore. All the
goods were so much wetted, that we were obliged
to halt for the night, and spread them out to dry.
While all this was exhibited, it was necessary to
place two sentinels over the merchandize, for we
found that the Indians, though kind and disposed
to give us every aid during our distress, could not
resist the temptation of pilfering some of the small
articles. We passed, during our route of twenty
miles to-day, several encampments of Indians on
the islands, and near the rapids, which places are
chosen as most convenient for taking salmon. At

one of these camps we found our two chiefs, who, after promising to descend the river with us, had left us; they, however, willingly came on board after we had gone through the ceremony of smoking.

Wednesday, 9. The morning was as usual cool; but as the weather both yesterday and to-day was cloudy, our merchandize dried but slowly. The boat, though much injured, was repaired by ten o'clock, so as to be perfectly fit for service; but we were obliged to remain during the day till the articles were sufficiently dry to be reloaded: the interval we employed in purchasing fish for the voyage and conversing with the Indians. In the afternoon we were surprised to hear that our old Shoshonee guide and his son had left us, and been seen running up the river several miles above. As he had never given any notice of his intention, nor had even received his pay for guiding us, we could not imagine the cause of his desertion, nor did he ever return to explain his conduct. We requested the chief to send a horseman after him to beg he would return and receive what we owed him. From this, however, he dissuaded us, and said very frankly, that his nation, the Chopunnish, would take from the old man any presents that he might have on passing their camp.

The Indians came about our camp at night, and were very gay and good humoured with the men. Among other exhibitions was that of a squaw, who appeared to be crazy: she sang in a wild incoherent manner, and would offer to the spectators all the little articles she possessed, scarifying herself in a horrid manner if any one refused her present: she seemed to be an object of pity among the Indians, who suffered her to do as she pleased without interruption.

Thursday, 10. A fine morning. We loaded the canoes and set off at seven o'clock. At the distance of two and a half miles we had passed three islands, the last of which is opposite to a small stream on the right. Within the following three and a half miles is another island and a creek on the left, with wide low grounds, containing willow and cotton-wood trees, on which were three tents of Indians. Two miles lower is the head of a large island, and six and a half miles further we halted at an encampment of eight lodges on the left, in order to view a rapid before us: we had already passed eight, and some of them difficult; but this was worse than any of them, being a very hazardous ripple strewed with rocks: we here purchased roots and dined with the Indians. Among them was a man from the Falls, who says that he saw white people at that place, and is very desirous of going down with us; an offer which however we declined. Just above this camp we had passed a tent, near which was an Indian bathing himself in a small pond or hole of water, warmed by throwing in hot stones. After finishing our meal, we descended the rapid with no injury, except to one of our boats which ran against a rock, but in the course of an hour was brought off with only a small split in her side. This ripple, from its appearance and difficulty, we named the Rugged rapid. We went on over five other rapids of a less dangerous kind, and at the distance of five miles reached a large fork of the river from the south ; and after coming twenty miles, halted below the junction on the right side of the river : our arrival soon attracted the attention of the Indians, who flocked in all directions to see us. In the evening the Indian from the Falls, whom we had seen at the Rugged rapid, joined us with his son in a small canoe, and insisted on accompanying us to the Falls. Being again reduced to fish and roots, we made an experiment to vary our food by purchasing a few dogs, and after having been accustomed to horse-flesh, felt no disrelish to this new dish. The Chopunnish have great numbers of dogs, which they employ for domestic purposes, but never eat ; and our using the flesh of that animal soon brought us into ridicule as dog-eaters.

The country at the junction of the two rivers is an open plain on all sides, broken towards the left by a distant ridge of highland, thinly covered with timber : this is the only body of timber which the country possesses : for at the Forks there is not a tree to be seen, and during almost the whole descent of sixty miles down the Kooskooskee, from its Forks, there are very few. This southern branch is in fact the main stream of Lewis's river, on which we encamped when among the

Shoshonees. The Indians inform us that it is navigable for sixty miles; that not far from its mouth it receives a branch from the south; and a second and larger branch, two days' march up, and nearly parallel to the first Chopunnish villages, we met near the mountains. This branch is called Pawnashte, and is the residence of a chief, who, according to their expression, has more horses than he can count. The river has many rapids, near which are situated several fishing camps; there being ten establishments of this kind before reaching the first southern branch; one on that stream, five between that and the Pawnashte; one on that river, and two above it; besides many other Indians who reside high up on the more distant waters of this river. All these Indians belong to the Chopunnish nation, and live in tents of an oblong form, covered with flat roofs.

At its mouth Lewis's river is about two hundred and fifty yards wide, and its water is of a greenish-blue colour. The Kooskooskee, whose waters are clear as crystal, is one hundred and fifty yards in width, and after the union the river enlarges to the space of three hundred yards: at the point of the union is an Indian cabin, and in Lewis's river a small island.

The Chopunnish or Pierce-nosed nation, who reside on the Kooskooskee and Lewis's rivers, are in person stout, portly, well-looking men: the women are small, with good features, and generally handsome, though the complexion of both

sexes is darker than that of the Tushepaws. In
dress they resemble that nation, being fond of
displaying their ornaments. The buffaloe or elk-
skin robe decorated with beads, sea-shells, chiefly
mother-of-pearl, attached to an otter-skin collar,
and hung in the hair, which falls in front in two
queues; feathers, paints of different kinds, principally white, green, and light blue, all of which
they find in their own country: these are the chief
ornaments they use. In the winter they wear a
short shirt of dressed skins, long painted leggings
and moccasins, and a plait of twisted grass round
the neck.

The dress of the women is more simple, consisting of a long shirt of argalia or ibex skin,
reaching down to the ankles without a girdle: to
this are tied little pieces of brass and shells, and
other small articles : but the head is not at all ornamented. The dress of the female is indeed more
modest, and more studiously so than any we have
observed, though the other sex is careless of the
indelicacy of exposure.

The Chopunnish have very few amusements, for
their life is painful and laborious; and all their exertions are necessary to earn even their precarious.
subsistence. During the summer and autumn they
are busily occupied in fishing for salmon, and collecting their winter store of roots. In the winter
they hunt the deer on snow-shoes over the plains,
and towards spring cross the mountains to the Missouri, for the purpose of trafficking for buffaloe

robes. The inconveniences of that comfortless life are increased by frequent encounters with their enemies from the west, who drive them over the mountains with the loss of their horses, and sometimes the lives of many of the nation. Though originally the same people, their dialect varies very perceptibly from that of the Tushepaws: their treatment of us differed much from the kind and disinterested services of the Shoshonees: they are indeed selfish and avaricious; they part very reluctantly with every article of food or clothing; and while they expect a recompense for every service, however small, do not concern themselves about reciprocating any presents we may give them.

They are generally healthy — the only disorders which we have had occasion to remark being of a scrophulous kind, and for these, as well as for the amusement of those who are in good health, hot and cold bathing is very commonly used.

The soil of these prairies is of a light yellow clay, intermixed with small smooth grass : it is barren, and produces little more than a bearded grass about three inches high, and a prickly pear, of which we now found three species : the first is of the broad-leafed kind, common to the Missouri. The second has the leaf of a globular form, and is also frequent on the upper part of the Missouri, particularly after it enters the Rocky mountains. The third is peculiar to this country, and is much more inconvenient than the other two : it consists of

small thick leaves of a circular form, which grow
from the margin of each other, as in the broad-leafed
pear of the Missouri : these leaves are armed with
a greater number of thorns, which are stronger,
and appear to be barbed ; and as the leaf itself is
very slightly attached to the stem, as soon as one
thorn touches the moccasin it adheres and brings
with it the leaf, which is accompanied by a rein-
forcement of thorns.

CHAPTER XVIII.

THE PARTY PROCEED IN CANOES — DESCRIPTION OF AN
INDIAN SWEATING BATH AND BURIAL PLACE — MANY
DANGEROUS RAPIDS PASSED — NARROW ESCAPE OF ONE
OF THE CANOES — IN THE PASSAGE DOWN THEY ARE
VISITED BY SEVERAL INDIANS, ALL OF WHOM MANIFEST
PACIFIC DISPOSITIONS — DESCRIPTION OF THE SOKULK
TRIBE — THEIR DRESS, AND MANNER OF BUILDING HOUSES
— THEIR PACIFIC CHARACTER — THEIR HABITS OF
LIVING — THEIR MODE OF BOILING SALMON — VAST
QUANTITIES OF SALMON AMONGST THE SOKULK — COUN-
CIL HELD WITH THIS TRIBE — THE TERROR AND CON-
STERNATION EXCITED BY CAPTAIN CLARKE, CONCERNING
WHICH AN INTERESTING CAUSE IS RELATED — SOME
ACCOUNT OF THE PISQUITPAWS — THEIR MODE OF BURY-
ING THEIR DEAD.

FRIDAY, October 11, 1805. This morning
the wind was from the east, and the weather
cloudy. We set out early, and at the distance of
a mile and a half, reached a point of rocks in a
bend of the river towards the left, near to which
was an old Indian house, and a meadow on the opposite bank. Here the hills came down towards
the water, and formed by the rocks, which have
fallen from their sides, a rapid over which we
dragged the canoes. We passed, a mile and a half
further, two Indian lodges in a bend towards the

right, and at six miles from our camp of last evening reached the mouth of a brook on the left. Just above this stream we stopped for breakfast at a large encampment of Indians on the same side : we soon began to trade with them for a stock of provisions, and were so fortunate as to purchase seven dogs and all the fish they would spare : while this traffic was going on, we observed a vapour bath or sweating house in a different form from that used on the frontiers of the United States, or in the Rocky mountains. It was a hollow square of six or eight feet deep, formed in the river bank by damming up with mud the other three sides, and covering the whole completely, except an aperture about two feet wide at the top. The bathers descend by this hole, taking with them a number of heated stones, and jugs of water ; and after being seated round the room, throw the water on the stones till the steam becomes of a temperature sufficiently high for their purposes. The baths of the Indians in the Rocky mountains are of different sizes, the most common being made of mud and sticks like an oven, but the mode of raising the steam is exactly the same. Among both these nations it is very uncommon for a man to bathe alone, he is generally accompanied by one, or sometimes several of his acquaintances ; indeed it is so essentially a social amusement, that to decline going in to bathe when invited by a friend, is one of the highest indignities which can be offered to him. The Indians on the frontiers generally use a bath which will accommodate only one person, and is formed of a wickered work of willows about four feet high, arched at the top, and covered with skins. In this the patient sits till by means of the heated stones and water he has perspired sufficiently. Almost universally these baths are in the neighbourhood of running water, into which the Indians plunge immediately on coming out of the vapour bath, and sometimes return again, and subject themselves to a second perspiration. This practice is, however, less frequent among our neighbouring nations than those to the westward. This bath is employed either for pleasure or for health, and is used indiscriminately for rheumatism, venereal, or in short for all kinds of diseases.

On leaving this encampment we passed two more rapids, and some swift water, and at the distance of four and a half miles reached one which was much more difficult to pass. Three miles beyond this rapid, are three huts of Indians on the right, where we stopped, and obtained in exchange for a few trifles some pashequa roots, five dogs, and a small quantity of dried fish. We made our dinner of part of each of these articles, and then proceeded on without any obstruction, till, after making twelve and a half miles, we came to a stony island on the right side of the river, opposite to which is a rapid, and a second at its lower point. About three and a half miles beyond the island is a small brook which empties itself into a bend on the right, where we encamped at two Indian huts, which are

now inhabited. Here we met two Indians belonging to a nation who reside at the mouth of this
river. We had made thirty-one miles to-day, although the weather was warm, and we found the
current obstructed by nine different rapids, more
or less difficult to pass. All these rapids are fishing places of great resort in the season, and as we
passed we observed near them slabs and pieces of
split timber raised from the ground, and some entire houses, which are vacant at present, but will
be occupied as soon as the Indians return from the
plains on both sides of the river, where our chief
informs us they are now hunting the antelope.
Near each of these houses is a small collection of
graves, the burial places of those who frequent
these establishments. The dead are wrapped up
in robes of skins, and deposited in graves, which
are covered over with earth, and marked or secured
by little pickets or pieces of wood, stuck promiscuously over and around it. The country on both
sides, after mounting a steep ascent of about two
hundred feet, becomes an open, level, and fertile
plain, which is, however, as well as the borders of
the river itself, perfectly destitute of any kind of
timber ; and the chief growth which we observed,
consisted of a few low black-berries. We killed
some geese and ducks. The wind in the after
part of the day changed to the south-west, and became high, but in the morning,

Saturday, 12, it shifted to the east, and we had
a fair cool morning. After purchasing all the pro-

visions these Indians would spare, which amounted
to only three dogs and a few fish, we proceeded.
We soon reached a small island, and, in the course
of three miles, passed three other islands, nearly
opposite to each other, and a bad rapid on the left
in the neighbourhood of them. Within the following seven miles we passed a small rapid, and an
island on the left, another stony island, and a rapid on the right, just below which a brook comes
in on the same side, and came to a bend towards the
right, opposite to a small island. From this place
we saw some Indians on the hills, but they were
too far off for us to have any intercourse, and
shewed no disposition to approach us. After going on two miles to a bend towards the left, we
found the plains, which till now had formed rugged
cliffs over the river, leaving small and narrow bottoms, become much lower on both sides; and the
river itself widens to the space of four hundred
yards, and continues for the same width, the country rising by a gentle ascent towards the high
plains. At two and a half miles is a small creek
on the left, opposite to an island. For the three
following miles the country is low, and open on
both sides, after which it gradually rises, till we
reached a bend of the river towards the right,
three and a half miles further, in the course of
which we passed a rapid and an island. The wind
now changed to the south-west, and became violent. We passed an island at the distance of four
miles, another one mile beyond it, where the wa-

9

ter was swift and shallow; and two miles further, a rapid at the upper point of a small stony island. We went along this island by the mouth of a brook on the right, and encamped on the same side, opposite to a small island close under the left shore. Our day's journey had been thirty miles, and we might have gone still farther, but as the evening was coming on, we halted at the head of a rapid, which the Indians represented as dangerous to pass, for the purpose of examining it before we set out in the morning. The country has much the same appearance as that we passed yesterday, consisting of open plains, which, when they approach the water, are faced with a dark-coloured rugged stone. The river is, as usual, much obstructed by islands and rapids, some of which are difficult to pass. Neither the plains nor the borders of the river possess any timber, except a few hack-berry bushes and willows; and as there is not much driftwood, fuel is very scarce.

Sunday, 13. The morning was windy and dark, and the rain, which began before day-light, continued till near twelve o'clock. Having viewed very accurately the whole of this rapid, we set out, the Indians going on before us to pilot the canoes. We found it, as had been reported, a very dangerous rapid, about two miles in length, and strewed with rocks in every direction, so as to require great dexterity to avoid running against them. We, however, passed through the channel, which is towards the left, without meeting with any accident. Two miles below it we had another bad rapid, a mile beyond which is a large creek in a bend to the left. This we called Kimooenim creek.

On leaving it the river soon became crowded with rough black rocks, till at the distance of a mile it forms a rapid, which continues for four miles, and during the latter part of it, for a mile and a half, the whole river is compressed into a narrow channel, not more than twenty-five yards wide. The water happened to be low as we passed, but during the high waters the navigation must be very difficult. Immediately at the end of this rapid, is a large stream in a bend to the right, which we called Drewyer's river, after George Drewyer, one of the party. A little below the mouth of this river is a large fishing establishment, where there are the scaffolds and timbers of several houses piled up against each other; and the meadow adjoining contains a number of holes, which seem to have been used as places of deposit for fish for a great length of time. There were no entire houses standing, and we saw only two Indians who had visited the narrows; but we were overtaken by two others, who accompanied us on horseback down the river, informing us that they meant to proceed by land down to the great river. Nine and a half miles below Drewyer's river, we passed another rapid, and three and a half miles farther, reached some high cliffs in a bend to the left. Here, after passing the timbers of a house, which were preserved on forks, we encamped on the right side, near a collection of graves, such as we had seen above. The country was still an open plain without timber, and our day's journey had no variety, except the fishing-houses, which are scattered near the situations convenient for fishing, but are now empty. Our two Indian companions spent the night with us.

Monday, 14. The wind was high from the south-west during the evening, and this morning it changed to the west, and the weather became very cold until about twelve o'clock, when it shifted to the south-west, and continued in that quarter during the rest of the day. We set out early, and after passing some swift water, reached at two and a half miles a rock of a very singular appearance. It was situated on a point to the left, at some distance from the ascending country, very high and large, and resembling in its shape the hull of a ship. At five miles we passed a rapid; at eight another rapid, and a small island on the right, and at ten and a half a small island on the right. We halted a mile and a half below, for the purpose of examining a much larger and more dangerous rapid than those we had yet passed. It is three miles in length, and very difficult to navigate. We had scarcely set out, when three of the canoes stuck fast in endeavouring to avoid the rocks in the channel; soon after in passing two small rocky islands, one of the canoes struck a rock, but was prevented from upsetting; and, fortunately, we all arrived safe at the lower end of the rapid. Here we dined, and then proceeded, and soon reached another rapid on both sides of the river, which was divided by an island.

As we were descending it one of the boats was driven crosswise against a rock in the middle of the current. The crew attempted to get her off, but the waves dashed over her, and she soon filled: they got out on the rock and held her above water, with great exertion, till another canoe was unloaded and sent to her relief, but they could not prevent a great deal of her baggage from floating down the stream. As soon as she was lightened, she was hurried down the channel, leaving the crew on the rock. They were brought off by the rest of the party, and the canoe itself, and nearly all that had been washed overboard, were recovered. The chief loss was the bedding of two of the men, a tomahawk, and some small articles. But all the rest were wetted, and though by drying we were able to save the powder, all the loose packages of which were in this boat, yet we lost all the roots and other provisions, which were spoilt by the water. In order to diminish the loss as far as was in our power, we halted for the night on an island, and exposed every thing to dry. On landing we found some split timber for houses which the Indians had very securely covered with stone, and also a place where they had deposited their fish. We have hitherto abstained scrupulously from taking any thing belonging to the Indians; but on this occasion we were compelled to depart from this rule; and as there was no other timber to be found in any direction for fire-wood, and no owner appeared from whom it could be purchased, we used a part of these split planks, bearing in mind our obligation to repay the proprietor whenever we should discover him. The only game which we observed were geese and ducks; of the latter we killed some, and a few of the blue-winged teal. Our journey was fifteen miles in length.

Tuesday, 15. The morning was fair, and being obliged to remain for the purpose of drying the baggage, we sent out the hunters to the plains, but they returned at ten o'clock, without having seen even the tracks of any large game, but brought in three geese and two ducks. The plains are waving, and as we walked in them, we could plainly discover a range of mountains bearing south-east and north-west, becoming higher as they advanced towards the north, the nearest point, bearing south about sixty miles from us. Our stores being sufficiently dry to be reloaded, and as we shall be obliged to stop for the purpose of making some celestial observations at the mouth of the river, which cannot be at a great distance, we concluded to embark and complete the drying at that place: we therefore set out at two o'clock. For the first four miles we passed three islands, at the lower points of which were the same number of rapids, besides a fourth at a distance from them. During the next ten miles we passed eight islands and

three more rapids, and reached a point of rocks
on the left side. The islands were of various sizes,
but were all composed of round stone and sand:
the rapids were in many places difficult and dangerous to pass. About this place the country becomes lower than usual, the ground over the river
not being higher than ninety or a hundred feet, and
extending back into a waving plain. Soon after
leaving this point of rocks, we entered a narrow
channel formed by the projecting cliffs of the
bank, which rise nearly perpendicular from the
water. The river is not however rapid, but gentle
and smooth during its confinement, which lasts
for three miles, when it falls, or rather widens into
a kind of basin, nearly round, and without any perceptible current. After passing through this basin,
we were joined by the three Indians who had
piloted us through the rapids since we left the
forks, and who, in company with our two chiefs, had
gone before us. They had now halted here to warn
us of a dangerous rapid, which begins at the lower
point of the basin. As the day was too far spent to
descend it, we determined to examine before we
attempted it, and therefore landed near an island
at the head of the rapid, and studied particularly
all its narrow and difficult parts. The spot where we
landed was an old fishing establishment, of which
there yet remained the timbers of a house carefully
raised on scaffolds to protect them against the
spring tide. Not being able to procure any other
fuel, and the night being cold, we were again

obliged to use the property of the Indians, who still remain in the plains hunting the antelope. Our progress was only twenty miles, in consequence of the difficulty of passing the rapids. Our game consisted of two teal.

Wednesday, 16. Having examined the rapids, which we found more difficult than the report of the Indians had induced us to believe, we set out early, and putting our Indian guide in front, our smallest canoe next, and the rest in succession, began the descent : the passage proved to be very disagreeable ; as there is a continuation of shoals extending from bank to bank for the distance of three miles, during which the channel is narrow and crooked, and obstructed by large rocks in every direction, so as to require great dexterity to avoid being dashed on them. We got through the rapids with no injury to any of the boats except the hindmost, which ran on a rock ; but by the assistance of the other boats, and of the Indians, who were very alert, she escaped, though the baggage she contained was wetted. Within three miles after leaving the rapid we passed three small islands, on one of which were the parts of a house put on scaffolds as usual, and soon after came to a rapid at the lower extremity of three small islands ; and a second at the distance of a mile and a half below them ; reaching, six miles below the great rapid, a point of rocks at a rapid opposite to the upper point of a small island on the left. Three miles further is another rapid ; and two miles beyond this a very bad rapid, or rather a fall of the river : this, on examination, proved so difficult to pass, that we thought it imprudent to attempt it, and therefore unloaded the canoes and made a portage of three quarters of a mile. The rapid, which is of about the same extent, is much broken by rocks and shoals, and has a small island in it on the right side. After crossing by land, we halted for dinner, and whilst we were eating were visited by five Indians, who came up the river on foot in great haste : we received them kindly, smoked with them, and gave them a piece of tobacco to smoke with their tribe : on receiving the present they set out to return, and continued running as fast as they could while they remained in sight. Their curiosity had been excited by the accounts of our two chiefs, who had gone on in order to apprise the tribes of our approach and of our friendly dispositions towards them. After dinner we reloaded the canoes and proceeded : we soon passed a rapid opposite to the upper point of a sandy island on the left, which has a smaller island near it. At three miles is a gravelly bar in the river : four miles beyond this, the Kimooenim empties itself into the Columbia, and at its mouth has an island just below a small rapid. We halted above the point of junction on the Kimooenim to confer with the Indians, who had collected in great numbers to receive us. On landing, we were met by our two chiefs, to whose good offices we were indebted for this reception, and also the two Indians

who had passed us a few days since on horseback ; one of whom appeared to be a man of
influence, and harangued the Indians on our arrival. After smoking with the Indians, we formed
a camp at the point where the two rivers unite,
near to which we found some drift-wood, and were
supplied by our two old chiefs with the stalks of
willows and some small bushes for fuel. We had
scarcely fixed the camp and got the fires prepared,
when a chief came from the Indian camp about a
quarter of a mile up the Columbia, at the head of
nearly two hundred men: they formed a regular
procession, keeping time to the noise, rather than
the music, of their drums, which they accompanied with their voices. As they advanced they
formed a semicircle round us, and continued singing for some time : we then smoked with them all,
and communicated, as well as we could by signs,
our friendly intentions towards all nations, and our
joy at finding ourselves surrounded by our children :
we then proceeded to distribute presents to them,
giving the principal chief a large medal, a shirt and
handkerchief; to the second chief, a medal of a
smaller size ; and to a third chief, who came down
from some of the upper villages, a small medal and
a handkerchief. This ceremony being concluded
they left us ; but in the course of the afternoon,
several of them returned and remained with us till
a late hour. After they had dispersed, we proceeded to purchase provisions, and were enabled
to collect seven dogs, to which some of the Indians

added small presents of fish, and one of them gave us twenty pounds of fat dried horse-flesh.

Thursday, October 17. The day being fair, we were occupied in making the necessary observations for determining our longitude, and obtained a meridian altitude, from which it appeared that we were in latitude 46° 15' 13" 9'''. We also measured the two rivers by angles, and found that at the junction the Columbia is nine hundred and sixty yards wide, and Lewis's river five hundred and seventy-five; but soon after they unite, the former widens to the space of from one to three miles, including the islands. From the point of junction the country is a continued plain, which is low near the water, from which it rises gradually, and the only elevation to be seen is a range of high country running from the north-east towards the south-west, where it joins a range of mountains from the south-west, and is on the opposite side about two miles from the Columbia. There is through this plain no tree and scarcely any shrub, except a few willow bushes; and even of smaller plants there is not much more than the prickly pear, which is in great abundance, and is even more thorny and troublesome than any we have yet seen. During this time, the principal chief came down with several of his warriors and smoked with us: we were also visited by several men and women, who offered dogs and fish for sale, but as the fish was out of season, and at present abundant in the river, we contented ourselves with purchasing all the dogs

we could obtain. The nation among which we
now are, call themselves Sokulks ; and with them
are united a few of another nation, who reside on
a western branch, emptying itself into the Columbia a few miles above the mouth of the latter river,
and whose name is Chimnapum. The languages
of these nations, of each of which we obtained a
vocabulary, differ but little from each other, or
from that of the Chopunnish who inhabit the Kooskooskee and Lewis's rivers. In their dress and
general appearance also, they resemble much those
nations ; the men wearing a robe of deer or antelope skin, under which a few of them have a short
leathern shirt. The most striking difference between
them is among the females, the Sokulk women being
more inclined to corpulency than any we have yet
seen : their stature is low, their faces broad, and
their heads flattened in such a manner, that the
forehead is in a straight line from the nose to the
crown of the head : their eyes are of a dirty sable,
their hair, too, is coarse and black, and braided as
above, without ornament of any kind : instead of
wearing, as do the Chopunnish, long leathern
shirts, highly decorated with beads and shells, the
Sokulk females have no other covering but a truss
or piece of leather tied round the hips, and then
drawn tight between the legs. The ornaments
usually worn by both sexes are large blue or white
beads, either pendant from their ears, or round the
necks, wrists, and arms ; they have likewise bracelets of brass, copper, and horn, and some trinkets

of shells, fish-bones, and curious feathers. The houses of the Sokulks are made of large mats of rushes, and are generally of a square or oblong form, varying in length from fifteen to sixty feet, and supported in the inside by poles or forks about six feet high ; the top is covered with mats, leaving a space of twelve or fifteen inches, the whole length of the house, for the purpose of admitting the light and suffering the smoke to pass through : the roof is nearly flat, which seems to indicate that rains are not common in this open country, and the house is not divided into apartments, the fire being in the middle of the large room, and immediately under the hole in the roof: the rooms are ornamented with their nets, gigs, and other fishing tackle, as well as the bow for each inhabitant, and a large quiver of arrows, which are headed with flint and stones.

The Sokulks seem to be of a mild and peaceable disposition, and live in a state of comparative happiness. The men, like those on the Kimooenim, are said to content themselves with a single wife, with whom we observe the husband shares the labours of procuring subsistence much more than is usual among savages. What may be considered as an unequivocal proof of their good disposition, is the great respect which was shown to old age. Among other marks of it, we observed in one of the houses an old woman perfectly blind, and who, we were informed, had lived more than a hundred winters. In this state of decrepitude, she occupied the best position in the house, seemed to be treated with great kindness, and whatever she said was listened to with much attention. They are by no means intrusive, and as their fisheries supply them with a competent, if not an abundant sub-sistence, although they receive thankfully whatever we choose to give, they do not importune us by begging. The fish is, indeed, their chief food, except the roots, and the casual supplies of the antelope, which, to those who have only bows and arrows, must be very scanty. This diet may be the direct or remote cause of the chief disorder which prevails among them, as well as among the Flatheads, on the Kooskooskee and Lewis's rivers. With all these Indians a bad soreness of the eyes is a very common disorder, which is suffered to ripen by neglect, till many are deprived of one of their eyes, and some have totally lost the use of both. This dreadful calamity may reasonably, we think, be imputed to the constant reflection of the sun on the waters where they are continually fishing in the spring, summer, and fall, and during the rest of the year on the snows of a country which affords no object to relieve the sight. Among the Sokulks too, and indeed among all the tribes whose chief subsistence is fish, we have observed that bad teeth are very general : some have the teeth, particularly those of the upper jaw, worn down to the gums, and many of both sexes, and even of middle age, have lost them almost entirely. This decay of the teeth is a circumstance very unusual among the

Indians, either of the mountains or the plains, and
seems peculiar to the inhabitants of the Columbia.
We cannot avoid regarding as one principal cause
of it, the manner in which they eat their food.
The roots are swallowed as they are dug from the
ground, frequently nearly covered with a gritty
sand : so little idea have they that this is offensive,
that all the roots they offer us for sale are in the
same condition. A second and a principal cause
may be their great use of the dried salmon, the
bad effects of which are most probably increased
by their mode of cooking it, which is simply to
warm, and then swallow the rind, scales, and flesh,
without any preparation. The Sokulks possess but
few horses, the greater part of their labours being
performed in canoes. Their amusements are similar to those of the Missouri Indians.

In the course of the day Captain Clarke, in a
small canoe with two men, ascended the Columbia.
At the distance of five miles he passed an island in
the middle of the river, at the head of which is a
small and not a dangerous rapid. On the left
bank of the river, opposite to this river, is a fishing-
place, consisting of three mat-houses. Here were
great quantities of salmon drying on scaffolds ;
and, indeed, from the mouth of the river upwards,
he saw immense numbers of dead salmon strewed
along the shore or floating on the surface of
the water, which is so clear that the salmon
may be seen swimming in it at the depth of
fifteen or twenty feet. The Indians, who had

collected on the banks to view him, now joined him in eighteen canoes, and accompanied him up the river. A mile above the rapids he came to the lower point of an island, where the course of the river, which had been from its mouth N. 83° W. now became due west. He proceeded in that direction, when observing three houses of mats at a short distance, he landed to visit them. On entering one of the houses he found it crowded with men, women, and children, who immediately provided a mat for him to sit on, and one of the party undertook to prepare something to eat. He began by bringing in a piece of pine wood that had drifted down the river, which he split into small pieces, with a wedge made of the elk's horn, by means of a mallet of stone curiously carved. The pieces were then laid on the fire, and several round stones placed upon them ; one of the squaws now brought a bucket of water, in which was a large salmon about half dried, and as the stones became heated, they were put into the bucket till the salmon was sufficiently boiled for use. It was then taken out, put on a platter of rushes neatly made, and laid before Captain Clarke, and another was boiled for each of his men. During these preparations he smoked with those about him who would accept of tobacco, but very few were desirous of smoking, a custom which is not general among them, and chiefly used as a matter of form in great ceremonies. After eating the fish, which was of an excellent flavour, Captain Clarke set out, and at the distance of four miles from the last island, came to the lower point of another near the left shore, where he halted at two large mat-houses. Here, as at the three houses below, the inhabitants were occupied in splitting and drying salmon. The multitudes of this fish are almost inconceivable. The water is so clear that they can readily be seen at the depth of fifteen or twenty feet; but at this season they float in such quantities down the stream, and are drifted ashore, that the Indians have only to collect, split and dry them on the scaffolds. Where they procure the timber of which these scaffolds are composed he could not learn; but as there is nothing but willow bushes to be seen for a great distance from the place, it rendered very probable, what the Indians assured him by signs, that they often used dried fish as fuel for the common occasions of cooking. From this island they shewed him the entrance of a western branch of the Columbia, called the *Tapteal,* which, as far as could be seen, bears nearly west, and empties itself about eight miles above into the Columbia; the general course of which is north-west: towards the southwest a range of highland runs parallel to the river, at the distance of two miles on the left, while on the right side the country is low and covered with the prickly pear, and a weed or plant two or three feet high, resembling whins. To the eastward is a range of mountains about fifty or sixty miles distant, which bear north and south; but neither in the low grounds, nor in the highlands, is any tim-

ber to be seen. The evening coming on, he determined not to proceed further than the island, and
therefore returned to camp, accompanied by three
canoes, which contained twenty Indians. In the
course of his excursion he shot several grouse and
ducks, and received some presents of fish, for
which he gave in return small pieces of ribband.
He also killed a prairie cock, an animal of the
pheasant kind, but about the size of a small turkey.
It measured from the beak to the end of the toe
two feet six inches and three quarters, from the
extremity of the wings three feet six inches, and
the feathers of the tail were thirteen inches long.
This bird we have seen nowhere except on this
river. Its chief food is the grasshopper, and the
seed of the wild plant, which is peculiar to this
river and the upper parts of the Missouri.

The men availed themselves of this day's rest to
mend their clothes, dress skins, and put their
arms in complete order, an object always of pri-
mary concern, but particularly at a moment when
we are surrounded by so many strangers.

Friday, 18. We were visited this morning by
several canoes of Indians, who joined those who
were already with us, and soon opened a numerous
council. We informed them, as we had done all
the other Indian nations, of our friendship for
them, and of our desire to promote peace among
all our red children in this country. This was
conveyed by signs through the means of our two
chiefs, and seemed to be perfectly understood.

We then made a second chief, and gave to all the chiefs a string of wampum, in remembrance of what we had said. Whilst the conference was going on, four men came in a canoe from a large encampment on an island about eight miles below, but after staying a few minutes returned without saying a word to us. We now procured from the principal chief and one of the Cuimnapum nation a sketch of the Columbia, and the tribes of his nation living along its banks and those of the Tapteal. They drew it with a piece of coal on a robe, and as we afterwards transferred it to paper, it exhibited a valuable specimen of Indian delineation.

Having completed the purposes of our stay, we now began to lay in our stores, and fish being out of season, purchased forty dogs, for which we gave small articles, such as bells, thimbles, knitting-needles, brass wire, and a few beads, an exchange with which they all seemed perfectly satisfied. These dogs, with six prairie cocks killed this morning, formed a plentiful supply for the present. We here left our guide and the two young men who had accompanied him, two of the three not being willing to go any further, and the third could be of no use, as he was not acquainted with the river below. We therefore took no Indians but our two chiefs, and resumed our journey in the presence of many of the Sokulks, who came to witness our departure. The morning was cool and fair, and the wind from the south-east. Soon after proceeding,

We passed the island in the mouth of Lewis's river, and at eight miles reached a larger island, which extends three miles in length. On going down by this island there is another on the right, which commences about the middle of it, and continues for three and a half miles. While they continue parallel to each other, they occasion a rapid near the lower extremity of the first island, opposite to which on the second island are nine lodges built of mats, and intended for the accommodation of the fishermen, of whom we saw great numbers, and vast quantities of dried fish on their scaffolds.

On reaching the lower point of the island, we landed to examine a bad rapid, and then undertook the passage, which is very difficult, as the channel lies between two small islands, with two others still smaller, near the left side of the river. Here are two Indian houses, the inhabitants of which were, as usual, drying fish. We passed the rapid without injury, and fourteen and a half miles from the mouth of Lewis's river, came to an island near the right shore, on which were two other houses of Indians, pursuing the customary occupation. One mile and a half beyond this place, is a mouth of a small brook, under a high hill, on the left. It seems to run during its whole course through the high country, which at this place begins, and rising to the height of two hundred feet, forms cliffs of rugged black rocks which project a considerable distance into the river. At this place too we observed a mountain to the S. W. the form of which is conical, and its top covered with snow. We followed the river as it entered these islands, and at the distance of two miles reached three islands, one on each side of the river, and a third in the middle, on which were two houses, where the Indians were drying fish opposite a small rapid. Near these a fourth island begins, close to the right shore, where were nine lodges of Indians, all employed about their fish. As we passed they called to us to land, but as night was coming on, and there was no appearance of wood in the neighbourhood, we went on about a mile further, till observing a log that had drifted down the river, we landed near it on the left side, and formed our camp under a high hill, after having made twenty miles to-day. Directly opposite to us are five houses of Indians, who were drying fish on the same island where we had passed the nine lodges, and on the other side of the river we saw a number of horses feeding. Soon after landing, we were informed by our chiefs that the large camp of nine houses belonged to the first chief of all the tribes in this quarter, and that he had called to request us to land and pass the night with him, as he had plenty of wood for us. This intelligence would have been very acceptable if it had been explained sooner, for we were obliged to use dried willows for fuel to cook with, not being able to burn the drift-log which had tempted us to land. We now sent the two chiefs along the left side of the river, to invite the great chief down to spend the night with us. He came at a late hour, accompanied by twenty men, bringing a basket of mashed berries, which he left as a present for us, and formed a camp at a short distance from us. The next morning,

Saturday, 19, the great chief, with two of his inferior chiefs, and a third belonging to a band on the river below, made us a visit at a very early hour. The first of these is called *Yelleppit*, a hand-some well-proportioned man, about five feet eight inches high, and thirty-five years of age, with a bold and dignified countenance ; the rest were not distinguished in their appearance. We smoked with them, and after making a speech, gave a medal, a handkerchief, and a string of wampum to Yelleppit, and a string of wampum only to the inferior chiefs. He requested us to remain till the middle of the day, in order that all his nation might come and see us, but we excused ourselves by telling him that on our return we would spend two or three days with him. This conference detained us till nine o'clock, by which time great numbers of the Indians had come down to visit us. On leaving them, we went on for eight miles, when we came to an island near the left shore, which continued six miles in length. At the lower extremity of it is a small island, on which are five houses, at present vacant, though the scaffolds of fish are, as usual, abundant.

A short distance below are two more islands, one of them near the middle of the river. On this there were seven houses; but as soon as the Indians, who were drying fish, saw us, they fled to their houses, and not one of them appeared till we had passed, when they came out in greater numbers than is usual for houses of that size, which induced us to think that the inhabitants of the five lodges had been alarmed at our approach, and taken refuge with them. We were very desirous of landing, in order to relieve their apprehensions, but as there was a bad rapid along the island, all our care was necessary to prevent injury to the canoes. At the foot of this rapid is a rock, on the left shore, which is fourteen miles from our camp of last night, and resembles a hat in its shape.

Four miles beyond this island we came to a rapid, from the appearance of which it was judged prudent to examine it. After landing for that purpose on the left side, we began to enter the channel, which is close under the opposite shore. It is a very dangerous rapid, strewed with high rocks and rocky islands, and in many places obstructed by shoals, over which the canoes were to be hauled, so that we were more than two hours in passing through the rapids, which extend for the same number of miles. The rapid has several small islands, and banks of muscle-shells are spread along the river in several places. In order to lighten the boats, Captain Clarke, with the two chiefs, the interpreter, and his wife, had walked across the low grounds on the left, to the foot of the rapids. On the way, Captain Clarke ascended a cliff, about two hundred feet above the water, from which he saw that the country on both sides of the river, immediately from its cliffs, was low, and spreads itself into a level plain, extending for a great distance on all sides. To the west, at the distance of about one hundred and fifty miles, is a very high mountain covered with snow, which, from its direction and appearance, he supposed to be the Mount St. Helen's, laid down by Vancouver as visible from the mouth of the Columbia : there is also another mountain of a conical form, whose top is covered with snow in a south-west direction. As Captain Clarke arrived at the lower end of the rapid before any, except one of the small canoes, he sat down on a rock to wait for them, and seeing a crane fly across the river, shot it, and it fell near him. Several Indians had been before this passing on the opposite side towards the rapids, and some few who had been nearly in front of him, being either alarmed at his appearance, or the re-port of the gun, fled to their houses. Captain Clarke was afraid that these people had not yet heard that white men were coming, and therefore, in order to allay their uneasiness before the whole party should arrive, he got into the small canoe with three men, and rowed over towards the houses, and while crossing shot a duck, which fell into the water. As he approached, no person was to be seen, except three men in the plains, and they too

fled as he came near the shore. He landed before
five houses close to each other, but no one
appeared, and the doors, which were of mat,
were closed. He went towards one of them
with a pipe in his hand, and pushing aside the
mat entered the lodge, where he found thirty-
two persons, chiefly men and women, with a
few children, all in the greatest consternation ;
some hanging down their heads, others crying and
wringing their hands. He went up to them all
and shook hands with them in the most friendly
manner ; but their apprehensions, which had for a
moment subsided, revived on his taking out a
burning glass, as there was no roof to the house,
and lighting his pipe : he then offered it to several
of the men, and distributed among the women and
children some small trinkets which he carried about
with him, and gradually restored some tranquillity
among them. He then left this house, and direct-
ing each of the men to go into a house, went himself to a second : here he found the inhabitants
more terrified than those he had first seen ; but he
succeeded in pacifying them, and then visited the
other houses, where the men had been equally
successful. After leaving the houses, he went
out to sit on a rock, and beckoned to some of
the men to come and smoke with him ; but none
of them ventured to join him till the canoes arrived
with the two chiefs, who immediately explained
our pacific intentions towards them. Soon after
the interpreter's wife landed, and her presence

dissipated all doubts of our being well-disposed, since in this country no woman ever accompanies a war party: they therefore all came out and seemed perfectly reconciled; nor could we indeed blame them for their terrors, which were perfectly natural. They told the two chiefs that they knew we were not men, for they had seen us fall from the clouds : in fact, unperceived by them, Captain Clarke had shot the white crane, which they had seen fall just before he appeared to their eyes : the duck which he had killed also fell close by him, and as there were a few clouds flying over at the moment, they connected the fall of the birds and his sudden appearance, and believed that he had himself dropped from the clouds; the noise of the rifle, which they had never heard before, being considered merely as a sound to announce so extraordinary an event. This belief was strengthened when on entering the room he brought down fire from the heavens by means of his burning-glass. We soon convinced them satisfactorily, that we were only mortals, and after one of our chiefs had explained our history and objects, we all smoked together in great harmony. These people do not speak precisely the same language as the Indians above, but understand them in conversation. In a short time we were joined by many of the inhabitants from below, several of them on horse-back, and all pleased to see us, and to exchange their fish and berries for a few trinkets. We remained here to dine, and then proceeded. At half a mile, the hilly country on the right side of the river ceased : at eleven miles we found a small rapid, and a mile further came to a small island on the left, where there are some willows. Since we had left the five lodges, we passed twenty more, dispersed along the river, at different parts of the valley on the right ; but as they were now apprised of our coming, they showed no signs of alarm. On leaving the island we passed three miles further along a country which is low on both sides of the river, and encamped under some willow-trees on the left, having made thirty-six miles to-day. Immediately opposite to us is an island close to the left shore, and another in the middle of the river, on which are twenty-four houses of Indians, all engaged in drying fish. We had scarcely landed before about a hundred of them came over in their boats to visit us, bringing with them a present of some wood, which was very acceptable : we received them in as kind a manner as we could — smoked with all of them, and gave the principal chief a string of wampum ; but the highest satisfaction they enjoyed was from the music of two of our violins, with which they seemed much delighted : they remained all night at our fires. This tribe is a branch of the nation called Pishquitpaws, and can raise about three hundred and fifty men. In dress they resemble the Indians near the forks of the Columbia, except that their robes are smaller and do not reach lower than the waist ; indeed, three-fourths of them have scarcely any robes at all. The dress of the females is equally scanty; for they wear only a small piece of a robe which covers their shoulders and neck, and reaches down the back to the waist, where it is attached by a piece of leather tied tight round the body: their breasts, which are thus exposed to view, are large, ill-shaped, and are suffered to hang down very low: their cheek-bones high, their heads flattened, and their persons, in general, adorned with scarcely any ornaments. Both sexes are employed in curing fish, of which they have great quantities on their scaffolds.

Sunday, 20. The morning was cool, the wind from the south-west. Our appearance had excited the curiosity of the neighbourhood so much, that before we set out, about two hundred Indians had collected to see us, and as we were desirous of conciliating their friendship, we remained to smoke and confer with them till breakfast. We then took our repast, which consisted wholly of dog-flesh, and proceeded. We passed three vacant houses near our camp, and at six miles reached the head of a rapid, on descending which we soon came to another, very difficult and dangerous. It is formed by a chain of large black rocks, stretching from the right side of the river, and with several small islands on the left, nearly choaking the channel of the river. To this place we gave the name of the Pelican rapid, from seeing a number of pelicans and black cormorants about it. Just below it is a small island near the right shore, where are four

houses of Indians, all busy in drying fish. At sixteen miles from our camp, we reached a bend to
the left opposite to a large island, and at one
o'clock halted for dinner on the lower point of an
island on the right side of the channel. Close to
this was a larger island on the same side, and on
the left bank of the river a small one, a little below.
We landed near some Indian huts, and counted on
this cluster of three islands, seventeen of their
houses filled with inhabitants, resembling in every
respect those higher up the river; like the inhabitants above, they were busy in preparing fish. We
purchased of them some dried fish, which were not
good, and a few berries, on which we dined; and
then walked to the head of the island, for the purpose of examining a vault, which we had marked
in coming along. This place, in which the dead
are deposited, is a building about sixty feet long,
and twelve feet wide, and is formed by placing in
the ground poles or forks six feet high, across
which a long pole is extended the whole length of
the structure. Against this ridge-pole are placed
broad boards, and pieces of canoes, in a slanting
direction, so as to form a shed. It stands east and
west, and neither of the extremities is closed. On
entering the western end we observed a number of
bodies wrapped carefully in leathern robes, and arranged in rows on boards, which were then covered
with a mat. This was the part destined for those
who had recently died: a little farther on, the
bones half decayed were scattered about, and in

the centre of the building was a large pile of them heaped promiscuously on each other. At the eastern extremity was a mat, on which twenty-one skulls were placed in a circular form ; the mode of interment being first to wrap the body in robes, and as it decays, the bones are thrown into the heap, and the skulls placed together. From the different boards and pieces of canoes which form the vault, were suspended, on the inside, fishing-nets, baskets, wooden-bowls, robes, skins, trenchers, and trinkets of various kinds, obviously intended as offerings of affection to deceased relatives. On the outside of the vault were the skeletons of several horses, and great quantities of bones in the neighbourhood, which induced us to believe that these animals were most probably sacrificed at the funeral rites of their masters.

Having dined, we proceeded past a small island, where were four huts of Indians, and at the lower extremity a bad rapid. Half a mile beyond this, and at the distance of twenty-four from our camp, we came to the commencement of the highlands on the right, which are the first we have seen on that side since near the Muscleshell rapids, leaving a valley forty miles in extent. Eight miles lower, we passed a large island in the middle of the river ; below which are eleven small islands, five on the right, the same number on the left, and one in the middle of the stream. A brook falls in on the right side, and a small rivulet empties itself behind one of the islands. The country on the right consists of high and rugged hills; the left is a low plain with no timber on either side, except a few small willow-brushes along the banks; though a few miles after leaving these islands, the country on the left rises to the same height with that opposite to it, and becomes an undulating plain. Two miles after passing a small rapid, we reached a point of highland in a bend towards the right, and encamped for the evening, after a journey of forty-two miles. The river has been about a quarter of a mile in width, with a current much more uniform than it had during the last two days. We killed two speckled gulls, and several ducks of a delicious flavour.

CHAPTER XIX.

MONDAY, 21. The morning was cool, and the wind from the south-west. At five and a half miles we passed a small island, and one mile and a half further, another, in the middle of the river, which has some rapid water near its head, and opposite to its lower extremity are eight cabins of Indians, on the right side. We landed near them to breakfast; but such is the scarcity of wood, that last evening we had not been able to collect any thing except dry willows, and of these not more than barely sufficient to cook our supper, and this morning we could not find enough even to prepare breakfast. The Indians received us with great kindness, and examined every thing they saw with much attention. In their appearance and employments, as well as in their language, they do not differ from those higher up the river. The dress, too, is nearly the same; that of the men consisting of nothing but a short robe of deer or goat-skin; while the women wear only a piece of dressed skin, falling from the neck so as to cover the front of the body as low as the waist; a bandage tied round the body and passing between the legs; and over this a short robe of deer and antelope skin is occasionally thrown. Here we saw two blankets of scarlet, and one of blue cloth, and also a sailor's round jacket; but we obtained only a few pounded roots, and some fish, for which we of course paid them. Among other things, we observed some acorns, the fruit of the white oak. These they use as food, either raw or roasted; and, on inquiry, informed us that they were procured from the Indians who live near the Great Falls. This place they designate by a name very commonly applied to it by the Indians, and highly expressive, the word *Timm*, which they pronounce so as to make it perfectly represent the sound of a distant cataract. After breakfast we resumed our journey, and in the course of three miles passed a rapid where large rocks were strewed across the river, and at the head of which, on the right shore, were two huts of Indians. We stopped here for the purpose of examining it, as we always do whenever any danger is to be apprehended, and send round by land all those who cannot swim. Five miles further is another rapid, formed by large rocks projecting from each side, above which were five huts of Indians on the right side, occupied, like those we had already seen, in drying fish. One mile below this is the lower point of an island, close to the right side; opposite to which, on that shore, are two Indian huts.

On the left side of the river, at this place, are immense piles of rocks, which seem to have slipped from the cliffs under which they lie; they continue till spreading still farther into the river, at the distance of a mile from the island, they occasion a very dangerous rapid; a little below which, on the right side, are five huts. For many miles the river is now narrow, and obstructed with very large rocks thrown into its channel; the hills continue high and covered, as is very rarely the case, with a few low pine trees on their tops. Between three and four miles below the last rapid, occurs a second, which is also difficult, and, three miles below it, is a small river, which seems to rise in the open plains to the south-east, and falls in on the left. It is forty yards wide at its mouth; but discharges only a small quantity of water at present: we gave it the name of Lepage's river, from Lepage, one of our company. Near this little river, and immediately below it, we had to encounter a new rapid.

The river is crowded, in every direction, with large
rocks and small rocky islands : the passage crooked
and difficult, and for two miles we were obliged to
wind with great care along the narrow channels
and between the huge rocks.   At the end of this
rapid are four huts of Indians on the same side.
Here we landed and passed the night, after making
thirty-three miles.   The inhabitants of these huts
explained to us that they were the relations of those
who live at the Great Falls.   They appear to be of
the same nation with those we have seen above,
whom, indeed, they resemble in every thing, except
that their language, although the same, has some
words different.   They have all pierced noses, and
the men, when in full dress, wear a long tapering
piece of shell or bead put through the nose.   These
people did not, however, receive us with the cordiality to which we have been accustomed.   They
are poor ; but we are able to purchase from them
some wood to make a fire for supper, of which they
have but little, and which they say they bring
from the Great Falls.   The hills in this neighbourhood are high and rugged, and a few scattered
trees, either small pine or scrubby white oak, are
occasionally seen on them.   From the last rapids
we also observed the conical mountain towards the
south-west, which the Indians say is not far to the
left of the Great Falls.   From its vicinity to that
place we called it the Timm or Falls mountain.
The country through which we passed is furnished
with several fine springs, which rise either high up

the sides of the hills or else in the river meadows, and discharge themselves into the Columbia. We could not help remarking, that almost universally the fishing establishments of the Indians, both on the Columbia and the waters of Lewis's river, are on the right bank. On inquiry, we were led to believe that the reason may be found in their fear of the Snake Indians ; between whom and themselves, considering the warlike temper of that people, and the peaceful habits of the river tribes, it is very natural that the latter should be anxious to interpose so good a barrier. These Indians are described as residing on a great river to the south, and always at war with the people in this neighbourhood. One of our chiefs pointed out, to-day, a spot on the left where, not many years ago, a great battle was fought, in which numbers of both nations were killed. We were agreeably surprised this evening by a present of some very good beer, made out of the remains of the bread, composed of the Pashecoquamash, part of the stores we had laid in at the head of the Kooskooskee, and which by frequent exposure becomes sour and moulded.

Tuesday, 22. The morning was fair and calm. We left our camp at nine o'clock, and after going on for six miles, came to the head of an island, and a very bad rapid, where the rocks are scattered nearly across the river. Just above this, and on the right side, are six huts of Indians. At the distance of two miles below are five more huts ; the inhabitants of which are all engaged in drying fish, and some of them in their canoes, killing fish with gigs; opposite to this establishment is a small island in a bend towards the right, on which there were such quantities of fish, that we counted twenty stacks of dried and pounded salmon. This small island is at the upper point of one much larger, the sides of which are high uneven rocks, jutting over the water; here there is a bad rapid. The island continues for four miles, and at the middle of it is a large river, which appears to come from the south-east, and empties itself on the left. We landed just above its mouth, in order to examine it, and soon found the route intercepted by a deep narrow channel, running into the Columbia above the large entrance, so as to form a dry and rich island about four hundred yards wide and eight hundred long. Here, as along the grounds of the river, the natives had been digging large quantities of roots, as the soil was turned up in many places. We reached the river about a quarter of a mile above its mouth, at a place where a large body of water is compressed within a channel of about two hundred yards in width, where it foams over rocks, many of which are above the surface of the water. These narrows are the end of a rapid, which extends two miles back, where the river is closely confined between two high hills, below which it is divided by numbers of large rocks and small islands, covered with a low growth of timber. This river, which is called by the Indians Towahnahiooks, is two hundred yards wide at its mouth, has a very rapid current, and contributes about one-fourth as much water as the Columbia possesses before the junction. Immediately at the entrance are three sand islands, and near it the head of an island which runs parallel to the large rocky island. We now returned to our boats, and passing the mouth of the Towahnahiooks, went between the islands. At the distance of two miles we reached the lower end of this rocky island, where were eight huts of Indians. Here, too, we saw some large logs of wood, which were most probably rafted down the Towahnahiooks; and a mile below, on the right bank, were sixteen lodges of Indians, with whom we stopped to smoke. Then at the distance of about a mile passed six more huts on the same side, nearly opposite the lower extremity of the island, which has its upper end in the mouth of Towahna-hiooks. Two miles below we came to seventeen huts on the right side of the river, situated at the commencement of the pitch which includes the great Falls. Here we halted, and immediately on landing walked down, accompanied by an old Indian from the huts, in order to examine the Falls, and ascertain on which side we could make a portage most easily. We soon discovered that the nearest route was on the right side, and there-fore dropped down to the head of the rapid, un-loaded the canoes, and took all the baggage over by land to the foot of the rapid. The distance is twelve hundred yards. On setting out we crossed a solid rock, about one-third of the whole distance; then reached a space of two hundred yards wide, which forms a hollow, where the loose sand from the low grounds has been driven by the winds, and is steep and loose, and therefore disagreeable to pass: the rest of the route is over firm and solid ground. The labour of crossing would have been very inconvenient, if the Indians had not assisted us in carrying some of the heavy articles on their horses; but for this service they repaid themselves so adroitly, that on reaching the foot of the rapids we formed a camp in a position which might secure us from the pilfering of the natives, which we apprehend much more than we do their hostilities. Near our camp are five large huts of Indians engaged in drying fish, and preparing it for the market. The manner of doing this is by first opening the fish, and exposing it to the sun on their scaffolds. When it is sufficiently dried it is pounded fine between two stones till it is pulverized, and is then placed in a basket about two feet long, and one in diameter, neatly made of grass and rushes, and lined with the skin of a salmon stretched and dried for the purpose. Here they are pressed down as hard as possible, and the top covered with skins of fish, which are secured by cords through the holes of the basket. The baskets are then placed in some dry situation, the corded part up-wards, seven being usually placed as close as they can be put together, and five on the top of them. The whole is then wrapped up in mats, and made fast by cords, over which mats are again thrown.

T 2

Twelve of these baskets, each of which contains from ninety to a hundred pounds, form a stack, which is now left exposed till it is sent to market; the fish thus preserved is kept sound and sweet for several years, and great quantities of it, they inform us, are sent to the Indians who live below the Falls, whence it finds its way to the whites who visit the mouth of the Columbia. We observe, both near the lodges and on the rocks of the river, great numbers of stacks of these pounded fish.

Besides fish, these people supplied us with filberts and berries, and we purchased a dog for supper; but it was with much difficulty that we were able to buy wood enough to cook it. In the course of the day we were visited by many Indians, from whom we learnt that the principal chiefs of the bands residing in this neighbourhood, are now hunting in the mountains towards the south-west. On that side of the river none of the Indians have any permanent habitations, and on enquiry we were confirmed in our belief, that it was for fear of attacks from the Snake Indians, with whom they are at war. This nation they represent as very numerous, and residing in a great number of villages on the Towahnahiooks, where they live principally on salmon. That river, they add, is not obstructed by rapids above its mouth, but there becomes large, and reaches to a considerable distance : the first village of the Snake Indians on that river being twelve days' journey, on a course about south-east from this place.

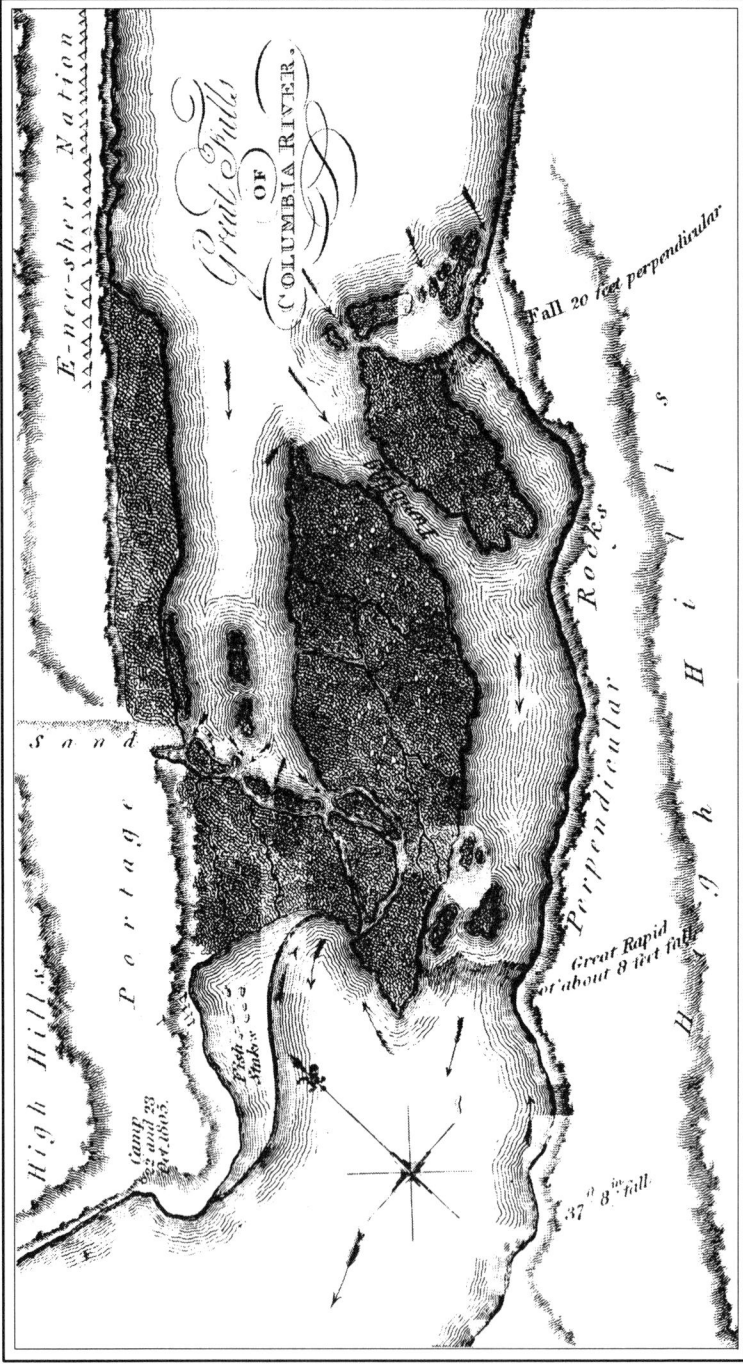

Great Falls
OF
COLUMBIA RIVER

E-nee-shur Nation

High Hills

Portage

Sand

Camp 22
and 23
Oct. 1805.

Fish Stakes

Rocks

Perpendicular

High Hills

Fall 20 feet perpendicular

Great Rapid
of about 8 feet fall

37° 8 in fall

Published April 28th 1814 by Longman & Cᵒ Paternoster Row.

Yeele sc. Strand.

Wednesday, 23. Having ascertained from the
Indians, and by actual examination, the best mode
of bringing down the canoes, it was found necessary, as the river was divided into several narrow
channels by rocks and islands, to follow the route
adopted by the Indians themselves. This operation
Captain Clarke began this morning, and after
crossing to the other side of the river, hauled the
canoes over a point of land, so as to avoid a perpendicular fall of twenty feet. At the distance of
four hundred and fifty-seven yards we reached the
water, and embarked at a place where a long
rocky island compresses the channel of the river
within the space of a hundred and fifty yards, so
as to form nearly a semicircle. On leaving this
rocky island the channel is somewhat wider, but
a second and much larger island of hard black
rock still divides it from the main stream, while
on the left shore it is closely bordered by perpendicular rocks. Having descended in this way for
a mile, we reached a pitch of the river, which
being divided by two large rocks, descends with
great rapidity down a fall eight feet in height: as
the boats could not be navigated down this steep
descent, we were obliged to land and let them
down as slowly as possible by strong ropes of elk-
skin, which we had prepared for the purpose.
They all passed in safety except one, which being
loosed by the breaking of the ropes, was driven
down, but was recovered by the Indians below.
With this rapid ends the first pitch of the great

T 3

Falls, which is not great in point of height, and remarkable only for the singular manner in which the rocks have divided its channel. From the marks every where perceivable at the Falls, it is obvious that in high floods, which must be in the spring, the water below the Falls rises nearly to a level with that above them. Of this rise, which is occasioned by some obstructions which we do not as yet know, the salmon must avail themselves to pass up the river in such multitudes, that that fish is almost the only one caught in great abundance above the Falls; but below that place, we observe the salmon trout, and the heads of a species of trout smaller than the salmon trout, which is in great quantities, and which they are now burying to be used as their winter food. A hole of any size being dug, the sides and bottom are lined with straw, over which skins are laid : on these the fish, after being well dried, are laid, covered with other skins, and the hole closed with a layer of earth twelve or fifteen inches deep. About three o'clock we reached the lower camp, but our joy at having accomplished this object was somewhat diminished, by the persecution of a new acquaintance. On reaching the upper point of the portage, we found that the Indians had been encamped there not long since, and had left behind them multitudes of fleas. These sagacious animals were so pleased to exchange the straw and fish-skins, in which they had been living, for some better residence, that we were soon covered with them, and during the portage the men were obliged to strip to the skin, in order to brush them from their bodies. They were not, however, so easily dislodged from our clothes, and accompanied us in great numbers to our camp.

We saw no game except a sea-otter, which was shot in the narrow channel as we came down, but we could not get it. Having, therefore, scarcely any provisions, we purchased eight small fat dogs, a food to which we are now compelled to have recourse, for the Indians are very unwilling to sell us any of their good fish, which they reserve for the market below. Fortunately, however, the habit of using this animal has completely overcome the repugnance which we felt at first, and the dog, if not a favourite dish, is always an acceptable one. The meridian altitude of to-day gives 45° 42' 57" 3-10 north, as the latitude of our camp.

On the beach near the Indian huts, we observed two canoes of a different shape and size from any which we had hitherto seen : one of these we got in exchange for our smallest canoe, giving a hatchet and a few trinkets to the owner, who said he had purchased it from a white man below the Falls, by giving him a horse. These canoes are very beautifully made ; they are wide in the middle and tapering towards each end, with curious figures carved on the bow. They are thin, but being strengthened by cross bars, about an inch in diameter, which are tied with strong pieces of bark through holes in the sides, are able to bear very heavy burdens, and seem calculated to live in the roughest water.

A great number of Indians, both from above and below the Falls, visited us to-day, and towards evening we were informed by one of the chiefs who had accompanied us, that he had overheard that the Indians below intended to attack us as we went down the river. Being at all times ready for any attempt of that sort, we were not under greater apprehensions than usual at this intelligence : we, therefore, only re-examined our arms, and increased the ammunition to one hundred rounds. Our chiefs, who had not the same motives of confidence, were by no means so much at their ease, and when at night they saw the Indians leave us earlier than usual, their suspicions of an intended attack were confirmed, and they were very much alarmed. The next morning,

Thursday, 24, the Indians approached us with apparent caution, and behaved with more than usual reserve. Our two chiefs, by whom these circumstances were not unobserved, now told us that they wished to return home ; that they could be no longer of any service to us, and they could not understand the language of the people below the Falls; that those people formed a different nation from their own; that the two people had been at war with each other; and as the Indians had expressed a resolution to attack us, they would cer-

tainly kill them. We endeavoured to quiet their
fears, and requested them to stay two nights longer,
in which time we would see the Indians below, and
make a peace between the two nations. They
replied that they were anxious to return and see
their horses; we however insisted on their remaining with us, not only in hopes of bringing about an
accommodation between them and their enemies,
but because they might be able to detect any hostile
designs against us, and also assist us in passing the
next Falls, which are not far off, and represented as
very difficult: they at length agreed to stay with
us two nights longer. About nine o'clock we proceeded, and on leaving our camp near the lower
Fall, found the river about four hundred yards
wide, with a current more rapid than usual, though
with no perceptible descent. At the distance of
two and a half miles, the river widened into a large
bend or basin on the right, at the beginning of
which are three huts of Indians. At the extremity
of this basin stands a high black rock, which, rising
perpendicularly from the right shore, seems to run
wholly across the river: so totally indeed does it
appear to stop the passage, that we could not see
where the water escaped, except that the current
appeared to be drawn with more than usual velocity
to the left of the rock, where was a great roaring.
We landed at the huts of the Indians, who went
with us to the top of this rock, from which we saw
all the difficulties of the channel. We were no
longer at a loss to account for the rising of the

5

river at the Falls, for this tremendous rock stretches
across the river, to meet the high hills of the left
shore, leaving a channel of only forty-five yards
wide, through which the whole body of the Columbia must press its way. The water, thus forced
into so narrow a channel, is thrown into whirls, and
swells and boils in every part with the wildest agi-
tation. But the alternative of carrying the boats
over this high rock was almost impossible in our
present situation; and as the chief danger seemed
to be not from any rocks in the channel, but from
the great waves and whirlpools, we resolved to try
the passage in our boats, in hopes of being able,
by dextrous steering, to escape. This we attempted,
and with great care were able to get through, to the
astonishment of all the Indians of the huts we had
just passed, who now collected to see us from the
top of the rock. The channel continues thus confined within a space of about half a mile, when the
rock ceased. We passed a single Indian hut at
the foot of it, where the river again enlarges itself
to the width of two hundred yards, and at the distance of a mile and a half stopped to view a very
bad rapid; this is formed by two rocky islands,
which divide the channel, the lower and larger of
which is in the middle of the river. The appearance
of this place was so unpromising, that we unloaded
all the most valuable articles, such as guns, ammunition, our papers, &c. and sent them by land, with
all the men that could not swim, to the extremity
of the rapids. We then descended with the canoes

two at a time, and though the canoes took in some water, we all went through safely; after which we made two miles, and stopped in a deep bend of the river towards the right, and encamped a little above a large village of twenty-one houses. Here we landed, and as it was late before all the canoes joined us, we were obliged to remain here this evening, the difficulties of the navigation having permitted us to make only six miles. This village is situated at the extremity of a deep bend towards the right, and immediately above a ledge of high rocks, twenty feet above the marks of the highest flood, but broken in several places, so as to form channels which are at present dry, extending nearly across the river; this forms the second Fall, or the place most probably which the Indians indicate by the word Timm. While the canoes were coming on, Captain Clarke walked with two men down to examine these channels. On these rocks the Indians are accustomed to dry fish, and as the season for that purpose is now over, the poles which they use are tied up very securely in bundles, and placed on the scaffolds. The stock of fish dried and pounded was so abundant, that he counted one hundred and seven of them, making more than ten thousand pounds of that provision. After examining the Narrows as well as the lateness of the hour would permit, he returned to the village through a rocky open country, infested with polecats. This village, the residence of a tribe called the Echeloots, consists of twenty-one houses, scattered promiscuously over an elevated situation, near a mound about thirty feet above the common level, which has some remains of houses on it, and bears every appearance of being artificial.

The houses, which are the first wooden buildings we have seen since leaving the Illinois country, are nearly equal in size, and exhibit a very singular appearance. A large hole, twenty feet wide, and thirty in length, is dug to the depth of six feet. The sides are then lined with split pieces of timber, rising just above the surface of the ground, which are smoothed to the same width by burning, or shaved with small iron axes. These timbers are secured in their erect position by a pole, stretched along the side of the building near the eaves, and supported on a strong post fixed at each corner. The timbers at the gable ends rise gradually higher, the middle pieces being the broadest. At the top of these is a sort of semicircle, made to receive a ridge-pole, the whole length of the house, propped by an additional post in the middle, and forming the top of the roof. From this ridge-pole to the eaves of the house, are placed a number of small poles, or rafters, secured at each end by the fibres of the cedar. On these poles, which are connected by small transverse bars of wood, is laid a covering of the white cedar, or arbor vitæ, kept on by the strands of the cedar fibres: but a small distance along the whole length of the ridge-pole is left uncovered for the purpose of light, and permitting the smoke to pass through. The roof thus formed has a descent about equal to that common amongst us, and near the eaves is perforated with a number of small holes, made most probably to discharge their arrows in case of an attack. The only entrance is by a small door at the gable end, cut out of the middle piece of timber, twenty-nine and a half inches high, and fourteen inches broad, and reaching only eighteen inches above the earth. Before this hole is hung a mat, and on pushing it aside, and crawling through, the descent is by a small wooden ladder, made in the form of those used amongst us. One-half of the inside is used as a place of deposit for their dried fish, of which there are large quantities stored away, and with a few baskets of berries, form the only family provisions; the other half, adjoining the door, remains for the accommodation of the family. On each side are arranged, near the walls, small beds of mats, placed on little scaffolds or bedsteads, raised from eighteen inches to three feet from the ground, and in the middle of the vacant space is the fire, or sometimes two or three fires, when, as is indeed usually the case, the house contains three families.

The inhabitants received us with great kindness — invited us to their houses, and in the evening, after our camp had been formed, came in great numbers to see us: accompanying them was a principal chief, and several of the warriors of the nation below the Great Narrows. We made use of this opportunity to attempt a reconciliation be-

tween them and our two chiefs, and to put an end
to the war which had disturbed the two nations.
By representing to the chiefs the evils which the
war inflicted on them, and the wants and privations to which it subjects them, they soon became
disposed to conciliate with each other, and we had
some reason to be satisfied with the sincerity of the
mutual professions, that the war should no longer
continue, and that in future they would live in
peace with each other. On concluding this negociation, we proceeded to invest the chief with the
insignia of command, a medal and some small articles of clothing; after which the violin was produced, and our men danced to the great delight
of the Indians, who remained with us till a late
hour.

Friday, 25. We walked down with several of
the Indians to view the part of the Narrows, which
they represented as most dangerous: we found it
very difficult, but, as with our large canoes the
portage was impracticable, we concluded on carrying our most valuable articles by land, and then
hazarding the passage. We therefore returned to
the village, and after sending some of the party
with our best stores to make a portage, and fixed
others on the rock to assist with ropes the canoes
that might meet with any difficulty, we began the
descent, in the presence of great numbers of Indians, who had collected to witness this exploit.
The channel for three miles is worn through a hard
rough black rock from fifty to one hundred yards

wide, in which the water swells and boils in a tremendous manner. The three first canoes escaped very well; the fourth, however, had nearly filled with water; the fifth passed through with only a small quantity of water over her. At half a mile we had got through the worst part, and having reloaded our canoes, went on very well for two and a half miles, except that one of the boats was nearly lost by running against a rock. At the end of this channel of three miles, in which the Indians inform us they catch as many salmon as they wish, we reached a deep basin, or bend of the river towards the right, near the entrance of which are two rocks. We crossed the basin, which has a quiet and gentle current, and at the distance of a mile from its commencement, and a little below where the river resumes its channel, reached a rock which divides it. At this place we met our old chiefs, who, when we began the portage, had walked down to a village below, to smoke a pipe of friendship on the renewal of peace. Just after our meeting, we saw a chief of the village above, with a party who had been out hunting, and were then crossing the river with their horses on their way home. We landed to smoke with this chief, whom we found a bold looking man of a pleasing appearance, about fifty years of age, and dressed in a war jacket, a cap, leggings, and moccasins: we presented him with a medal and other small articles, and he gave us some meat, of which he had been able to procure but little; for on his route he had

met with a war party of Indians from the Towahnahiooks, with whom he had had a battle. We here
smoked a parting pipe with our two faithful friends,
the chiefs who had accompanied us from the heads
of the river, and who now had each bought a
horse, intending to go home by land.

On leaving this rock the river is gentle, but
strewed with a great number of rocks for a few
miles, when it becomes a beautiful still stream
about half a mile wide. At five miles from the
large bend we came to the mouth of a creek
twenty yards wide, heading in the range of mountains which run S.S.W. and S.W. for a long distance, and discharging a considerable quantity of
water : it is called by the Indians Quenett. We
halted below it under a high point of rocks on the
left ; and as it was necessary to make some celestial observations, we formed a camp on the top of
these rocks. This situation is perfectly well calculated for defence in case the Indians should incline to attack us, for the rocks form a sort of
natural fortification with the aid of the river and
creek, and is convenient to hunt along the
foot of the mountains to the west and south-west,
where there are several species of timber which
form fine coverts for game. From this rock, the
pinnacle of the round mountain covered with
snow, which we had seen a short distance below
the forks of the Columbia, and which we had
called the Falls, or Timm mountain, is south 43°
west, and about thirty-seven miles distant. The

face of the country on both sides of the river above and below the Falls is steep, rugged, and rocky, with a very small proportion of herbage, and no timber, except a few bushes: the hills, however, to the west, have some scattered pine, white oak, and other kinds of trees. All the timber used by the people at the upper Falls is rafted down the Towahnahiooks; and those who live at the head of the Narrows we have just passed, bring their wood in the same way from this creek to the lower part of the Narrows, from which it is carried three miles by land to their habitations.

Both above and below, as well as in the Narrows, we saw a great number of sea-otter or seals, and this evening one deer was killed, and great signs of that animal seen near the camp. In the creek we shot a goose, and saw much appearance of beaver, and one of the party also saw a fish, which he took to be a drum-fish. Among the willows we found several snares, set by the natives for the purpose of catching wolves.

Saturday, 26. The morning was fine: we sent six men to hunt and to collect rosin to pitch the canoes, which, by being frequently hauled over rocks, have become very leaky. The cargoes were also brought out to dry, and on examination it was found that many of the articles had become spoiled by being repeatedly wetted. We were occupied with the observations necessary to determine our longitude, and with conferences among the Indians, many of whom came on horseback to the opposite shore in the forepart of the day, and showed some anxiety to cross over to us: we did not however think it proper to send for them, but towards evening two chiefs, with fifteen men, came over in a small canoe. They proved to be the two principal chiefs of the tribes at and above the Falls, who had been absent on a hunting excursion as we passed their residence: each of them, on their arrival, made us a present of deer's flesh, and small white cakes made of roots. Being anxious to ingratiate ourselves in their favour, so as to ensure a friendly reception on our return, we treated them with all the kindness we could show: we acknowledged the chiefs, gave a medal of the small size, a red silk handkerchief, an arm-band, a knife, and a piece of paint to each chief, and small presents to several of the party, and half a deer: these attentions were not lost on the Indians, who appeared very well pleased with them. At night a fire was made in the middle of our camp, and as the Indians sat round it our men danced to the music of the violin, which so delighted them, that several resolved to remain with us all night: the rest crossed the river. All the tribes in this neighbourhood are at war with the Snake Indians, whom they all describe as living on the Towahnahiooks, and whose nearest town is said to be four days' march from this place, and in a direction nearly south-west: there has lately been a battle between these tribes, but we could not ascertain the loss on either side. The water rose to-day eight inches, a rise which

we could only ascribe to the circumstance of the
wind's having been up the river for the last twenty-
four hours, since the influence of the tide cannot
be sensible here on account of the falls below.
The hunters returned in the evening; they had
seen the tracks of elk and bear in the mountains,
and killed five deer, four very large grey squirrels,
and a grouse : they inform us that the country off
the river is broken, stony, and thinly timbered
with pine and white oak. Besides these delicacies,
one of the men killed with a gig a salmon trout,
which, being fried in some bear's oil, which had
been given to us by the chief whom we had met
this morning below the Narrows, furnished a dish
of a very delightful flavour. A number of white
cranes were also seen flying in different directions,
but at such a height that we could not procure
any of them.

The fleas, with whom we had contracted an intimacy at the Falls, are so unwilling to leave us,
that the men are obliged to throw off all their
clothes, in order to relieve themselves from their
persecution.

Sunday, 27. The wind was high from the westward during last night and this morning, but the
weather being fair, we continued our celestial observations. The two chiefs who remained with us,
were joined by seven Indians, who came in a canoe
from below. To these men we were very particular in our attentions; we smoked and ate with
them; but some of them, who were tempted by

the sight of our goods exposed to dry, wished to take liberties with them; to which we were under the necessity of putting an immediate check : this restraint displeased them so much, that they returned down the river in a very ill humour. The two chiefs however remained with us till the evening, when they crossed the river to their party. Before they went we procured from them a vocabulary of the Echeloot, their native language, and on comparison were surprised at its difference from that of the Eneeshur tongue. In fact, although the Echeloots, who live at the Great Narrows, are not more than six miles from the Eneeshurs or residents at and above the Great Falls, the two people are separated by a broad distinction of language. The Eneeshurs are understood by all the tribes residing on the Columbia, above the Falls, but at that place they meet with the unintelligible language of the Echeloots, which then descends the river to a considerable distance. Yet the variation may possibly be rather a deep shade of dialect than a radical difference, since among both many words are the same, and the identity cannot be accounted for by supposing that their neighbourhood has interwoven them into their daily conversations, because the same words are equally familiar among all the Flathead bands which we have passed. To all these tribes too the strange clucking or guttural noise which first struck us is common. They also flatten the heads of the children in nearly the same manner, but we now begin to observe that the heads of the males, as well as of the other sex, are subjected to this operation, whereas among the mountains custom has confined it almost to the females. The hunters brought home four deer, one grouse, and a squirrel.

Monday, 28. The morning was again cool and windy. Having dried our goods, we were about setting out, when three canoes came from above to visit us, and at the same time two others from below arrived for the same purpose. Among these last was an Indian who wore his hair in a queue, and had on a round hat, and a sailor's jacket, which he said he had obtained from the people below the Great Rapids, who bought them from the whites. This interview detained us till nine o'clock, when we proceeded down the river, which is now border-ed with cliffs of loose dark-coloured rocks about ninety feet high, with a thin covering of pine and other small trees. At the distance of four miles we reached a small village of eight houses under some high rocks on the right, with a small creek on the opposite side of the river. We landed and found the houses similar to those we had seen at the Great Narrows: on entering one of them we saw a British musket, a cutlass, and several brass tea-kettles, of which they seemed to be very fond. There were figures of men, birds, and different animals, which were cut and painted on the boards which form the sides of the room, and though the workmanship of these uncouth figures was very rough, they were as highly esteemed by the Indians

as the finest frescoes of more civilized people.
This tribe is called the Chilluckittequaw, and their
language, although somewhat different from that
of the Echeloots, has many of the same words,
and is sufficiently intelligible to the neighbouring
Indians. We procured from them a vocabulary,
and then after buying five small dogs, some dried
berries, and a white bread or cake made of roots,
we left them. The wind however rose so high,
that we were obliged, after going one mile, to land
on the left side, opposite to a rocky island, and
pass the day there. We formed our camp in a
niche above a point of high rocks, and as it was
the only safe harbour we could find, submitted to
the inconvenience of lying on the sand, exposed
to the wind and rain during all the evening. The
high wind, which obliged us to consult the safety
of our boats by not venturing further, did not
at all prevent the Indians from navigating the river.
We had not been long on shore, before a canoe,
with a man, his wife, and two children, came from
below through the high waves with a few roots to
sell; and soon after we were visited by many
Indians from the village above, with whom we
smoked and conversed. The canoes used by these
people are like those already described, built of
white cedar or pine, very light, wide in the middle,
and tapering towards the ends, the bow being raised
and ornamented with carvings of the heads of
animals. As the canoe is the vehicle of transport-
ation, the Indians have acquired great dexterity in

4

the management of it, and guide it safely over the highest waves. They have, among their utensils, bowls and baskets very neatly made of small bark and grass, in which they boil their provisions. The only game seen to-day were two deer, of which only one was killed, the other was wounded but escaped.

Tuesday, 29. The morning was still cloudy, and the wind from the west, but as it had abated its violence, we set out at day-light. At the distance of four miles, we passed a creek on the right, one mile below which is a village of seven houses, on the same side. This is the residence of the principal chief of the Chilluckittequaw nation, whom we now found to be the same between whom and our two chiefs we had made a peace at the Echeloot village. He received us very kindly, and set before us pounded fish, filberts, nuts, the berries of the Sacacommis, and white bread made of roots. We gave in return a bracelet of ribband to each of the women of the house, with which they were very much pleased. The chief had several articles, such as scarlet and blue cloth, a sword, a jacket and hat, which must have been procured from the whites, and on one side of the room were two wide split boards placed together, so as to make space for a rude figure of a man cut and painted on them. On pointing to this and asking them what it meant, he said something, of which all we understood was " good," and then stepped to the image and brought out his bow and quiver, which, with some other warlike instruments, were kept behind it.

The chief then directed his wife to hand him his medicine-bag, from which he brought out fourteen fore-fingers, which he told us had once belonged to the same number of his enemies, whom he had killed in fighting with the nations to the south-east, to which place he pointed, alluding, no doubt to the Snake Indians, the common enemy of the nations on the Columbia. This bag is about two feet in length, containing roots, pounded dirt, &c. which the Indians only know how to appreciate. It is suspended in the middle of the lodge, and it is supposed to be a species of sacrilege to be touched by any but the owner. It is an object of religious fear, and it is from its sanctity the safest place to deposit their medals and their more valuable articles. The Indians have likewise small bags, which they preserve in their great medicine bag, from whence they are taken and worn around their waists and necks, as amulets against any real or imaginary evils. This was the first time we had ever known the Indians to carry from the field any other trophy except the scalp. They were shown with great exultation, and after an harangue, which we were left to presume was in praise of his exploits, the fingers were carefully replaced among the valuable contents of the red medicine-bag.

This village being part of the same nation with the village we passed above, the language of the two is the same, and their houses of similar form and materials, and calculated to contain about thirty souls. The inhabitants were unusually hospitable and good humoured, so that we gave to the place the name of the Friendly village. We breakfasted here, and after purchasing twelve dogs, four sacks of fish, and a few dried berries, proceeded on our journey. The hills, as we passed, are high, with steep and rocky sides, and some pine and white oak, and an undergrowth of shrubs scattered over them. Four miles below this village is a small river on the right side; immediately below is a village of Chilluckittequaws, consisting of eleven houses. Here we landed and smoked a pipe with the inhabitants, who were very cheerful and friendly. They, as well as the people of the last village, inform us, that this river comes a considerable distance from the N. N. E. that it has a great number of falls, which prevent the salmon from passing up, and that there are ten nations residing on it, who subsist on berries, or such game as they can procure with their bows and arrows. At its mouth the river is sixty yards wide, and has a deep and very rapid channel. From the number of falls of which the Indians spoke, we gave it the name of Cataract river. We purchased four dogs, and then proceeded. The country as we advance, is more rocky and broken, and the pine and low white oak on the hills increase in great quantity. Three miles below Cataract river we passed three large rocks in the river; that in the middle is larger and longer than the rest, and from the circumstance of its having several square vaults on it, obtained the name of Sepulchre island. A

short distance below are two huts of Indians on
the right : the river now widens, and in three miles
we came to two more houses on the right ; one
mile beyond which is a rocky island in a bend of
the river towards the left. Within the next six
miles we passed fourteen huts of Indians, scattered
on the right bank, and then reached the entrance
of a river on the left, which we called Labieshe's
river, after Labieshe one of our party. Just above
this river is a low ground more thickly timbered
than usual, and in front are four huts of Indians
on the bank, which are the first we have seen on
that side of the Columbia. The exception may be
occasioned by this spot's being more than usually
protected from the approach of their enemies, by
the creek, and the thick wood behind.

We again embarked, and at the distance of a
mile passed the mouth of a rapid creek on the right
eighteen yards wide : in this creek the Indians
whom we left take their fish, and from the number
of canoes which were in it, we called it Canoe
creek. Opposite to this creek is a large sand-bar,
which continues for four miles along the left side
of the river. Just below this a beautiful cascade
falls in on the left over a precipice of rock one
hundred feet in height. One mile further are four
Indian huts in the low ground on the left : and two
miles below this a point of land on the right, where
the mountains become high on both sides, and
possess more timber and greater varieties of it than
hitherto, and those on the left are covered with

snow. One mile from this point we halted for the night at three Indian huts on the right, having made thirty-two miles. On our first arrival they seemed surprised, but not alarmed at our appearance, and we soon became intimate by means of smoking, and our favourite entertainment for the Indians, the violin. They gave us fruit, some roots, and root-bread, and we purchased from them three dogs. The houses of these people are similar to those of the Indians above, and their language the same : their dress also, consisting of robes or skins of wolves, deer, elk, and wild cat; is nearly after the same model : their hair is worn in plaits down each shoulder, and round their neck is put a strip of some skin, with the tail of the animal hanging down over the breast : like the Indians above they are fond of otter skins, and give a great price for them. We here saw the skin of a mountain sheep, which they say live among the rocks in the mountains : the skin was covered with white hair, the wool long, thick, and coarse, with long coarse hair on the top of the neck, and the back resembling somewhat the bristles of a goat. Immediately behind the village is a pond, in which were great numbers of small swan.

Wednesday, 30. A moderate rain fell during all last night, but the morning was cool, and after taking a scanty breakfast of deer, we proceeded. The river is now about three quarters of a mile wide, with a current so gentle, that it does not exceed one mile and a half an hour; but its course

is obstructed by the projection of large rocks,
which seemed to have fallen promiscuously from
the mountains into the bed of the river. On the
left side four different streams of water empty
themselves in cascades from the hills: what is,
however, most singular is, that there are stumps of
pine trees scattered to some distance in the river,
which has the appearance of being dammed below,
and forced to encroach on the shore: these obstructions continue till at the distance of twelve
miles, when we came to the mouth of a river on
the right, where we landed: we found it sixty
yards wide, and its banks possess two kinds of
timber which we had not hitherto seen: one is a
very large species of ash; the other resembling in
its bark the beach; but the tree itself, as also the
leaves, are smaller. We called this stream Crusatte's
river, after Crusatte, one of our men: opposite to
its mouth the Columbia widens to the distance
of a mile, with a large sand-bar, and large stones
and rocks scattered through the channel. We
here saw several of the large buzzards, which are
of the size of the largest eagle, with the under part
of their wings white: we also shot a deer and three
ducks; on part of which we dined, and then
continued down the Columbia. Above Crusatte's
river the low grounds are about three quarters of
a mile wide, rising gradually to the hills, and with
a rich soil covered with grass, fern, and other
small undergrowth; but below, the country rises
with a steep ascent, and soon the mountains ap-

proach to the river with steep rugged sides, covered
with a very thick growth of pine, cedar, cotton-
wood, and oak. The river is still strewed with
large rocks. Two and a half miles below Crusatte's
river is a large creek on the right, with a small
island in the mouth. Just below this creek we
passed along the right side of three small
islands on the right bank of the river, with a
larger island on the opposite side, and landed on
an island very near the right shore at the head of
the great shoot, and opposite to two smaller islands
at the fall or shoot itself. Just above the island on
which we were encamped is a small village of eight
large houses in a bend on the right, where the
country, from having been very mountainous, becomes low for a short distance. We had made
fifteen miles to-day, during all which time we were
kept constantly wet with the rain ; but as we were
able to get on this island some of the ash which
we saw for the first time to-day, and which makes
a tolerable fire, we were as comfortable as the
moistness of the evening would permit. As soon
as we landed, Captain Lewis went with five men
to the village, which is situated near the river,
with ponds in the low grounds behind. The greater
part of the inhabitants were absent collecting roots
down the river : the few, however, who were at
home, treated him very kindly, and gave him berries, nuts, and fish ; and in the house were a gun
and several articles which must have been procured
from the whites ; but not being able to procure any

information he returned to the island. Captain Clarke had in the mean time gone down to examine the shoot, and to discover the best route for a portage. He followed an Indian path, which, at the distance of a mile, led to a village on an elevated situation, the houses of which had been large, but built in a different form from any we had yet seen, but which had been lately abandoned, the greater part of the boards being put into a pond near the village: this was most probably for the purpose of drowning the fleas, which were in immense quantities near the houses. After going about three miles the night obliged him to return to camp: he resumed his search in the morning,

Thursday, 31st, through the rain. At the extremity of the basin, in which is situated the island where we are encamped, several rocks and rocky islands are interspersed through the bed of the river. The rocks on each side have fallen down from the mountains; that on the left being high, and on the right the hill itself, which is lower, slipping into the river; so that the current is here compressed within a space of one hundred and fifty yards. Within this narrow limit it runs for the distance of four hundred yards with great rapidity, swelling over the rocks, with a fall of about twenty feet: it then widens to two hundred paces, and the current for a short distance becomes gentle; but at the distance of a mile and a half, and opposite to the old village mentioned yesterday, it is obstructed by a very bad rapid, where the waves

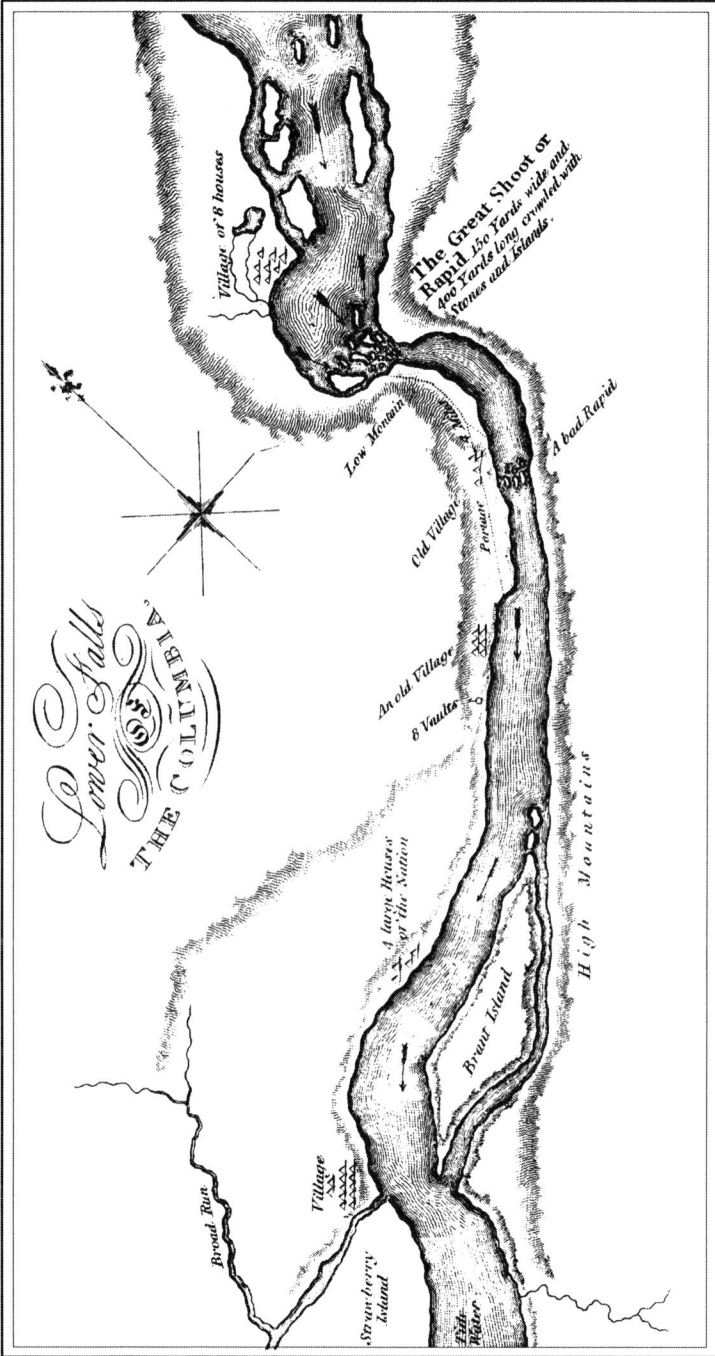

Lower Falls
of
THE COLUMBIA

The Great Shoot or
Rapid 150 Yards wide and
400 Yards long crouded with
Stones and Islands.

Village of 8 houses

Low Mountain

A bad Rapid

Old Village

Portage

An old Village

8 Vaults

A large Houses
for the Nation

High Mountains

Brant Island

Village

Broad Run

Strawberry Island

Tide Water

are unusually high, the river being confined between large rocks, many of which are at the surface of the water, Captain Clarke proceeded along
the same path he had taken before, which led him
through a thick wood and along a hill side, till
two and a half miles below the shoots, he struck
the river at the place whence the Indians make
their portage to the head of the shoot : he here
sent Crusatte, the principal waterman, up the
stream, to examine if it were practicable to bring
the canoes down the water. In the meantime, he,
with Joseph Fields, continued his route down the
river, along which the rapids seem to stretch as
far as he could see. At half a mile below the end
of the portage, he came to a house, the only rem-
nant of a town, which, from its appearance, must
have been of great antiquity. The house was un-
inhabited, and being old and decayed, he felt no
disposition to encounter the fleas, which abound in
every situation of that kind, and therefore did not
enter. About half a mile below this house, in a
very thick part of the woods, is an ancient burial
place : it consists of eight vaults made of pine, or
cedar boards, closely connected, about eight feet
square and six in height ; the top secured, covered
with wide boards sloping a little, so as to convey
off the rain : the direction of all of them is east and
west, the door being on the eastern side, and partially stopped with wide boards, decorated with
rude pictures of men and other animals. On entering we found in some of them four dead bodies,

carefully wrapped in skins, tied with cords of grass
and bark, lying on a mat, in a direction east and
west : the other vaults contained only bones, which
were in some of them piled to the height of four
feet: on the tops of the vaults, and on poles attached to them, hung brass kettles and frying-pans,
with holes in their bottoms, baskets, bowls, sea-
shells, skins, pieces of cloth, hair, bags of trinkets,
and small bones, the offerings of friendship or
affection, which have been saved by a pious ve-
neration from the ferocity of war, or the more
dangerous temptations of individual gain. The
whole of the walls as well as the door were decorated with strange figures cut and painted on them ;
and besides these were several wooden images of
men, some of them so old and decayed as to have
almost lost their shape, which were all placed
against the sides of the vaults. These images as
well as those in the houses we have lately seen, do
not appear to be at all the objects of adoration :
in this place they were most probably intended as
resemblances of those whose decease they indicate ; and when we observe them in houses, they
occupy the most conspicuous part ; but are treated
more like ornaments than objects of worship. Near
the vaults which are standing, are the remains of
others on the ground, completely rotted and covered with moss ; and as they are formed of the
most durable pine and cedar timber, there is every
appearance, that for a very long series of years
this retired spot has been the depository for the

Indians near this place. After examining this place Captain Clarke went on, and found the river, as before, strewed with large rocks, against which the water ran with great rapidity. Just below the vaults, the mountain, which is but low on the right side, leaves the river, and is succeeded by an open stony level, which extends down the river, while on the left the mountain is still high and rugged. At two miles distance he came to a village of four houses, which were now vacant and the doors barred up ; on looking in he saw the usual quantity of utensils still remaining, from which he concluded that the inhabitants were at no great distance collecting roots, or hunting, in order to lay in their supply of food for the winter : he left them, and went on three miles to a difficult rocky rapid, which was the last in view. Here, on the right, are the remains of a large and ancient village, which could be plainly traced by the holes for the houses, and the deposits for fish. After he had examined these rapids, and the neighbouring country, he returned to camp by the same route : the only game he had obtained was a sandhill crane.

In the meantime we had been occupied in preparations for making the portage, and in conference with the Indians, who came down from the village to visit us. Towards evening two canoes arrived from the village at the mouth of Cataract river, loaded with fish and bears' grease, for the market below : as soon as they landed they unloaded the canoes, turned them upside down on the beach, and encamped under a shelving rock near our camp. We had an opportunity of seeing to-day the hardihood of the Indians of the neighbouring village : one of the men shot a goose, which fell into the river, and was floating rapidly towards the great shoot, when an Indian observing it, plunged in after it ; the whole mass of the waters of the Columbia, just preparing to descend its narrow channel, carried the animal down with great rapidity ; the Indian followed it fearlessly, to within one hundred and fifty feet of the rocks, where he would inevitably have been dashed to pieces ; but seizing his prey, he turned round and swam a-shore with great composure. We very willingly relinquished our right to the bird in favour of the Indian who had thus saved it at the imminent hazard of his life : he immediately set to work, and picked off about half the feathers, and then, without opening it, ran a stick through it, and carried it off to roast.

Friday, November 1, 1805. The morning was cool and the wind high from the north-east. The Indians who arrived last night took their empty canoes on their shoulders, and carried them below the great shoot, where they put them in the water and brought them down the rapid, till at the distance of two and a half miles they stopped to take in their loading, which they had been afraid to trust in the last rapid, and had therefore carried by land from the head of the shoot.

After their example we carried our small canoe,

and all the baggage, across the slippery rocks to the foot of the shoot. The four large canoes were next brought down, by slipping them along poles, placed from one rock to another, and in some places by using partially streams which escaped along-side of the river. We were not, however, able to bring them across without three of them receiving injuries, which obliged us to stop at the end of the shoot to repair them. At this shoot we saw great numbers of sea-otters; but they are so shy that it is difficult to reach them with the musket: one of them that was wounded to-day sunk and was lost. Having by this portage avoided the rapid and shoot of four hundred yards in length, we re-embarked, passed at a mile and a half the bad rapid opposite to the old village on the right, and making our way through the rocks, saw the house just below the end of the portage; the eight vaults near it; and at the distance of four miles from the head of the shoot, reached a high rock, which forms the upper part of an island near the left shore. Between this island and the right shore we proceeded, leaving at the distance of a mile and a half, the village of four houses on our right, and a mile and a half lower came to the head of a rapid near the village on the right. Here we halted for the night, having made only seven miles from the head of the shoot. During the whole of the passage the river is very much obstructed by rocks. The island, which is about three miles long, reaches to the rapid which its lower extremity continues to form.

The meridian altitude of to-day, gave us the latitude of 45° 44' 3" north. As we passed the village of four houses, we found that the inhabitants had returned, and stopped to visit them. The houses are similar to those already described, but larger, from thirty-five to fifty feet long, and thirty feet wide, being sunk in the ground about six feet, and raised the same height above. Their beds are raised about four feet and a half from the floor, and the ascent is by a new painted ladder, with which every family is provided, and under them are stored their dried fish, while the space between the part of the bed on which they lie and the wall of the house is occupied by the nuts, roots, berries, and other provisions, which are spread on mats. The fire-place is about eight feet long, and six feet wide, sunk a foot below the floor, secured by a frame, with mats placed around for the family to sit on. In all of the houses are images of men of different shapes, and placed as ornaments in the parts of the house where they are most seen. They gave us nuts, berries, and some dried fish to eat, and we purchased, among other articles, a hat made after their own taste, such as they wear, without a brim. They ask high prices for all that they sell, observing that the whites below pay dearly for all which they carry there. We cannot learn precisely the nature of the trade carried on by the Indians with the inhabitants below. But as their knowledge of the whites seems to be very imperfect, and the only articles which they carry to market, such as pounded fish, bear-grease, and roots, cannot be an object of much foreign traffic, their intercourse appears to be an intermediate trade with the natives near the mouth of the Columbia; from them these people obtain in exchange for their fish, roots, and bear-grease, blue and white beads, copper tea-kettles, brass arm-bands, some scarlet and blue robes, and a few articles of old European clothing. But their great object is to obtain beads, an article which holds the first place in their ideas of relative value, and to procure which they will sacrifice their last article of clothing, or the last mouthful of food. Independently of their fondness for them as an ornament, these beads are the medium of trade, by which they obtain from the Indians still higher up the river, robes, skins, chappelel bread, bear-grease, &c. Those Indians, in turn, employ them to procure from the Indians in the rocky mountains bear-grease, pachico, roots, robes, &c.

These Indians are rather below the common size, with high cheek-bones, their noses pierced, and in full dress ornamented with a tapering piece of white shell or wampum, about two inches long. Their eyes are exceedingly sore and weak, many of them have only a single eye, and some are perfectly blind; their teeth prematurely decayed, and in frequent instances altogether worn away. Their general health, however, seems to be good, the only disorder we have remarked, being tumours in different parts of the body. The women are small

x 3

and homely in their appearance, their legs and thighs much swelled, and their knees remarkably large; deformities, which are no doubt owing to the manner in which they sit on their hams. They go nearly naked, having only a piece of leather tied round the breast, falling thence, nearly as low as the waist; a small robe about three feet square, and a piece of leather, which ill supplies the place of a cover, tied between their legs. Their hair is suffered to hang loose in every direction; and in their persons, as well as in their cookery, they are filthy to a most disgusting degree. We here observe, that the women universally have their heads flattened, and in many of the villages we have lately seen the female children undergo the operation.

CHAPTER XX.

FIRST APPEARANCE OF TIDE WATER IN THE COLUMBIA RIVER
— DESCRIPTION OF THE QUICKSAND RIVER—SOME ACCOUNT
OF THE SKILLOOT INDIANS — THE PARTY PASS THE RIVER
COWELISKE—SOME ACCOUNT OF THE WASHKIACUM INDIANS
— ARRIVAL ON THE BORDERS OF THE PACIFIC — DISAGREE-
ABLE AND CRITICAL SITUATION OF THE PARTY WHEN FIRST
ENCAMPED — THEIR DISTRESS OCCASIONED BY THE INCES-
SANT TORRENTS OF RAIN — EXPOSED FOR THIRTY DAYS
TO THIS DRENCHING DELUGE, DURING WHICH TIME
THEIR PROVISIONS ARE SPOILED, AND MOST OF THEIR
FEW ARTICLES OF MERCHANDISE DESTROYED — DISTRESS
OF THE PARTY — ADVENTURE OF SHANNON, AND HIS
DANGER FROM THE WASHKIACUMS — DIFFICULTY OF FIND-
ING A PLACE SUITABLE FOR A PERMANENT ENCAMPMENT —
VISITED BY SEVERAL INDIANS OF DIFFERENT TRIBES, ON
WHOM MEDALS ARE BESTOWED.

SATURDAY, November 2. We now examined the rapid below more particularly, and the danger appearing to be too great for the loaded canoes, all those who could not swim were sent with the baggage by land. The canoes then passed safely, and were re-loaded ; at the foot of the rapid we took a meridian altitude of 59° 45′ 45″. Just as we were setting out seven squaws arrived across the portage loaded with dried fish and bear-grease, neatly packed in bundles, and soon after four

x 4

Indians came down the rapid in a large canoe. After breakfasting we left our camp at one o'clock, passed the upper point of an island which is separated from the right shore by a narrow channel, through which, in high tides, the water passes. But at present it contains no running water, and a creek which falls into it from the mountains on the right, is in the same dry condition, though it has the marks of discharging immense torrents at some seasons. The island thus made is three miles in length, and about one in width; its situation is high and open, the land rich, and at this time covered with grass and a great number of strawberry vines, from which we gave it the name of Strawberry island. In several places we observed that the Indians had been digging for roots, and indeed the whole island bears every appearance of having been at some period in a state of cultivation. On the left side of the river the low ground is narrow and open: the rapid which we have just passed is the last of all the descents of the Columbia. At this place the first tide-water commences, and the river in consequence widened immediately below the rapid. As we descended, we reached, at the distance of one mile from the rapid, a creek under a bluff on the left; at three miles is the lower point of Strawberry island. To this immediately succeed three small islands covered with wood; in the meadow to the right, and at some distance from the hills, stands a high perpendicular rock, about eight hundred feet high,

and four hundred yards round the base ; this we
called the Beacon rock. Just below is an Indian
village of nine houses, situated between two small
creeks.

At this village the river widens to nearly a mile
in extent, the low grounds too become wider, and
they, as well as the mountains on each side, are
covered with pine, spruce-pine, cotton-wood, a species of ash, and some alder. After being so long
accustomed to the dreary nakedness of the country
above, the change is as grateful to the eye, as it is
useful in supplying us with fuel. Four miles from
the village is a point of land on the right, where the
hills become lower, but are still thickly timbered.
The river is now about two miles wide, the current
smooth and gentle, and the effect of the tide has
been sensible since leaving the rapid. Six miles
lower is a rock rising from the middle of the river,
to the height of one hundred feet, and about eighty
yards at its base. We continued six miles further,
and halted for the night under a high projecting
rock on the left side of the river opposite the point
of a large meadow. The mountains, which, from
the great shoot to this place, are high, rugged, and
thickly covered with timber, chiefly of the pine
species, here leave the river on each side ; the
river becomes two and a half miles in width, and
the low grounds are extensive and well supplied
with wood. The Indians, whom we left at the
portage, passed us, on their way down the river,
and seven others, who were descending in a canoe

for the purpose of trading below, encamped with us. We had made from the foot of the great shoot twenty-nine miles to-day. The ebb-tide rose at our camp about nine inches, the flood must rise much higher. We saw great numbers of water-fowl, such as swan, geese, ducks of various kinds, gulls, plover, and the white and grey brant, of which last we killed eighteen.

Sunday, 3. We were detained until ten o'clock by a fog so thick that a man could not be discerned at the distance of fifty steps. As soon as it cleared off we set out in company with our new Indian acquaintances, who came from a village near the Great Falls. The low grounds along the river are covered so thickly with rushes, vines, and other small growth, that they are almost impassable. At the distance of three miles we reached the mouth of a river on the left, which seemed to lose its waters in a sand-bar opposite; the stream itself being only a few inches in depth. But on attempting to wade across, we discovered that the bed was a very bad quicksand, too deep to be passed on foot. We went up a mile and a half to examine this river, and found it to be at this distance a very considerable stream, one hundred and twenty yards wide at its narrowest part, with several small islands. Its character resembles very much that of the river Platte. It drives its quick-sand over the low grounds with great impetuosity; and such is the quantity of coarse sand which it discharges, that the accumulation has formed a large sand-bar or island three miles long, and a mile and a half wide, which divides the waters of the Quicksand river into two channels. This sand island compresses the Columbia within a space of half a mile, and throws its whole current against the right shore. Opposite to this river, which we call Quicksand river, is a large creek, to which we gave the name of Seal river. The first appears to pass through the low country, at the foot of the high range of mountains towards the south-east, while the second, as well as all the large creeks on the right side of the Columbia, rises in the same ridge of mountains N.N.E. from this place. The mountain which we have supposed to be the Mount Hood of Vancouver, bears S. 85° E. about forty-seven miles from the mouth of the Quicksand river. After dinner we proceeded, and at the distance of three miles reached the lower mouth of Quicksand river. On the opposite side a large creek falls in near the head of an island, which extends for three miles and a half down the river; it is a mile and a half in width, rocky at the upper end, has some timber round its borders, but in the middle is open and has several ponds. Half a mile lower is another island in the middle of the river, to which, from its appearance, we gave the name of Diamond island. Here we met fifteen Indians ascending the river in two canoes, but the only information we could procure from them was, that they had seen three vessels, which we presume to be European, at the mouth of the Columbia. We went along its right side for three miles, and encamped opposite to it, after making to-day thirteen miles. A canoe soon after arrived from the village at the foot of the last rapid, with an Indian and his family, consisting of a wife, three children, and a woman, who had been taken prisoner from the Snake Indians, living on a river from the south, which we afterwards found to be the Multnomah. Sacajaweah was immediately introduced to her, in hopes that being a Snake Indian also, they might understand each other, but their language was not sufficiently intelligible to permit them to converse together. The Indian had a gun with a brass barrel and cock, which he appeared to value very highly.

Below Quicksand river the country is low, rich, and thickly wooded on each side of the river; the islands have less timber, but are furnished with a number of ponds, near which are vast quantities of fowls, such as swan, geese, brants, cranes, storks, white gulls, cormorants, and plover. The river is wide, and contains a great number of sea-otters.

In the evening the hunters brought in game for a sumptuous supper, which we shared with the Indians, both parties of whom spent the night with us.

Monday, 4. The weather was cloudy and cool, and the wind from the west. During the night, the tide rose eighteen inches near our camp. We set out about eight o'clock, and at the distance of three miles came to the lower end of Diamond island. It is six miles long, nearly three in width, and like the other islands thinly covered with timber, and has a number of ponds, or small lakes, scattered over its surface. Besides the animals already mentioned, we shot a deer on it this morning. Near the end of Diamond island are two others, separated by a narrow channel filled at high tides only, which continue on the right for the distance of three miles, and like the adjacent low grounds are thickly covered with pine. Just below the last, we landed on the left bank of the river, at a village of twenty-five houses; all of these were thatched with straw, and built of bark, except one, which was about fifty feet long, built of boards, in the form of those higher up the river, from which it differed, however, in being completely above ground, and covered with broad split boards; this village contains about two hundred men of the Skilloot nation, who seem well provided with canoes, of which there were at least fifty-two, and some of them very large, drawn up in front of the village. On landing we found the Indian from above, who had left us this morning, and who now invited us into a lodge of which he appeared to own a part. Here he treated us with a root, round in shape, and about the size of a small Irish potatoe, which they call wappatoo; it is the common arrow-head or sagittifolia, so much cultivated by the Chinese, and when roasted in the embers till it becomes soft, has an agreeable taste, and is a very good substitute for bread. After purchasing some more of this root, we resumed our journey, and at seven miles distance came to the head of a large island near the left. On the right shore is a fine open prairie for about a mile, back of which the country rises, and is supplied with timber, such as white oak, pine of different kinds, wild crab, and several species of under-growth, while along the borders of the river there are only a few cotton-wood and ash trees. In this prairie were also signs of deer and elk. When we landed for dinner, a number of Indians from the last village came down, for the purpose, as we supposed, of paying us a friendly visit, as they had put on their favourite dresses. In addition to their usual covering, they had scarlet and blue blankets, sailors' jackets and trowsers, shirts, and hats. They had all of them either war-axes, spears, and bow arrows, or muskets and pistols, with tin powder flasks. We smoked with them and endeavoured to show them every attention, but we soon found them very assuming and disagreeable companions. While we were eating, they stole the pipe with which they were smoking, and the great coat of one of the men. We immediately searched them all, and discovered the coat stuffed under the root of a tree near where they were sitting; but the pipe we could not recover. Finding us determined not to suffer any imposition, and discontented with them, they showed their displeasure in the only way which they dared, by returning in an ill humour to their village. We then proceeded, and soon met two canoes with twelve men of the same Skilloot nation, who were on their way from below. The larger of the canoes was ornamented with the figure of a bear in the bow, and a man in the stern, both nearly as large as life, both made of painted wood, and very neatly fixed to the boat. In the same canoe were two Indians finely dressed, and with round hats. This circumstance induced us to give the name of Image-canoe to the large island, the lower end of which we now passed, at the distance of nine miles from its head. We had seen two smaller islands to the right, and three more near its lower extremity. The Indians in the canoe here made signs that there was a village behind those islands, and indeed we presumed there was a channel on that side of the river, for one of the canoes passed in that direction between the small islands, but we were anxious to press forward, and therefore did not stop to examine more minutely. The river was now about a mile and a half in width, with a gentle current, the bottoms extensive and low, but not subject to be overflowed. Three miles below the Image-canoe island we came to four large houses on the left side, at which place we had a full view of the mountain, which we first saw on the 19th of October, from the Muscle-shell rapid, and which we now find to be the Mount St. Helen of Vancouver. It bears north 25° east, about ninety miles distant; it rises, in the form of a sugar-loaf, to a very great height, and is covered with snow. A mile lower we passed a single house on the left, and another on the right. The Indians had now learnt so much of us, that their curiosity was without any mixture

10

of fear, and their visits became very frequent and troublesome. We therefore continued on till after night, in hopes of getting rid of them ; but after passing a village on each side, which, on account of the lateness of the hour, we saw indistinctly, we found there was no escaping from their importunities. We therefore landed at the distance of seven miles below Image-canoe island, and encamped near a single house on the right, having made during the day twenty-nine miles.

The Skilloots whom we passed to-day, speak a language somewhat different from that of the Echeloots or Chilluckittequaws, near the Long Narrows. Their dress is similar, except that the Skilloots possess more articles procured from the white traders ; and there is a further difference between them ; inasmuch as the Skilloots, both males and females, have the head flattened. Their principal food is fish, and wappatoo roots, and some elk and deer, in killing which with their arrows, they seem very expert, for during the short time we remained at the village, three deer were brought in. We also observed there a tame brairo.

As soon as we landed, we were visited by two canoes loaded with Indians, from whom we purchased a few roots. The grounds along the river continue low and rich, and among the shrubs which cover them is a large quantity of vines resembling the raspberry. On the right the low grounds are terminated at the distance of five miles by a range of high hills covered with tall timber, and running south-east and north-west. The game, as usual, very abundant; and among other birds we observe some white geese with a part of their wings black.

Tuesday, 5. Our choice of a camp had been very unfortunate; for on a sand island opposite to us were immense numbers of geese, swan-ducks, and other wild fowl, who, during the whole night, serenaded us with a confusion of noises which completely prevented our sleeping. During the latter part of the night it rained, and we therefore willingly left our encampment at an early hour. We passed at three miles a small prairie, where the river is only three quarters of a mile in width, and soon after two houses on the left, half a mile distant from each other; from one of which three men came in a canoe merely to look at us, and having done so, returned home. At eight miles we came to the lower point of an island, separated from the right side by a narrow channel, on which, a short distance above the end of the island, is situated a large village: it is built more compactly than the generality of the Indian villages, and the front has fourteen houses, which are ranged for a quarter of a mile along the channel. As soon as we were discovered, seven canoes came out to see us; and after some traffic, during which they seemed well-disposed and orderly, accompanied us a short distance below. The river here again widens to the space of a mile and a half. As we descended we soon observed, behind a sharp point of rocks, a

channel a quarter of a mile wide, which we suppose must be the one taken by the canoes yesterday, on leaving Image-canoe island. A mile below
the channel are some low cliffs of rocks, near
which is a large island on the right side, and two
small islands a little farther on. Here we met two
canoes ascending the river. At this place the
shore on the right becomes bold and rocky, and
the bank is bordered by a range of high hills
covered with a thick growth of pine : on the other
side is an extensive low island, separated from the
left side by a narrow channel. Here we stopped
to dine, and found the island open, with an abundant growth of grass, and a number of ponds well
supplied with fowls ; and at the lower extremity are
the remains of an old village. We procured a swan,
several ducks, and a brant, and saw some deer on
the island. Besides this island, the lower extremity
of which is seventeen miles from the channel just
mentioned, we passed two or three smaller ones in
the same distance. Here the hills on the right retire from the river, leaving a high plain, between
which, on the left bank, a range of high hills running south-east, and covered with pine, forms a
bold and rocky shore. At the distance of six
miles, however, these hills again return, and close
the river on both sides. We proceeded on, and at
four miles reached a creek on the right, about
twenty yards in width, immediately below which
is an old village. Three miles further, and at the
distance of thirty-two miles from our camp of last

night, we halted under a point of highland, with thick pine trees on the left bank of the river. Before landing we met two canoes, the largest of which had at the bow the image of a bear, and that of a man on the stern: there were twenty-six Indians on board, but they all proceeded upwards, and we were left, for the first time since we reached the waters of the Columbia, without any of the natives with us during the night. Besides the game already mentioned, we killed a grouse much larger than the common size, and observed along the shore a number of striped snakes. The river is here deep, and about a mile and a half in width. Here too the ridge of low mountains running north-west and south-east, cross the river, and form the western boundary of the plain through which we have just passed. This great plain or valley begins above the mouth of Quicksand river, and is about sixty miles wide in a straight line, while on the right and left it extends to a great distance: it is a fertile and delightful country, shaded by thick groves of tall timber, watered by small ponds, and running on both sides of the river. The soil is rich, and capable of any species of culture; but in the present condition of the Indians, its chief production is the wappatoo root, which grows spontaneously and exclusively in this region. Sheltered as it is on both sides, the temperature is much milder than that of the surrounding country; for even at this season of the year we observe very little appearance of frost. During its whole extent it is inhabited by numerous tribes of Indians, who either reside in it permanently, or visit its waters in quest of fish, and wappatoo roots: we gave it the name of the Columbia valley.

Wednesday, 6. The morning was cool, wet, and rainy. We proceeded, at an early hour, between the high hills on both sides of the river, till at the distance of four miles we came to two tents of Indians in a small plain on the left, where the hills on the right recede a few miles from the river, and a long narrow island stretches along the right shore. Behind this island is the mouth of a large river, a hundred and fifty yards wide, and called by the Indians Coweliske. We halted for dinner on the island, but the red wood and green briars are so interwoven with the pine, alder, ash, a species of beech, and other trees, that the woods form a thicket, which our hunters could not penetrate. Below the mouth of the Coweliske a very remarkable knob rises from the water's edge, to the height of eighty feet, being two hundred paces round the base; and as it is in a low part of the island, and some distance from the high grounds, the appearance of it is very singular. On setting out after dinner, we overtook two canoes going down to trade: one of the Indians, who spoke a few words of English, mentioned, that the principal person who traded with them was a Mr. Haley, and he shewed a bow of iron, and several other things, which he said Mr. Haley had given him. Nine miles below that river is a creek on the same ; and between them three smaller islands; one on the left shore, the other about the middle of the river ; and a third near the lower end of the long narrow island, and opposite a high cliff of black rocks on the left, sixteen miles from our camp. Here we were overtaken by the Indians from the two tents we passed in the morning, from whom we now purchased wappatoo roots, salmon, trout, and two beaver skins, for which last we gave five small fish-hooks. At these cliffs the mountains, which had continued high and rugged on the left, retired from the river, and as the hills on the other side had left the water at the Coweliske, a beautiful extensive plain now presented itself before us. For a few miles we passed alongside of an island, a mile in width and three miles long, below which is a smaller island, where the high rugged hills, thickly covered with timber, border the right bank of the river, and terminate the low grounds ; these were supplied with common rushes, grass, and nettles ; in the moister parts with bull-rushes and flags, and along the water's edge some willows. Here also were two ancient villages, now abandoned by their inhabitants, of whom no vestige remains, except two small dogs, almost starved, and a prodigious quantity of fleas. After crossing the plain, and making five miles, we proceeded through the hills for eight miles. The river is about a mile in width, and the hills so steep that we could not, for several miles, find a place sufficiently level to suffer us to sleep in a level position : at length, by removing the large stones, we cleared a place fit for our purpose above the reach of the tide, and after a journey of twenty-nine miles, slept among the smaller stones under a mountain to the right. The weather was rainy during the whole day : we therefore made large fires to dry our bedding, and to kill the fleas, who have accumulated upon us at every old village we have passed.

Thursday, 7. The morning was rainy, and the fog so thick that we could not see across the river. We observed, however, opposite to our camp, the upper point of an island, between which and the steep hills on the right we proceeded for five miles. Three miles lower is the beginning of an island separated from the right shore by a narrow channel; down this we proceeded, under the direction of some Indians whom we had just met going up the river, and who returned in order to show us their village. It consists of four houses only, situated on this channel behind several marshy islands formed by two small creeks. On our arrival they gave us some fish, and we afterwards purchased wappatoo roots, fish, three dogs, and two otter skins, for which we gave fish-hooks chiefly, that being an article of which they are very fond.

These people seem to be of a different nation from those we have just passed : they are low in stature, ill-shaped, and all have their heads flattened. They call themselves Wahkiacum, and their language differs from that of the tribes above, with whom they trade for wappatoo roots. The houses too are built in a different style, being raised entirely above ground, with the eaves about five feet high, and the door at the corner. Near the end opposite to this door is a single fire-place, round which are the beds, raised four feet from the floor of earth; over the fire are hung the fresh fish, and when dried they are stowed away with the wappatoo roots under the beds. The dress of the men is like that of the people above, but the women are clad in a peculiar manner, the robe not reaching lower than the hip, and the body being covered in cold weather by a sort of corset of fur, curiously plaited, and reaching from the arms to the hip; added to this is a sort of petticoat, or rather tissue of white cedar bark, bruised or broken into small strands, and woven into a girdle by several cords of the same materials. Being tied round the middle, these strands hang down as low as the knee in front, and to midleg behind; and are of sufficient thickness to answer the purpose of concealment, whilst the female stands in an erect position, but in any other attitude is but a very ineffectual defence. Sometimes the tissue is formed of strings of silk-grass, twisted and knotted at the end.

After remaining with them about an hour, we proceeded down the channel with an Indian dressed in a sailor's jacket for our pilot, and on reaching the main channel were visited by some Indians, who have a temporary residence on a marshy island in the middle of the river, where is a great abun-

dance of water fowl. Here the mountainous country again approaches the river on the left, and a
higher mountain is distinguished towards the south-
west. At a distance of twenty miles from our
camp we halted at a village of Wahkiacums, consisting of seven ill-looking houses, built in the same
form with those above, and situated at the foot of
the high hills on the right, behind two small
marshy islands. We merely stopped to purchase
some food and two beaver skins, and then proceeded. Opposite to these islands the hills on
the left retire, and the river widens into a kind of
bay crowded with low islands, subject to be overflowed occasionally by the tide. We had not gone
far from this village when the fog cleared off, and
we enjoyed the delightful prospect of the ocean;
that ocean, the object of all our labours, the reward of all our anxieties. This cheering view ex-
hilarated the spirits of all the party, who were still
more delighted on hearing the distant roar of the
breakers. We went on with great cheerfulness
under the high mountainous country which continued along the right bank ; the shore was however so bold and rocky, that we could not, until
after going fourteen miles from the last village,
find any spot fit for an encampment. At that distance, having made during the day thirty-four miles,
we spread our mats on the ground, and passed the
night in the rain. Here we were joined by our
small canoe, which had been separated from us
during the fog this morning. Two Indians from

the last village also accompanied us to the camp, but, having detected them in stealing a knife, they were sent off.

Friday, 8. It rained this morning ; and having changed the clothing which had been wetted during yesterday's rain, we did not set out till nine o'clock. Immediately opposite our camp is a rock at the distance of a mile in the river, about twenty feet in diameter and fifty in height, and towards the south-west some high mountains, one of which is covered with snow at the top. We proceeded past several low islands in the bay or bend of the river to the left, which is here five or six miles wide. We were here overtaken by three Indians in a canoe, who had a. salmon to sell. On the right side we passed an old village, and then, at the distance of three miles, entered an inlet or niche, about six miles across, and making a deep bend of nearly five miles into the hills on the right shore, where it receives the waters of several creeks. We coasted along this inlet, which, from its little depth, we called Shallow bay, and at the bottom of it halted to dine near the remains of an old village, from which, however, we kept at a cautious distance, as it was occupied by great numbers of fleas. At this place we observed a number of fowl, among which we killed a goose and two ducks, exactly resembling in appearance and flavour the canvas-back duck of the Susque-hannah. After dinner the three Indians left us, and we then took advantage of the returning tide,

to go on about three miles to a point on the right,
eight miles distant from our camp; but here the
waves ran so high, and dashed about our canoes
so much, that several of the men became sea-sick.
It was therefore judged imprudent to go on in the
present state of the weather, and we landed at the
point. The situation was extremely uncomfortable; the high hills jutted in so closely that there
was not room for us to lie level, nor to secure our
baggage free from the tide; and the water of the
river is too salt to be used : but the waves increasing every moment so much, that we could not
move from the spot with safety; we therefore
fixed ourselves on the beach left by the ebb-tide,
and having raised the baggage on poles, passed a
disagreeable night, the rain during the day having
wetted us completely, as indeed we have been for
some days past.

Saturday, 9. Fortunately for us, the tide did
not rise as high as our camp during the night; but
being accompanied by high winds from the south,
the canoes, which we could not place beyond its
reach, were filled with water, and were saved with
much difficulty : our position was very uncomfortable, but as it was impossible to move from it, we
waited for a change of weather. It rained, however, during the whole day, and at two o'clock in
the afternoon, the flood tide set in, accompanied
by a high wind from the south, which, about four
o'clock, shifted to the south-west, and blew almost
a gale directly from the sea. The immense waves

now broke over the place where we were encamped, and the large trees, some of them five or six feet thick, which had lodged at the point, were drifted over our camp, and the utmost vigilance of every man could scarcely save our canoes from being crushed to pieces. We remained in the water and drenched with rain during the rest of the day : our only food being some dried fish, and some rain-water which we caught. Yet, though wet and cold, and some of them sick from using the salt-water, the men are cheerful and full of anxiety to see more of the ocean. The rain continued all night, and,

Sunday, 10th, the following morning, the wind having lulled, and the waves not being so high, we loaded our canoes and proceeded. The mountains on the right are high, covered with timber, chiefly pine, and descend in a bold and rocky shore to the water. We went through a deep niche and several inlets on the right, while on the opposite side is a large bay, above which the hills are close on the river. At the distance of ten miles the wind rose from the north-west, and the waves became so high that we were forced to return for two miles to a place where we could with safety unload. Here we landed at the mouth of a small run, and having placed our baggage on a pile of drifted logs waited until low water. The river then appeared more calm : we therefore started, but after going a mile found the waves too high for our canoes, and were obliged to put to shore. We unloaded the canoes, and having placed the baggage on a rock above the reach of the tide, encamped on some drift logs, which formed the only place where we could lie, the hills rising steep over our heads to the height of five hundred feet. All our baggage as well as ourselves was thoroughly wetted with the rain, which did not cease during the day; it continued violently during the night, in the course of which the tide reached the logs on which we lay, and set them afloat.

Monday, 11. The wind was still high from the south-west, and drove the waves against the shore with great fury : the rain too fell in torrents, and not only drenched us to the skin, but loosened the stones on the hill sides, which then came rolling down upon us. In this comfortless situation we remained all day, wet, cold, with nothing but dried fish to satisfy our hunger; the canoes in one place at the mercy of the waves; the baggage in another; and all the men scattered on floating logs, or sheltering themselves in the crevices of the rocks and hill sides. A hunter was dispatched in hopes of finding some fresh meat, but the hills were so steep, and covered with under-growth and fallen timber, that he could not penetrate them, and he was forced to return. About twelve o'clock we were visited by five Indians in a canoe : they came from above this place on the opposite side of the river, and their language much resembles that of the Wahkiacum : they called themselves *Cathlamahs*. In person they are small, ill-made, and badly clothed : though one of them had on a sailor's round jacket and pantaloons, which, as he explained by signs, he had received from the whites below the point : we purchased from them thirteen red char, a fish which we found very excellent. After some time they went on board the boat, and crossed the river, which is here five miles wide, through a very heavy sea.

Tuesday, 12. About three o'clock a tremendous gale of wind arose, accompanied with lightning, thunder, and hail : at six it became light for a short time, but a violent rain soon began and lasted during the day. During this storm one of our boats, secured by being sunk with great quantities of stone, got loose, but drifting against a rock, was recovered without having receiving much injury. Our situation became now much more dangerous, for the waves were driven with fury against the rocks and trees, which till now had afforded us refuge : we therefore took advantage of a low tide, and moved about half a mile round a point to a small brook, which we had not observed till now, on account of the thick bushes and driftwood which concealed its mouth. Here we were more safe ; but still cold and wet, our clothes and bedding rotten as well as wet, our baggage at a distance, and the canoes, our only means of escape from this place, at the mercy of the waves : we were, however, fortunate enough to enjoy good health, and even had the luxury of getting some fresh salmon, and three salmon trout in the brook.

Three of the men attempted to go round a point in our small Indian canoe, but the high waves rendered her quite unmanageable ; these boats requiring the seamanship of the natives themselves to make them live in so rough a sea.

Wednesday, 13. During the night we had short intervals of fair weather, but it began to rain in the morning, and continued through the day. In order to obtain a view of the country below, Captain Clarke followed up the course of the brook, and with much fatigue, and after walking three miles, ascended the first spur of the mountains. The whole lower country was covered with almost impenetrable thickets of small pine, with which is mixed a species of plant resembling arrow wood, twelve or fifteen feet high, with a thorny stem, almost interwoven with each other, and scattered among the fern and fallen timber : there is also a red berry, somewhat like the Solomon's seal, which is called by the natives solme, and used as an article of diet. This thick growth rendered travelling almost impossible, and it was rendered more fatiguing by the steepness of the mountain, which was so great as to oblige him to draw himself up by means of the bushes. The timber on the hills is chiefly of a large tall species of pine, many of them eight or ten feet in diameter at the stump, and rising sometimes more than one hundred feet in height. The hail, which fell two nights since, is still to be seen on the mountains ; there was no game, and no traces of any, except some old signs

6

of elk : the cloudy weather prevented his seeing to any distance, and he therefore returned to camp, and sent three men in the Indian canoe to try if they could double the point and find some safer harbour for our canoes. At every flood-tide the sea breaks in great swells against the rocks, and drifts the trees among our establishment, so as to render it very insecure. We were confined as usual to dried fish, which is our last resource.

Thursday, 14. It rained without intermission during last night and to-day : the wind too is very high, and one of our canoes much injured by being dashed against rocks. Five Indians from below came to us in a canoe, and three of them having landed, informed us they had seen the men sent down yesterday. At this moment one of them arrived, and informed us that these Indians had stolen his gig and basket : we therefore ordered the two women who remained in the canoe, to restore them; but this they refused, till we threatened to shoot, when they gave back the articles, and we then ordered them to leave us. They were of the Wahkiacum nation. The man now informed us that they had gone round the point as far as the high sea would suffer them, in the canoe, and then landed, and that in the night he had separated from his companions, who had gone further down : that at no great distance from where we are is a beautiful sand beach and a good harbour. Captain Lewis concluded to examine more minutely the lower part of the bay, and taking one of the large canoes was landed at the point, whence he proceeded by land with four men, and the canoe returned nearly filled with water.

Friday, 15. It continued raining all night, but in the morning the weather became calm and fair: we therefore began to prepare for setting out, but before we were ready, a high wind sprang up from the south-east, and obliged us to remain. The sun shone until one o'clock, and we were thus enabled to dry our bedding and examine our baggage. The rain, which has continued for the last ten days without an interval of more than two hours, has completely wetted all our merchandise, and spoiled some of our fish, destroyed the robes, and rotted nearly one half of our few remaining articles of clothing, particularly the leather dresses. About three o'clock the wind fell, and we instantly loaded the canoes, and left the miserable spot to which we have been confined the last six days. On turning the point we came to the sand beach, through which runs a small stream from the hills; at the mouth of which is an ancient village of thirty-six houses, which has at present no inhabitants except fleas. Here we met Shannon, who had been sent back to meet us by Captain Lewis. The day Shannon left us in the canoe, he and Willard proceeded on till they met a party of twenty Indians, who never having heard of us, did not know where they came from: they, however, behaved with so much civility, and seemed so anxious that the men should go with them towards the sea, that their

suspicions were excited, and they declined going
on; the Indians, however, would not leave them,
and the men being confirmed in their suspicions,
and fearful if they went into the woods to sleep
they would be cut to pieces in the night, thought
it best to pass the night in the midst of the Indians;
they therefore made a fire, and after talking with
them to a late hour, lay down with their rifles
under their heads. As they awoke this morning
they found that the Indians had stolen and concealed their guns: having demanded them in vain,
Shannon seized a club, and was about assaulting
one of the Indians whom he suspected as a thief,
when another Indian began to load a fowling piece
with an intention of shooting him. He therefore
stopped and explained by signs, that if they did
not give up the guns, a large party would come
down the river before the sun rose to such a height,
and put every one of them to death. Fortunately,
Captain Lewis and his party appeared at this time,
and the terrified Indians immediately brought the
guns, and five of them came on with Shannon.
To these men we declared, that if ever any of their
nation stole any thing from us he should be instantly shot. They reside to the north of this
place, and speak a language different from that of
the people higher up the river. It was now apparent that the sea was at all times too rough for us
to proceed further down the bay by water: we
therefore landed, and having chosen the best spot
we could select, made our camp of boards from

the old village. We were now situated comfortably, and being visited by four Wahkiacums with wappatoo roots, were enabled to make an agreeable addition to our food.

Saturday, 16. The morning was clear and beautiful. We therefore put out all our baggage to dry, and sent several of the party to hunt. Our camp is in full view of the ocean, on the bay laid down by Vancouver, which we distinguished by the name of Haley's bay, from a trader who visits the Indians here, and is a great favourite among them. The meridian altitude of this day gave 46° 19′ 11$\frac{7}{10}$″ as the latitude of our camp. The wind was strong from the south-west, and the waves very high, yet the Indians were passing up and down the bay in canoes, and several of them encamped near us. We smoked with them, but after our recent experience of their thievish disposition, treated them with caution. Though so much exposed to the bad weather, none of the party have suffered, except one, who has a violent cold, in consequence of sleeping for several nights in wet leather. The hunters brought in two deer, a crane, some geese and ducks, and several brant, three of which were white, except a black part of the wing, and much larger than the grey brant, which is itself a size beyond the duck.

Sunday, 17. A fair cool morning and easterly wind. The tide rises at this place eight feet six inches in height, and rolls over the beach in great waves.

Mouth OF COLUMBIA RIVER.

East to Point William

South 47° East to Point Meriwether

extended from

in 25 Nov. 1805

South 16° West 2 miles

South 88° West 11 Miles

Encampment

Point Round

Clatsop River

Published April 28th 1814 by Longman & C. Paternoster Row.

About one o'clock Captain Lewis returned, after having coasted down Haley's bay to Cape Disappointment, and some distance to the north along the sea-coast. He was followed by several Chinnooks, among whom were the principal chief and his family. They made us a present of a boiled root, very much like the common liquorice in taste and size, and called culwhamo : in return we gave double the value of their present, and now learnt the danger of accepting any thing from them, since no return, even if ten times the value of their gift, can satisfy them. We were chiefly occupied in hunting, and were able to procure three deer, four brant, and two ducks, and also saw some signs of elk. Captain Clarke now prepared for an excursion down the bay, and accordingly started,

Monday, 18, at daylight, accompanied by eleven men. He proceeded along the beach one mile to a point of rocks about forty feet high, where the hills retire, leaving a wide beach, and a number of ponds covered with water-fowl, between which and the mountain is a narrow bottom of alder and small balsam trees. Seven miles from the rocks is the entrance of a creek, or rather drain from the ponds and hills, where is a cabin of Chinnooks. The cabin contained some children, and four women, one of whom was in a most miserable state, covered with ulcers, proceeding, as we imagine, from the venereal disease, with which several of the Chinnooks we have seen appear to be afflicted. We were taken across in a canoe by two Squaws, to each of whom we gave a fish-hook, and then coasting along the bay, passed, at two miles, the low bluff of a small hill, below which are the ruins of some old huts, and close to it the remains of a whale. The country is low, open, and marshy; interspersed with some high pine and a thick undergrowth. Five miles from the creek, we came to a stream forty yards wide at low water, which we called Chinnook river. The hills up this river, and towards the bay, are not high, but very thickly covered with large pine of several species: in many places pine trees, three or four feet in thickness, are seen growing on the bodies of large trees, which, though fallen and covered with moss, were in part sound. Here we dined on some brant and plover, killed as we came along, and after crossing in a boat lying in the sand near some old houses, proceeded along a bluff of yellow clay and soft stone, to a little bay or harbour, into which a drain from some ponds empties: at this harbour the land is low, but as we went on, it rose to hills of eighty or ninety feet above the water. At the distance of one mile is a second bay, and a mile beyond it a small rocky island in a deep bend, which seems to afford a very good harbour, and where the natives inform us, European vessels anchor for the purpose of trading. We went on round another bay, in which is a second small island of rocks, and crossed a small stream, which rises in a pond near the sea-coast, and after running through a low isthmus, empties into the bay. This narrow

low ground, about two or three hundred yards
wide, separates from the main hills a kind of peninsula, the extremity of which is two miles from
the anchoring place; and this spot, which was
called Cape Disappointment, is an elevated, circular knob, rising with a steep ascent one hundred
and fifty, or one hundred and sixty feet above the
water, formed like the whole shore of the bay, as
well as of the sea-coast, and covered with thick
timber on the inner side, but open and grassy in
the exposure next the sea. From this cape a high
point of land bears south 20° west, about twenty-
five miles distant. In the range between these two
eminences, is the opposite point of the bay, a very
low ground, which has been variously called Cape
Rond by La Perouse, and Point Adams by Vancouver. The water for a great distance off the
mouth of the river, and within the mouth nearest
to Point Adams, is a large sand-bar, almost covered
at high tide. We could not ascertain the direction
of the deepest channel, for the waves break with
tremendous force the whole distance across the
bay, but the Indians point nearer to the opposite
side as the best passage. After remaining for some
time on this elevation, we descended across the low
isthmus, and reached the ocean at the foot of a
high hill, about a mile in circumference, and projecting into the sea. We crossed this hill, which
is open, and has a growth of high coarse grass, and
encamped on the north side of it, having made
nineteen miles. Besides the pounded fish and

brant, we had for supper a flounder, which we picked up on the beach.

Tuesday, 19. In the night it began to rain, and continued till eleven o'clock. Two hunters were sent on to kill something for breakfast, and the rest of the party, after drying their blankets, soon followed. At three miles we overtook the hunters, and breakfasted on a small deer, which they had been fortunate enough to kill. This, like all those we have seen on this coast, are much darker than our common deer. Their bodies, too, are deeper, their legs shorter, and their eyes larger. The branches of the horns are similar, but the upper part of the tail is black, from the root to the end, and they do not leap, but jump like a sheep frightened. We then continued over rugged hills and steep hollows, near the sea, on a course about north 20° west, in a direct line from the cape, till at the distance of five miles, we reached a point of high land, below which a sandy beach extends, in a direction north 10° west, to another high point about twenty miles distant. This eminence we distinguished by the name of Point Lewis. It is there that the high lands, which, at the commencement of the sandy beach, recede towards Chinnook river, again approach the ocean. The intermediate country is low, with many small ponds, crowded with birds and watered by the Chinnook, on the borders of which resides the nation of the same name. We went four miles along the sandy beach to a small pine tree, on which

Captain Clarke marked his name, with the year
and day, and then returned to the foot of the
hills, passing on the shore a sturgeon ten feet
long, and several joints of the back-bone of a
whale, both which seem to have been thrown
ashore and foundered. After dining on the remains of the small deer, we crossed in a south-
eastern direction to the bay, where we arrived at
the distance of two miles, then continued along
the bay, crossed Chinnook river, and encamped
on its upper side, in a sandy bottom.

Wednesday, 20. It rained in the course of the
night. A hunter, dispatched early to kill some
food, returned with eight ducks, on which we
breakfasted, and then followed the course of the
bay to the creek or outlet of the ponds. It was
now high tide, the stream three hundred yards
wide, and no person in the cabin to take us across.
We therefore made a small raft, on which one of
the men passed and brought a canoe to carry us
over. As we went along the beach, we were overtaken by several Indians, who gave us dried sturgeon and wappatoo roots, and soon met several
parties of Chinnooks returning from the camp.
When we arrived there we found many Chinnooks,
and two of them being chiefs, we went through
the ceremony of giving to each a medal, and to
the most distinguished a flag. Their names were
Concommoly and Chillahlawill. One of the Indians
had a robe made of two sea-otter skins, the fur of
which was the most beautiful we had ever seen;

the owner resisted every temptation to part with it, but at length could not resist the offer of a belt of blue beads which Chaboneau's wife wore round her waist. During our absence the camp had been visited by many Indians, and the men who had been employed in hunting killed several deer, and a variety of wild fowls.

Thursday, 21. The morning was cloudy, and from noon till night it rained. The wind too was high from the south-east, and the sea so rough that the water reached our camp. Most of the Chinnooks returned home, but we were visited in the course of the day by people of different bands in the neighbourhood, among whom are the Chiltz, a nation residing on the sea-coast near Point Lewis, and the Clatsops, who live immediately opposite on the south side of the Columbia. A chief from the Grand Rapid also came to see us, and we gave him a medal. To each of our visitors we made a present of a small piece of ribband, and purchased some cranberries and some articles of their manufacture, such as mats and household furniture, for all which we paid high prices. After we had been relieved from these Indians, we were surprised at a visit of a different kind; an old woman who is the wife of a Chinnook chief came with six young women, her daughters and nieces, and having deliberately encamped near us, proceeded to cultivate an intimacy between our men and her fair wards.

CHAPTER XXI.

EXTRAVAGANT PASSION OF THE NATIVES FOR BLUE BEADS, WHICH CONSTITUTE AMONGST THEM THE CIRCULATING MEDIUM OF THE COUNTRY — THE PARTY STILL IN SEARCH OF A SUITABLE PLACE FOR WINTER QUARTERS — STILL SUFFERING FROM THE CONSTANT DELUGES OF RAIN — ARE VISITED BY THE INDIANS, WITH WHOM THEY TRAFFIC BUT LITTLE, ON ACCOUNT OF THE EXTRAVAGANT PRICES THEY ASK FOR EVERY ARTICLE — RETURN OF CAPTAIN LEWIS, WHO REPORTS THAT HE HAS FOUND A SUITABLE PLACE FOR WINTER QUARTERS — THE RAIN STILL CONTINUES — THEY PREPARE TO FORM AN ENCAMPMENT ON A POINT OF HIGH LAND ON THE BANKS OF THE RIVER NEUTEL — CAPTAIN CLARKE GOES WITH A PARTY TO FIND A PLACE SUITABLE FOR THE MANUFACTURE OF SALT — HE IS HOSPITABLY ENTERTAINED BY THE CLATSOPS — THIS TRIBE ADDICTED TO THE VICE OF GAMBLING — SICKNESS OF SOME OF THE PARTY, OCCASIONED BY THE INCESSANT RAINS — THEY FORM, NOTWITHSTANDING, A PERMANENT ENCAMPMENT FOR THEIR WINTER QUARTERS.

FRIDAY, 22. It rained during the whole night, and about day-light a tremendous gale of wind rose from the S. S. E. and continued during the whole day with great violence. The sea runs so high that the water comes into our camp, which the rain prevents us from leaving. We purchased from the old squaw, for arm-bands and rings, a few wappatoo roots, on which we subsisted. They are nearly equal in flavour to the Irish potatoe, and afford a very good substitute for bread. The bad weather has driven several Indians to our camp, but they are still under the terrors of the threat which we made on first seeing them, and now behave with the greatest decency.

Saturday, 23. The rain continued through the night, but the morning was calm and cloudy. The hunters were sent out, and killed three deer, four brant, and three ducks. Towards evening, seven Clatsops came over in a canoe with two skins of the sea-otter. To this article they attach an extravagant value, and their demands for it were so high that we were fearful of reducing our small stock of merchandise, on which we must depend for subsistence as we return, to venture on purchasing. To ascertain, however, their ideas as to the value of different objects, we offered for one of the skins a watch, a handkerchief, an American dollar, and a bunch of red beads ; but neither the curious mechanism of the watch, nor even the red beads, could tempt him : he refused the offer, but asked for tiacomoshack or chief beads, the most common sort of coarse blue-coloured beads, the article beyond all price in their estimation. Of these blue beads we have but few, and therefore reserve them for more necessitous circumstances.

Sunday, 24. The morning being fair, we dried our wet articles and sent out the hunters, but they returned with only a single brant. In the evening a chief and several men of the Chinnooks came to see us; we smoked with them, and bought a sea-otter skin for some blue beads. Having now examined the coast, it becomes necessary to decide on the spot for our wintering quarters. The people of the country subsist chiefly on dried fish and roots; but of these there does not seem to be a sufficient quantity for our support, even were we able to purchase, and the extravagant prices, as well as our small store of merchandise, forbid us to depend on that resource. We must therefore rely for subsistence on our arms, and be guided in the choice of our residence by the abundance of game which any particular spot may offer. The Indians say that the deer is most numerous at some distance above on the river, but that the country on the opposite side of the bay is better supplied with elk, an animal much larger and more easily killed than deer, with a skin better fitted for clothing, and the meat of which is more nutritive during the winter, when they are both poor. The climate too is obviously much milder here than above the first range of mountains, for the Indians are thinly clad, and say they have little snow; indeed since our arrival the weather has been very warm, and sometimes disagreeably so; and dressed as we are altogether in leather, the cold would be very unpleasant, if not injurious. The neighbourhood of the sea is moreover recommended by the facility of supplying ourselves with salt, and the hope of meeting some

of the trading vessels, which are expected in about
three months, and from which we may procure a
fresh supply of trinkets for our route homewards.
These considerations induced us to determine on
visiting the opposite side of the bay, and if there
was an appearance of much game, to establish ourselves there during the winter. Next day,

Monday, 25, however, the wind was too high
to suffer us to cross the river, but as it blew generally from the east-south-east, the coast on the north
was in some degree sheltered by the highlands.
We therefore set out, and keeping near the shore,
halted for dinner in the shallow bay, and after dark,
reached a spot near a rock, at some distance in the
river, and close to our former camp of the 7th inst.
On leaving our camp, seven Clatsops accompanied
us in a canoe, but after going a few miles, crossed
the bay through immense high waves, leaving us
in admiration, at the dexterity with which they
threw aside each wave as it threatened to come
over their canoe. The evening was cloudy, and
in the morning,

Tuesday, 26, it rained. We set out with the
wind from east-north-east, and a short distance
above the rock, near our camp, began to cross the
river. We passed between some low, marshy
islands, which we called the Seal islands, and reached the south side of the Columbia at a bottom three
miles below a point, to which we gave the name of
Point Samuel. After going along the shore for
five miles, we entered a channel two hundred yards

in width, which separates from the main land a
large, but low island. On this channel, and at the
foot of some highlands, is a village, where we
landed. It consists of nine large wooden houses,
inhabited by a tribe called Cathlamahs, who seem
to differ neither in dress, language, nor manners,
from the Chinnooks and Wahkiacums : like whom
they live chiefly on fish and wappatoo roots. We
found, however, as we hoped, some elk meat : after
dining on some fresh fish and roots, which we purchased from them at an immoderate price, we
coasted along a deep bend of the river towards the
south, and at night encamped under a high hill.
All the way from the village the land is high, and
has a thick growth of pine balsam, and other timber ; but as it was still raining very hard, it was
with difficulty we procured wood enough to make
fires. Soon after we landed, three Indians from
the Cathlamah village came down with wappatoo
roots, some of which we purchased with fish-hooks.
At day-light the next morning,

Wednesday, 27, eleven more came down with
provisions, skins, and mats for sale, but the prices
were too high for our reduced finances, and we
bought nothing. As we were preparing to set out
we missed an axe, which was found under the robe
of one of the Indians, and they were all prohibited,
in consequence, from following us. We went on
in the rain, which had continued through the night,
and passing between a number of islands came to
a small river, called by the Indians Kekemahke.

We afterwards came to a very remarkable knob of land, projecting about a mile and a half towards Shallow bay, and about four miles round, while the neck of land which connects it to the main shore is not more than fifty yards wide. We went round this projection, which we named Point William; but the waves then became so high that we could not venture any farther, and we therefore landed on a beautiful shore of pebbles of various colours, and encamped near an old Indian hut on the isthmus. In drawing our canoes in shore, we had the misfortune to make a split two feet long in one of them. This isthmus opposed a formidable barrier to the sea, for we now found that the water below is salt, while that above is fresh and well tasted. It rained hard during the whole day; it continued all night, and in the morning,

Thursday, 28, began more violently, attended with a high wind from the south-west. It was now impossible to proceed on so rough a sea. We therefore sent several men to hunt, and the rest of us remained during the day, in a situation the most cheerless and uncomfortable. On this little neck of land we are exposed with a miserable covering, which does not deserve the name of a shelter, to the violence of the winds; all our bedding and stores, as well as our bodies, are completely wet, our clothes rotting with constant exposure, and no food, except the dried fish brought from the Falls, to which we are again reduced. The hunters all returned hungry, and drenched with rain, having seen neither deer nor elk, and the swan and brant too shy to be approached. At noon the wind shifted to the northwest, and blew with such tremendous fury, that many trees were blown down near us. This gale lasted, with short intervals, during the whole night; but towards morning,

Friday, 29th, the wind lulled, though the rain continued, and the waves were still high. Captain Lewis took the Indian canoe, which is better calculated for rough weather, and with five men went down to a small bay below us, where we expect to find elk. Three other men set out at the same time to hunt in different directions, and the rest remained round the smoke of our fires drying leather, in order to make some new clothes. The night brought only a continuation of rain and hail, with short intervals of fair weather, till in the morning,

Saturday, 30, it cleared up about nine o'clock, and the sun shone for several hours. Other hunters were now sent out, and we passed the remainder of the day in drying our merchandise so long exposed. Several of the men complain of disorders in their bowels, which can be ascribed only to their diet of pounded fish mixed with salt water; and they are therefore directed to use for its correction, the fresh water above the Point. The hunters had seen three elk, but could not obtain any of them: they, however, brought in three hawks and a few black ducks, of a species common in the United States, living in large flocks, and feeding on grass : they are distinguished by a sharp white beak, toes separated, and by having no craw. Besides these wild fowls, there are in this neighbourhood a large kind of buzzard with white wings, the grey and the bald eagle, the large red-tailed hawk, the blue magpye, and great numbers of ravens and crows. We observe, however, few small birds, the one which has most attracted our attention being a small brown bird, which seems to frequent logs and the roots of trees. Of other animals there is a great abundance. We see great quantities of snakes, lizards, worms, and spiders, as well as small bugs, flies, and insects of different kinds. The vegetable productions are also numerous. The hills along the coast are high and steep, and the general covering is a growth of lofty pines of different species, some of which rise more than two hundred feet, and are ten or twelve feet in diameter near the root. Beside these trees we observe on the Point a species of ash, the alder, the laurel, one species of the wild crab, and several kinds of underbrush, among which the rose-bushes are conspicuous.

Sunday, December 1, 1805. Again we had a cloudy day, and the wind so high from the east, that having ventured in a boat with a view to hunt at some distance, we were obliged to return. We resumed our occupation of dressing leather and mending our old clothes, in which we passed the day. The hunters came in with a report of their having seen two herds of elk, but they could kill nothing, and we therefore again fed upon dried fish. At sun-set it began to rain violently, and continued all night, and

Monday, 2d, the next day. This disagreeable food, pounded fish, has occasioned so much sickness among the men, that it is now absolutely necessary to vary it. Three hunters therefore set out, and three more were sent up the Kekemahke creek in search of fish or birds. Towards evening one of them returned: he had observed great appearances of elk, and even seen two herds of them; but it rained so hard that he could with difficulty get a shot; he had, however, at last killed one, at the distance of six miles from the camp, and a canoe was now sent to bring it. The party from Kekemahke creek were less successful: they had seen no fish, and all the birds, in consequence probably of being much hunted by the Indians, were too shy to be approached.

Tuesday, 3. The wind was from the east, and the morning fair; but, as if a whole day of fine weather was not permitted, towards night it began to rain. Even this transient glimpse of sun-shine revived the spirits of the party, who were still more pleased, when the elk killed yesterday was brought into camp. This was the first elk we had killed on the west side of the Rocky mountains, and condemned as we had been to the dried fish, forms a most nourishing food. After eating the marrow of the shank bones, the squaw chopped them fine, and by boiling, extracted a pint of grease, superior to the tallow itself of the animal. A canoe of eight Indians, who were carrying down wappatoo-roots to trade with the Clatsops, stopped at our camp : we bought a few roots for small fish-hooks, and they then left us : but accustomed as we are to the sight, we could not but view with admiration the wonderful dexterity with which they guide their canoes over the most boisterous seas ; for though the waves were so high, that before they had gone half a mile, the canoe was several times out of sight, they proceeded with the greatest calmness and security. Two of the hunters who set out yesterday had lost their way, and did not return till this evening : they had seen in their ramble great signs of elk, and had killed six elk, which they had butchered and left at a great distance. A party was sent in the morning,

Wednesday, Dec. 4, to carry the elk to a bay some distance below, to which place, if the weather permitted, we would all remove our camp this evening ; but the rain, which had continued during the night, lasted all next day, and was accompanied by so high a wind from the south-east and south, that we dared not risk our canoes on the water. It was high water at eleven o'clock, when the spring-tides rose two feet higher than the common flood-tides. We passed the day around our fires, and as we are so situated that the smoke will not immediately leave the camp, we are very much incommoded, and our eyes injured by it. No news has yet been received from Captain Lewis, and we begin to have much uneasiness for his safety.

Thursday, December 5. It rained during the whole night, and this morning the rain and high wind compelled us to remain at our camp. Besides the inconvenience of being thus stopped on our route, we now found that all our stores and bedding are again wet with rain. The high water was at twelve o'clock, and rose two inches beyond that of yesterday. In the afternoon we were rejoiced at the return of Captain Lewis, who came in a canoe with three of his men, the other two being left to guard six elk and five deer which they had killed: he had examined the coast, and found a river a short distance below, on which we might encamp during the winter, with a sufficiency of elk for our subsistence within reach. This information was very satisfactory, and we decided on going thither as soon as we could move from the point; but all night and the following day,

Friday, 6, it rained, and the wind blew hard from the south-west, so that the sea was still too rough for us to proceed. The high tide of to-day rose thirteen inches higher than it did yesterday, and obliged us to move our camp to a high situation. Here we remained, waiting for better weather, till about dark the wind shifted to the north, and the sky was clear. We had now some prospect of being able to leave our situation, and indeed although some rain fell in the course of the night, the next morning,

Saturday, 7, was fair ; we therefore loaded our canoes, and proceeded. But the tide was against us, and the waves very high, so that we were obliged to proceed slowly and cautiously. We at length turned a point, and found ourselves in a deep bay ; here we landed for breakfast, and were joined by the party sent out three days ago to look for the six elk. In seeking for the elk they had missed their way for a day and a half, and when they reached the place, found the elk so much spoiled, that they brought the skins only of four of them. After breakfast we coasted round the bay, which is about four miles across, and receives, besides several small creeks, two rivers, called by the Indians, the one Killhowanakel, the other Netul. We called it Meriwether's bay, from the Christian name of Captain Lewis, who was, no doubt, the first white man who surveyed it. As we went along the wind was high from the north-east, and in the middle of the day it rained for two hours, and then cleared off. On reaching the south side of the bay, we ascended the Netul for three miles to the first point of highland on its western bank, and formed our camp in a thick grove of lofty pines, about two hundred yards from the water, and thirty feet above the level of the high tides.

Sunday, 8. This seemed the most eligible spot for our winter establishment. In order, therefore, to find a place for making salt, and to examine the country further, Captain Clarke set out with five men, and pursuing a course south, 60° west, over a dividing ridge, through thick pine timber, much of which had fallen, passed the heads of two small brooks. In the neighbourhood of these the land was swampy and overflowed, and they waded knee-deep till they came to an open ridgy prairie, covered with the plant known on our frontier by the name of sacacommis. Here is a creek about sixty yards wide, and running towards Point Adams; they passed it on a small raft. At this place they discovered a large herd of elk, and after pursuing them for three miles over bad swamps, and small ponds, killed one of them. The agility with which the elk crossed the swamps and bogs, seems almost incredible; as we followed their track, the ground for a whole acre would shake at our tread, and sometimes we sunk to our hips without finding any bottom. Over the surface of these bogs is a species of moss, among which are great numbers of cranberries, and occasionally there rise from the swamp steep and small knobs of earth, thickly covered with pine and laurel. On one of these we halted at night, but it was scarcely large enough to suffer us to lie clear of the water, and had very little dry wood. We succeeded, however, in collecting enough to make a fire, and having stretched the elk-skin to keep off the rain, which still continued, slept till morning,

Monday, 9, when we rose perfectly wet with rain during the night. Three men were then sent in pursuit of the elk, while with the other three,

Captain Clarke proceeded westward towards the
sea. He passed over three swamps, and then arrived at a creek, which was too deep to ford, and
there was no wood to make a raft. He therefore
proceeded down it for a short distance, till he
found that he was between the forks of a creek.
One branch, which he had passed yesterday,
turns round towards the south-west to meet another
of equal size from the south, and together they
form a small river, about seventy yards wide. He
returned to the place where he had left the raft,
and having crossed, proceeded down about a mile,
when he met three Indians. They were loaded
with fresh salmon, which they had taken with a
gig, and were now returning to their village on
the sea-coast, where they invited him to accompany them. He agreed, and they brought out a
canoe hid along the banks of the creek. In this
they passed over the branch which he had just
crossed on a raft, and then carried the canoe a
quarter of a mile to the other fork, which they
crossed, and continued down to the mouth of the
river. At this place it makes a great bend, where
the river is seventy yards wide; just above, or to
the south of which is the village. We crossed
over, and found that it consisted of three houses,
inhabited by twelve families of Clatsops. They
were on the south exposure of a hill, and sunk
about four feet deep into the ground; the walls,
roof, and gable-ends being formed of split pine-
boards; the descent through a small door down

a ladder. There are two fires in the middle of the room, and the beds disposed round the walls two or three feet from the floor, so as to leave room under them for their bags, baskets, and household articles. The floor itself is covered with mats. Captain Clarke was received with much attention. As soon as he entered, clean mats were spread, and fish, berries, and roots, set before him on small neat platters of rushes. After he had eaten, the men of the other houses came and smoked with him. They all appeared much neater in their persons and diet than Indians generally are, and frequently wash their hands and faces, a ceremony by no means frequent elsewhere. While he was conversing with them, a flock of brant lighted on the water, and he, with a small rifle, shot one of them at a great distance. They immediately jumped in, and brought it on shore, very much astonished at the shot, which contributed to make them increase their attention. Towards evening it began to rain, and blow very violently from the south-west; and Captain Clarke, therefore, determined to remain during the night. When they thought his appetite had returned, an old woman presented him, in a bowl made of light-coloured horn, a kind of syrup, pleasant to the taste, and made from a species of berry common in this country, about the size of a cherry, and called by the Indians shelwel: of these berries a bread is also prepared, which being boiled with roots, forms a soup, which was served in neat wooden trenchers: this, with some cockles, was his repast. The men of the village now collected, and began to gamble. The most common game, was one in which one of the company was banker, and played against all the rest. He had a piece of bone, about the size of a large bean, and having agreed with any individual as to the value of the stake, would pass the bone from one hand to the other, with great dexterity, singing at the same time, to divert the attention of his adversary; and then holding it in his hands, his antagonist was challenged to guess in which of them the bone was, and lost or won as he pointed to the right or wrong hand. To this game of hazard they abandoned themselves with great ardour; sometimes every thing they possess is sacrificed to it, and this evening several of the Indians lost all the beads which they had with them. This lasted for three hours, when Captain Clarke appearing disposed to sleep, the man who had been most attentive, and whose name was Cuskalah, spread two new mats near the fire, and ordering his wife to retire to her own bed, the rest of the company dispersed at the same time. Captain Clarke then lay down, but the violence with which the fleas attacked him, did not leave his rest unbroken, and he rose,

Tuesday, 10, early. The morning was cloudy, with some rain: he walked out on the sea-shore, and observed the Indians walking up and down the creek and examining the shore: he was at a loss to understand their object, till one of them came to him, and explained that they were in search of fish which had been thrown on shore and left by the tide, adding in English, " sturgeon is very good." There is, indeed, every reason to suppose that these Clatsops depend for their subsistence during the winter, chiefly on the fish thus casually thrown on the coast. After amusing himself for some time on the beach, he returned towards the village, and shot on his way two brant. As he came near the village, one of the Indians asked him to shoot a duck about thirty steps distant : he did so, and having accidentally shot off its head, the bird was brought to the village by the Indians, all of whom came round in astonishment : they examined the duck, the musket, and the very small bullet, which were a hundred to the pound, and then exclaimed, " Clouch musquet, wake, commatax musquet : a good musquet, do not understand this kind of musquet." They now placed before him their best roots, fish, and syrup, after which he attempted to purchase a sea-otter skin with some red beads which he happened to have about him; but they declined trading, as they valued none except blue or white beads : he therefore bought nothing but a little berry bread and a few roots, in exchange for fish-hooks, and then set out to return by the same route on which he came. He was accompanied by Cuskalah and his brother as far as the third creek, and then proceeded to the camp through a heavy rain. The whole party had been occupied during his absence in cutting down trees to make huts, and in hunting.

Wednesday, 11. The rain continued last night and the whole of this day. We were, however, all employed in putting up our winter cabins, which we are anxious to finish, as several of the men are beginning to suffer from the excessive dampness: four of them have very violent colds; one has a dysentery, a third has tumours on his legs, and two have been injured by dislocation and straining of their limbs.

Thursday, 12. We continued to work in the rain at our houses. In the evening there arrived two canoes of Clatsops, among whom was a principal chief, called Comowool. We gave him a medal, and treated his companions with great attention; after which we began to bargain for a small sea-otter skin, some wappatoo-roots, and another species of root called shanataque. We readily perceived that they were close dealers, stickled much for trifles, and never closed the bargain until they thought they had the advantage. The wappatoo is dear, as they themselves are obliged to give a high price for it to the Indians above. Blue beads are the articles most in request; the white occupy the next place in their estimation; but they do not value much those of any other colour. We succeeded at last in purchasing their whole cargo for a few fish-hooks and a small sack of Indian tobacco, which we had received from the Shoshonees. The next morning,

Friday, 13, we treated them to a breakfast on elk meat, of which they seemed very fond, and having purchased from them two skins of the lucervia, and two robes made of the skin of an animal about the size of a cat, they left us. Two hunters returned with the pleasing intelligence of their having killed eighteen elk, about six miles off. Our huts begin to rise, for though it rains all day we continue our labours, and are rejoiced to find that the beautiful balsam-pine splits into excellent boards, more than two feet in width. In the evening three Indians came in a canoe, with provisions and skins for sale, and spent the night with us.

Saturday, 14. Again it rained all day, but by working constantly we finished the walls of our huts, and nearly completed a house for our provisions. The constant rains have completely spoiled our last supply of elk; but notwithstanding that scarcely a man has been dry for a great number of days, the sick are recovering. Four men were dispatched to guard the elk which were killed yesterday, till a larger party joined them. Accordingly,

Sunday, 15, Captain Clarke, with sixteen men, set out in three canoes, and having rowed for three miles up the river, turned up a large creek from the right, and after going three miles further, landed about the height of the tide water. The men were then dispatched, in small parties, to bring in the elk, each man returning with a quarter of the animal. In bringing the third and last load, nearly half the men missed their way, and did not return till after night; five of them indeed were not able to find their way at all. It had been cloudy all day, and in the night began to rain, and, as we had no cover, were obliged to sit up the greater part of the night; for as soon as we lay down, the rain would come under us, and compel us to rise. It was indeed a most uncomfortable situation, but the five men who joined us in the morning,

Monday, 16, had been more unlucky, for in addition to the rain which had poured down upon them all night, they had no fire; and drenched and cold as they were when they reached us, exhibited a most distressing sight. They had left their loads where they slept, and some men were sent after them, while others were dispatched after two more elk in another bend of the creek, who, after taking these last on board, proceeded to our camp. It rained and hailed during the day, and a high wind from the south-east not only threw down trees as we passed along, but made the river so rough that we proceeded with great risk. We had now the meat-house covered, and all our game carefully hung up in small pieces.

Tuesday, 17. It rained all night, and this morning there was a high wind, and hail, as well as rain, fell; and on the top of a mountain, about ten miles to the south-east of us, we observed some snow. The greater part of our stores is wet, and our leathern tent is so rotten that the slightest touch makes a rent in it, and it will now scarcely shelter a spot large enough for our beds. We were all busy in finishing the inside of the huts. The after part of the day was cool and fair. But this respite was of very short duration, for all night it continued raining and snowing alternately, and in the morning,

Wednesday, 18, we had snow and hail till twelve o'clock, after which it changed to rain. The air now became cool and disagreeable, the wind high and unsettled, so that being thinly dressed in leather, we were able to do very little on the houses.

Thursday, 19. The rain continued all night, with short intervals, but the morning was fair, and the wind from the south-west. Situated as we are, our only occupation is to work as diligently as we can on our houses, and to watch the changes of the weather, on which so much of our comfort depends. We availed ourselves of this glimpse of sun-shine, to send across Meriwether's bay, for the boards of an old Indian house; but before the party returned with them, the weather clouded, and we had hail and rain during the rest of the day. Our only visitors were two Indians, who spent a short time with us.

Friday, 20. A succession of rain and hail during the night. At ten o'clock it cleared off for a short time, but the rain soon recommenced; we now covered in four of our huts; three Indians came in a canoe with mats, roots, and the berries of the sacacommis. These people proceed with a dexterity and finesse in their bargains, which, if they have not learned from their foreign visitors, may show how nearly allied is the cunning of savages to the little arts of traffic. They begin by asking double or treble the value of what they have to sell, and lower their demand in proportion to the greater or less degree of ardour or knowledge of the purchaser, who with all his management is not able to procure the article for less than its real value, which the Indians perfectly understand. Our chief medium of trade consists of blue and white beads, files, with which they sharpen their tools, fish-hooks, and tobacco : but of all these articles, blue beads and tobacco are the most esteemed.

Saturday, 21. As usual it rained all night, and continued without intermission during the day. One of our Indian visitors was detected in stealing a horn-spoon, and turned out of the camp. We find that the plant called sacacommis forms an agreeable mixture with tobacco, and we therefore dispatched two men to the open lands near the ocean, in order to collect some of it, while the rest continued their work.

Sunday, 22. There was no interval in the rain last night and to-day ; so that we cannot go on rapidly with our buildings. Some of the men are indeed quite sick, others have received bruises, and several complain of biles. We discover too, that part of our elk meat is spoiling, in consequence of the warmth of the weather, though we have kept up a constant smoke under it.

Monday, 23. It continued raining the whole day, with no variation, except occasional thunder and hail. Two canoes of Clatsops came to us with various articles for sale; we bought three mats and bags, neatly made of flags and rushes, and also the skin of a panther seven feet long, including the tail. For all these we gave six small fish-hooks, a worn-out file, and some pounded fish, which had become so soft and mouldy by exposure, that we could not use it: it is, however, highly prized by the Indians of this neighbourhood. Although a very portable and convenient food, the mode of curing seems known, or at least practised only by the Indians near the Great Falls, and coming from such a distance, has an additional value in the eyes of these people, who are anxious to possess some food less precarious than their ordinary subsistence. Among these Clatsops was a second chief, to whom we gave a medal, and sent some pounded fish to Cuscalah, who could not come to see us, on account of sickness. The next day,

Tuesday, 24, however, he came in a canoe with his young brother and two squaws. Having treated Captain Clarke so kindly at his village, we were pleased to see him, and he gave us two mats and a parcel of roots. These we accepted, as it would have been offensive to decline the offer, but after-wards two files were demanded in return for the presents, and not being able to spare those articles, we restored the mats and roots. Cuscalah was a little displeased; in the evening, however, he offered each of us one of the squaws, and even this being declined, Cuscalah, as well as the whole party of the Indians, were highly offended: the females particularly seemed to be much incensed at our indifference about their favours. The whole stock of meat being now completely spoiled, our pounded fish became again our chief dependence. It had rained constantly all day, but we still continued working, and at last moved into our huts.

Wednesday, 25. We were awaked at day-light by a discharge of fire-arms, which was followed by a song from the men, as a compliment to us on the return of Christmas, which we have always been accustomed to observe as a day of rejoicing. After breakfast we divided our remaining stock of tobacco, which amounted to twelve carrots, into two parts; one of which we distributed among such of the party as made use of it, making a present of a handkerchief to the others. The remainder of the day was passed in good spirits, though there was nothing in our situation to excite much gaiety. The rain confined us to the house, and our only luxuries in honour of the season, were some poor elk, so much spoiled that we ate it through mere necessity, a few roots, and some spoiled pounded fish. The next day,

Thursday, 26, brought a continuation of rain, accompanied with thunder, and a high wind from the south-east. We were therefore still obliged to remain in our huts, and endeavoured to dry our wet articles before the fire. The fleas which annoyed us near the portage of the Great Falls, have taken such possession of our clothes, that we are obliged to have a regular search every day through our blankets, as a necessary preliminary to sleeping at night. These animals indeed are so numerous, that they are almost a calamity to the Indians of this country. When they have once obtained the mastery of any house, it is impossible to expel them, and the Indians have frequently different houses, to which they resort occasionally when the fleas have rendered their permanent residence intolerable; yet in spite of these precautions, every Indian is constantly attended by multitudes of them, and no one comes into our houses without leaving behind him swarms of these tormenting insects.

Friday, 27. The rain did not cease last night, nor the greater part of the day. In the evening we were visited by Comowool, the chief, and four men of the Clatsop nation, who brought a very timely supply of roots and berries. Among these was one called culhomo, resembling liquorice in size and taste, and which they roast like a potatoe ; there was also the shanataque, a root of which they are very fond. It is of a black colour, sweet to the taste, and is prepared for eating in a kiln, as the Indians up the Columbia dry the pasheco. These, as well as the shellwell berries, they value highly, but were perfectly satisfied with the return we made them, consisting of a small piece of sheepskin, to wear round the chief's head, a pair of ear-bobs for his son, a small piece of brass, and a little ribband. In addition to our old enemies the fleas, we observed two musquitoes, or insects so completely resembling them, that we can perceive no difference in their shape and appearance.

Saturday, 28. Again it rained during the greater part of last night, and continued all day. Five men were sent out to hunt, and five others dispatched to the sea-side, each with a large kettle, in order to begin the manufacture of salt. The route to the sea-coast is about seven miles in length, in a direction nearly west. Five miles of the distance is through thick wood varied with hills, ravines, and swamps; though the land in general possesses a rich black mould. The remaining two miles is formed of open waving prairies of sand, with ridges running parallel to the river, and covered with green grass. The rest of the men were employed in making pickets and gates for our new fort. Although we had no sun, the weather was very warm.

Sunday, 29. It rained the whole night, but ceased this morning, and but little rain fell in the course of the day; still the weather was cloudy, and the wind high from the south-east. The Clatsop chief and his party left us, after begging for a great number of articles, which, as we could not spare them, we refused, except a razor. We were employed all day in picketting the fort: in the evening a young Wahkiacum chief, with four men and two women, arrived with some dressed elkskin and wappatoo for sale. We purchased about a bushel and a half of those roots for some red beads, and small pieces of brass wire and old check. The chief, too, made us a present of half a bushel more, for which we gave him a medal, and a piece of ribband, to tie round his hat. These roots are extremely grateful, since our meat has become spoiled, and we were desirous of purchasing the remainder; but the chief would not dispose of any more, as he was on his way to trade with the Clatsops. They remained with us, however, till the next day,

Monday, 30, when they were joined by four more of their countrymen from the Wahkiacum village. These last began by offering us some roots; but as we had now learned that they always expect three or four times as much in return as the real value of the articles, and are even dissatisfied with that, we declined such dangerous presents. Towards evening the hunters brought in four elk, and after a long course of abstinence and miserable diet, we had a most sumptuous supper of elk's tongues and marrow. Besides this agreeable repast, the state of the weather had been quite exhilarating. It had rained during the night, but in the morning, though the high wind continued, we enjoyed the fairest and most pleasant weather since our arrival; the sun having shone at intervals, and there being only

three showers in the course of the day. By sun-set
we had completed the fortification, and now an-
nounced to the Indians that every day, at that hour,
the gates would be closed, and they must leave the
fort, and not enter it till sun-rise. The Wahkiacums,
who had remained with us, and who are very forward in their deportment, complied very reluctantly
with this order; but being excluded from our
houses, formed a camp near us.

Tuesday, 31. As if it were impossible to have
twenty-four hours of pleasant weather, the sky last
evening clouded, and the rain began and continued
through the day. In the morning there came down
two canoes, one from the Wahkiacum village, the
other contained three men and a squaw of the
Skilloot nation. They brought wappatoo and
shanataque roots, dried fish, mats made of flags
and rushes, dressed elk-skins, and tobacco; for
which, particularly the skins, they asked a very
extravagant price. We purchased some wappatoo,
and a little tobacco, very much like that we had
seen among the Shoshonees, put up in small neat
bags made of rushes. These we obtained in exchange for a few articles, among which fish-hooks
are the most esteemed. One of the Skilloots
brought a gun which wanted some repair, and
having put it in order, we received from him a
present of about a peck of wappatoo; we then
gave him a piece of sheep-skin and blue cloth, to
cover the lock, and he very thankfully offered a
further present of roots. There is, in fact, an

obvious superiority in these Skilloots over the Wahkiacums, who are intrusive, thievish, and imper-
tinent. Our new regulations, however, and the
appearance of the sentinel, have improved the
behaviour of all our Indian visitors. They left
the fort before sun-set, even without being ordered.

Besides the fleas, we observe a number of insects
in motion to-day. Snakes are yet to be seen;
snails, too, without covers, are common. On the
rivers, and along the shores of Meriwether's bay,
are many kinds of large water-fowls, but at this
period they are excessively wild. The early part of
the night was fair.

Wednesday, January 1, 1806. We were awaked
at an early hour by a discharge of a volley of small
arms, to salute the new year. This is the only
mode of doing honour to the day which our situation permits; for though we have reason to be
gayer than we were at Christmas, our only dainties
are the boiled elk and wappatoo, enlivened by
draughts of pure water. We were visited by a few
Clatsops, who came by water, bringing roots and
berries for sale. Among this nation we have observed a man about twenty-five years old, of a
much lighter complexion than the Indians generally: his face was even freckled, and his hair long,
and of a colour inclining to red. He was in habits
and manners perfectly Indian; but though he did
not speak a word of English, he seemed to understand more than the others of his party; and, as
we could obtain no account of his origin, we con-

cluded that one of his parents, at least, must have been completely white.

These Indians staid with us during the night, and left the fort next morning,

Thursday, 2, having disposed of their cargo for fishing-hooks and other trifling articles. The hunters brought in two elk, and we obtained from the traps another. This animal, as well as the beaver and the raccoon, are in plenty near the sea-coast, and along the small creeks and rivers as high as the Grand Rapids, and in this country possess an extremely good fur.

The birds which most strike our attention are the large as well as the small or whistling swan, the sandhill crane, the large and small geese, cormorants, brown and white brant, duckinmallard, the canvas and several other species of ducks. There is also a small crow, the blue-crested corvus, and the smaller corvus with a white breast, the little brown wren, a large brown sparrow, the bald eagle, and the beautiful buzzard of the Columbia. All these wild fowl continue with us, though they are not in such numbers as on our first arrival in this neighbourhood.

Friday, 3. At eleven o'clock we were visited by our neighbour the Fia, or chief Comowool, who is also called Coone, and six Clatsops. Besides roots and berries, they brought for sale three dogs and some fresh blubber. Having been so long accustomed to live on the flesh of dogs, the greater part of us have acquired a fondness for it, and our original aversion for it is overcome, by reflecting that while we subsisted on that food we were fatter, stronger, and in general enjoyed better health than at any period since leaving the buffaloe country eastward of the mountains. The blubber, which is esteemed by the Indians an excellent food, has been obtained, they tell us, from their neighbours the Killamucks, a nation who live on the sea-coast to the south-east, and near one of whose villages a whale had recently been thrown and foundered. Three of the hunters who had been dispatched on the 28th, returned about dark ; they had been fifteen miles up the river to the east of us, which falls into Meriwether's bay, and had hunted a considerable distance to the east ; but they had not been able to kill more than a single deer, and a few fowls, scarcely sufficient for their subsistence ; an incident which teaches us the necessity of keeping out several parties of hunters, in order to procure a supply against any exigency.

Saturday, 4. Comowool left us this morning with his party, highly pleased with a present of an old pair of sattin breeches. The hunters were all sent in different directions, and we are now becoming more anxious for their success since our store of wappatoo is all exhausted.

Sunday, 5. Two of the five men who had been dispatched to make salt returned. They had carefully examined the coast, but it was not till the fifth day after their departure that they discovered a convenient situation for their manufacture. At length

they formed an establishment about fifteen miles
south-west of the fort, near some scattered houses
of the Clatsop and Killamuck nations, where they
erected a comfortable camp, and had killed a stock
of provisions. The Indians had treated them very
kindly, and made them a present of the blubber of
the whale, some of which the men brought home.
It was white, and not unlike the fat of pork, though
of a coarser and more spungy texture; and on being
cooked was found to be tender and palatable, and
in flavour resembling the beaver. The men also
brought with them a gallon of salt, which was
white, fine, and very good, but not so strong as
the rock-salt common to the western parts of the
United States. It proves to be a most agreeable
addition to our food, and as the salt-makers can
manufacture three or four quarters a-day, we have
a prospect of a very plentiful supply. The appearance of the whale seemed to be a matter of importance to all the neighbouring Indians, and as
we might be able to procure some of it for ourselves, or at least purchase blubber from the Indians, a small parcel of merchandize was prepared,
and a party of men held in readiness to set out in
the morning. As soon as this resolution was known,
Chaboneau and his wife requested that they might
be permitted to accompany us. The poor woman
stated very earnestly that she had travelled a great
way with us to see the great water, yet she had
never been down to the coast, and now that this
monstrous fish was also to be seen, it seemed hard

that she should not be permitted to see neither the ocean nor the whale. So reasonable a request could not be denied; they were therefore suffered to accompany Captain Clarke, who,

Monday, 6, after an early breakfast, set out with twelve men in two canoes. He proceeded down the Netul into Meriwether bay, intending to go to the Clatsop town, and there procure a guide through the creeks, which there was reason to believe communicated, not only with the bay, but with a small river running towards the sea, near where our salt-makers were encamped. Before however he could reach the Clatsop village, the high wind from the north-west compelled him to put into a small creek. He therefore resolved to attempt the passage without a guide, and proceeded up the creek three miles to some high open land, where he found a road. He therefore left the canoes, and followed the path over three deep marshes to a pond about a mile long and two hundred yards wide. He kept on the left of this pond, and at length came to the creek which he had crossed on a raft, when he had visited Cuscalah's village on the ninth of December. He proceeded down it, till he found a small canoe, fit to hold three persons, in which the whole party crossed the creek. Here they saw a herd of elk, and the men were divided in small parties, and hunted them till after dark, when they met again at the forks of the river. Three of the elk were wounded, but night prevented their taking more

6

than one, which was brought to the camp, and cooked with some sticks of pine which had drifted down the creeks. The weather was beautiful, the sky clear, the moon shone brightly, a circumstance the more agreeable, as this is the first fair evening we have enjoyed for two months.

CHAPTER XXII.

A PARTY HEADED BY CAPTAIN CLARKE, GO IN QUEST OF A
WHALE DRIVEN ON THE SHORE OF THE PACIFIC TO OBTAIN
SOME OF THE OIL — THEY PASS CLATSOP RIVER, WHICH
IS DESCRIBED — THE PERILOUS NATURE OF THIS
JAUNT, AND THE GRANDEUR OF THE SCENERY DESCRIBED
— INDIAN MODE OF EXTRACTING WHALE-OIL — THE LIFE
OF ONE OF CAPTAIN CLARKE'S PARTY PRESERVED BY THE
KINDNESS OF AN INDIAN WOMAN — A SHORT ACCOUNT OF
THE CHINNOOKS, OF THE CLATSOPS, KILLAMUCKS, THE
LUCKTONS, AND AN ENUMERATION OF SEVERAL OTHER
TRIBES — THE MANNER OF SEPULCHRE AMONG THE
CHINNOOKS, CLATSOPS, &c. — DESCRIPTION OF THEIR
WEAPONS OF WAR AND HUNTING — THEIR MODE OF
BUILDING HOUSES — THEIR MANUFACTURES, AND COOK-
ERY — THEIR MODE OF MAKING CANOES — THEIR GREAT
DEXTERITY IN MANAGING THAT VEHICLE.

TUESDAY, 7. There was a frost this morning. We rose early, and taking eight pounds of flesh, which were all the remains of the elk, proceeded up the south fork of the creek. At the distance of two miles we found a pine tree, which had been felled by one of our salt-makers, and on which we crossed the deepest part of the creek, and waded through the rest. We then went over an open ridgy prairie, three-quarters of a mile, to the sea-beach; after following which for three miles, we came to the mouth of a beautiful river, with a bold, rapid current, eighty-five yards wide, and three feet deep in its shallowest crossings. On its north-east side are the remains of an old village of Clatsops, inhabited by only a single family, who appeared miserably poor and dirty. We gave a man two fish-hooks to ferry the party over the river, which, from the tribe on its banks, we called Clatsop river. The creek, which we had passed on a tree, approaches this river within about an hundred yards, and by means of a portage, supplies a communication with the villages near Point Adams. After going on for two miles, we found the salt-makers encamped near four houses of Clatsops and Killamucks, who, though poor, dirty, and covered with fleas, seemed kind and well-disposed. We persuaded a young Indian, by a present of a file, and a promise of some other articles, to guide us to the spot where the whale lay. He led us for two and a half miles over the round slippery stones at the foot of a high hill projecting into the sea, and then suddenly stopping, and uttering the word peshack, or bad, explained by signs that we could no longer follow the coast, but must cross the mountain. This promised to be a most laborious undertaking, for the side is nearly perpendicular, and the top lost in clouds. He, however, followed an Indian path which wound along as much as possible, but still the ascent was so steep, that at one place we drew ourselves for about an hundred feet by means of bushes and roots. At length, after two hours labour, we reached the top of the mountain, where we looked down with astonishment on the prodigious height of ten or twelve hundred feet, which we had ascended. Immediately below us, in the face of this precipice, is a stratum of white earth, used, as our guide informed us, as a paint by the neighbouring Indians. It obviously contains argile, and resembles the earth of which the French porcelaine is made, though whether it contains silex or magnesia, or in what proportions, we could not observe. We were here met by fourteen Indians, loaded with oil and blubber, the spoils of the whale, which they were carrying, in very heavy burdens, over this rough mountain. On leaving them, we proceeded over a bad road till night, when we encamped on a small run: we were all much fatigued, but the weather was pleasant, and, for the first time since our arrival here, an entire day has passed without rain. In the morning,

Wednesday, 8, we set out early, and proceeded to the top of the mountain, the highest point of which is an open spot facing the ocean. It is situated about thirty miles south-east of Cape Disappointment, and projects nearly two and a half miles into the sea. Here one of the most delightful views in nature presents itself. Immediately in front is the ocean, which breaks with fury on the coast, from the rocks of Cape Disappointment, as far as the eye can discern to the north-west, and against the high lands and irregular piles of rock which diversify the shore to the south-east. To this boisterous scene, the Columbia, with its tributary waters, widening into bays as it approaches the ocean, and studded on both sides with the Chinnook and Clatsop villages, forms a charming contrast; while immediately beneath our feet, are stretched the rich prairies, enlivened by three beautiful streams, which conduct the eye to small lakes at the foot of the hills. We stopped to enjoy the romantic view from this place, which we distinguished by the name of Clarke's Point of View, and then followed our guide down the mountain. The descent was steep and dangerous: in many places the hill sides, which are formed principally of yellow clay, have been washed by the late rains, and is now slipping into the sea, in large masses of fifty and an hundred acres. In other parts, the path crosses the rugged perpendicular rocks which overhang the sea, into which a false step would have precipitated us. The mountains are covered with a very thick growth of timber, chiefly pine and fir; some of which near Clarke's Point of View, perfectly sound and solid, rise to the height of two hundred and ten feet, and are from eight to twelve in diameter. Intermixed is the white cedar, or arbor vitæ, and a small quantity of black alder, two or three feet thick, and sixty or seventy in height. At length we reached a single house, the remains of an old Killamuck village, situated among some rocks, in a bay immediately on the coast. We then continued for two miles along the sand beach; and after crossing a creek, eighty yards in width, near which are five cabins, reached the place where the waves had thrown the whale on shore. The animal had been placed between two Killamuck villages, and such had been their industry, that there now remained nothing more than the skeleton, which we found to be one hundred and five feet in length. Captain Clarke then returned to the village of five huts, on the creek, to which he gave the name of Ecola, or Whale creek. The natives were all busied in boiling the blubber, in a large square trough of wood, by means of heated stones, and preserving the oil, thus extracted, in bladders and the entrails of the whale. The refuse of the blubber, which still contained a portion of oil, is hung up in large flitches, and when wanted for use, is warmed on a wooden spit before the fire, and eaten either alone, or dipped in oil, or with roots of the rush and shanataque. These Killamucks, though they had great quantities, parted with it reluctantly, and at such high prices, that our whole stock of merchandize was exhausted in the purchase of about three hundred pounds of blubber, and a few gallons of oil. With these we set out to return; and having crossed Ecola creek, encamped on its bank, where there was abundance of fine timber. We were soon joined by the men of the village, with whom we smoked, and who gave us all the information they possessed relative to their country. These Killamucks are part of a much larger nation of the same name, and they now reside chiefly in four villages, each at the entrance of a creek, all of which fall into a bay on the south-west coast; that at which we now are being the most northern, and at the distance of about forty-five miles south-east of Point Adams. The rest of the nation are scattered along the coast, and on the banks of a river, which, as we found it in their delineations, we called Killamuck river, emptying itself in the same direction. During the salmon season they catch great quantities of that fish in the small creeks; and when they fail, their chief resource was the sturgeon and other fish stranded along the coast. The elk were very numerous in the mountains, but they could not procure many of them with their arrows; and their principal communication with strangers was by means of the Killamuck river, up which they passed to the Shocatilcum (or Columbia), to trade for wappatoo roots. In their dress, appearance, and indeed every circumstance of life, they differ very little from the Chinnooks, Clatsops, and other nations in the neighbourhood. The chief variation we have observed, is in the manner of burying the dead; the bodies being secured in an oblong box of plank, which is placed in an open canoe, lying on the ground, with a paddle, and other small articles of the deceased by his side.

Whilst smoking with the Indians, Captain Clarke was surprised about ten o'clock by a loud shrill outcry from the opposite village; on hearing which, all the Indians immediately started up to cross the creek, and the guide informed him that some one had been killed. On examination, one of the men was discovered to be absent, and a guard dispatched, who met him crossing the creek in great haste. An Indian belonging to another band, and who happened to be with the Killamucks that evening, had treated him with much kindness, and walked arm in arm with him to a tent where our man found a Chinnook squaw, who was an old acquaintance. From the conversation and manner of the stranger, this woman discovered that his object was to murder the white man, for the sake of the few articles on his person; and when he rose, and pressed our man to go to another tent, where they would find something better to eat, she held M‘Neal by the blanket: not knowing her object, he freed himself from her, and was going on with his pretended friend, when she ran out and gave the shriek which brought the men of the village over, and the stranger ran off before M‘Neal knew what had occasioned the alarm.

Thursday, 9. The morning was fine, the wind from the north-east; and having divided our stock of the blubber, we began at sun-rise to retread our steps, in order to reach Fort Clatsop, at the distance of thirty-five miles. We met several parties of Indians on their way to trade for blubber and oil with the Killamucks (our route lay across the same mountains which we had already passed); we also overtook a party returning from the village, and could not but regard with astonishment the heavy loads which the women carry over these fatiguing and dangerous paths. As one of the women was descending a steep part of the mountain, her load slipped from her back, and she stood holding it by a strap with one hand, and with the other supporting herself by a bush : Captain Clarke being near her, undertook to replace the load, and found it almost as much as he could lift, and above one hundred pounds in weight. Loaded as they were, they kept pace with us, till we reached the salt-makers' tents, where we passed the night, while they continued their route.

Friday, 10. We proceeded across Clatsop river to the place where we had left our canoes ; and as the tide was coming in, immediately embarked for the fort, at which place we arrived about ten o'clock at night. During their absence, the men had been occupied in hunting and dressing skins, but in this they were not very successful, as the deer have become scarce, and are, indeed, seen chiefly near the prairies and open grounds along the coast. This morning, however, there came to the fort twelve Indians, in a large canoe. They are of the Cathlamah nation, our nearest neighbours above, on the south side of the river. The tia, or chief, whose name was Shahawacap, having been absent on a hunting excursion as we passed his village, had never yet seen us, and we therefore shewed him the honours of our country, as well as our

reduced finances would permit. We invested him
with a small medal, and received a present of Indian tobacco and a basket of wappatoo in return,
for which we gave him a small piece of our tobacco,
and thread for a fishing net. They had brought
dried salmon, wappatoo, dogs, and mats made of
rushes and flags : but we bought only some dogs
and wappatoo. These Cathlamahs speak the same
language as the Chinnooks and Clatsops, whom
they also resemble in dress and manners.

Saturday, 11. A party was sent out out to bring
in some elk killed yesterday, and several were dispatched after our Indian canoe, which drifted away
last night : but, though the whole neighbourhood
was diligently searched, we were unable to find it.
This is a serious loss, as she is much superior to
our own canoes, and so light, that four men can
carry her readily without fatigue, though she will
carry from ten to twelve hundred pounds, besides
a crew of four. In the evening the Cathlamahs
left us, on their way to barter their wappatoo with
the Clatsops, for some blubber and oil, which these
last have procured from the Killamucks, in exchange
for beads and other articles.

Sunday, 12. Our meat is now becoming scarce ;
we therefore determined to jerk it, and issue it in
small quantities, instead of dividing it among the
four messes, and leaving to each the care of its
own provisions ; a plan by which much is lost, in
consequence of the improvidence of the men. Two
hunters had been dispatched in the morning, and

one of them, Drewyer, had before evening killed seven elk. We should scarcely be able to subsist, were it not for the exertions of this most excellent hunter. The game is scarce, and nothing is now to be seen, except elk, which, to almost all the men, are very difficult to be procured: but Drewyer, who is the offspring of a Canadian Frenchman, and an Indian woman, has passed his life in the woods, and unites, in a wonderful degree, the dexterous aim of the frontier huntsman, with the intuitive sagacity of the Indian, in pursuing the faintest tracks through the forest. All our men, however, have indeed become so expert with the rifle, that we are never under apprehensions as to food, since, whenever there is game of any kind, we are almost certain of procuring it.

Monday, 13. Captain Lewis took all the men who could be spared, and brought in the seven elk, which they had found untouched by the wolves, of which there are a few in the neighbourhood. The last of the candles which we brought with us being exhausted, we now began to make others of elk-tallow. From all that we have seen and learnt of the Chinnooks, we have been induced to estimate the nation at about twenty-eight houses, and four hundred souls. They reside chiefly along the banks of a river, to which we gave the same name ; and which, running parallel to the sea-coast, waters a low country with many stagnant ponds, and then empties itself into Haley's bay. The wild fowl of these ponds, and the elk and deer of the neighbourhood, furnish them with occasional luxuries; but their chief subsistence is derived from the salmon, and other fish, which are caught in the small streams by means of nets and gigs, or thrown on shore by the violence of the tide. To these are added some roots, such as the wild liquorice, which is the most common, the shanataque, and the wappatoo, brought down the river by the traders.

The men are low in stature, rather ugly, and ill made; their legs being small and crooked, their feet large, and their heads like those of the women, flattened in a most disgusting manner. These deformities are in part concealed by robes, made of sea-otter, deer, elk, beaver, or fox skins. They also employ in their dress, robes of the skin of a cat peculiar to this country, and of another animal of the same size, which is light and durable, and sold at a high price by the Indians, who bring it from above. In addition to these are worn blankets, wrappers of red, blue, or spotted cloth, and some sailors' old clothes, which are very highly prized. The greater part of the men have guns, powder, and ball.

The women have, in general, handsome faces, but are low and disproportioned, with small feet, and large legs and thighs, occasioned, probably, by strands of beads, or various strings, drawn so tight above the ankles as to prevent the circulation of the blood. Their dress, like that of the Wahkiacums, consists of a short robe, and a tissue of cedar bark. Their hair hangs loosely down the shoulders and back; and their ears, neck, and wrists, are ornamented with blue beads. Another decoration which is very highly prized, consists of figures, made by puncturing the arms or legs; and on the arm of one of the squaws, we observed the name of J. Bowman, executed in the same way. In language, habits, and in almost every other particular, they resemble the Clatsops, Cathlamahs, and indeed all the people near the mouth of the Columbia. They, however, seem to be inferior to their neighbours in honesty as well as spirit. No ill-treatment or indignity, on our part, seems to excite any feeling, except fear; nor, although better provided than their neighbours with arms, have they enterprise enough to use them advantageously against the animals of the forest, nor offensively against their neighbours; who owe their safety more to the timidity than the forbearance of the Chinnooks. We had heard instances of pilfering whilst we were amongst them, and therefore had a general order, excluding them from our encampment; so that whenever an Indian wished to visit us, he began by calling out "No Chinnook." It may be probable that this first impression left a prejudice against them, since, when we were among the Clatsops, and other tribes at the mouth of the Columbia, the Indians had less opportunity of stealing, if they were so disposed.

Tuesday, 14. We were employed in jerking the meat of the elk, and searching for one of the canoes which had been carried off by the tide last night. Having found it, we now had three of them drawn up out of reach of the water, and the other secured by a strong cord, so as to be ready for any emergency.

After many inquiries, and much observation, we were at length enabled to obtain a connected view of the nations who reside along the coast, on both sides of the Columbia.

To the south, our personal observation has not extended beyond the Killamucks; but we obtained from those who were acquainted with the sea-coast, a list of the Indian tribes, in the order in which they succeed each other, to a considerable distance. The first nation to the south are the Clatsops, who reside on the southern side of the bay, and along the sea-coast, on both sides of Point Adams. They are represented as the remains of a much larger nation; but about four years ago, a disorder, to which till then they were strangers, but which seems, from their description, to have been the small-pox, destroyed four chiefs, and several hundreds of the nation. These are deposited in canoes, a few miles below us on the bay, and the survivors do not number more than fourteen houses, and about two hundred souls. Next to them, along the south-east coast, is a much larger nation, the Killamucks, who number fifty houses, and a thousand souls. Their first establishment are the four huts at the mouth of Ecola creek, thirty-five miles from Point Adams; and two miles below are a few more huts; but the principal town is situated twenty miles lower, at the entrance of a creek, called Nielee, into the bay, which we designate by the name of Killamuck's bay. Into the same bay empties a second creek, five miles further, where is a Killamuck village, called Kilherhurst; at two miles a third creek, and a town called Kilherner; and at the same distance a town called *Chishuck*, at the mouth of Killamuck river. Towerquotton and *Chuctin*, are the names of two other towns, situated on creeks which empty into the bottom of the bay, the last of which is seventy miles from Point Adams. The Killamuck river is about one hundred yards wide, and very rapid; but having no perpendicular fall, is the great avenue for trade. There are two small villages of Killamucks settled above its mouth, and the whole trading part of the tribe ascend it, till by a short portage, they carry their canoes over to the Columbian valley, and descend the Multnomah to Wappatoo island. Here they purchase roots, which they carry down the Chockalilum or Columbia; and, after trafficking with the tribes on its banks for the various articles which they require, either return up the Columbia, or cross over through the country of the Clatsops. This trade, however, is obviously little more than a loose and irregular barter, on a very small scale; for the materials for commerce are so extremely scanty and precarious, that the stranding of a whale was an important commercial incident, which interested all the adjoining country. The Killamucks have little peculiar, either in character or manners, and resemble, in almost every particular, the Clatsops and Chinnooks.

Adjoining the Killamucks, and in a direction S.S.E., are the Lucktons, a small tribe inhabiting the sea-coast. They speak the same language as the Killamucks, but do not belong to the same nation. The same observation applies to the Kahunkle nation, their immediate neighbours, who are supposed to consist of about four hundred souls.

The Lickawis, a still more numerous nation, who have a large town of eight hundred souls.

The Youkone nation, who live in very large houses, and number seven hundred souls.

The Necketo nation, of the same number of persons.

The Ulseah nation, a small town of one hundred and fifty souls.

The Youitts, a tribe who live in a small town, containing not more than one hundred and fifty souls.

The Shiastuckle nation, who have a large town of nine hundred souls.

The Killawats nation, of five hundred souls collected into one large town.

With this last nation ends the language of the Killamucks: and the coast, which then turns towards the south-west, is occupied by nations whose languages vary from that of the Killamucks, and from each other. Of these, the first in order are,

The Cookoose, a large nation of one thousand five hundred souls, inhabiting the shore of the Pacific and the neighbouring mountains. We have seen several of this nation, who were taken prisoners by the Clatsops and Killamucks. Their complexion was much fairer than that of the Indians near the mouth of the Columbia, and their heads were not flattened. Next to these are,

The Shalalahs, of whom we know nothing, except their numbers, which are computed at twelve hundred souls. Then follow

The Luckasos, of about the same number, and

The Hannakalals, whom we estimate at six hundred souls.

This is the extent of the Indian information, and judging, as we can do, with considerable accuracy, from the number of sleeps, or days' journey, the distance which these tribes occupy along the coast, may be estimated at three hundred and sixty miles.

On the north of the Columbia we have already seen the Chinnooks, of four hundred souls, along the shores of Haley's bay, and the low grounds on Chinnook river. Their nearest neighbours to the north-east are,

The Killaxthokle, a small nation on the coast, of not more than eight houses, and a hundred souls. To these succeed

The Chilts, who reside above Point Lewis, and who are estimated at seven hundred souls, and

thirty-eight houses. Of this nation we saw, tran-
siently, a few among the Chinnooks, from whom
they did not appear to differ. Beyond the Chilts
we have seen none of the north-west Indians, and
all that we learnt, consisted of an enumeration of
their names and numbers. The nations next to
the Chilts, are

The Clamoitomish, of twelve houses, and two
hundred and sixty souls.

The Potoashees, of ten houses, and two hundred
souls.

The Pailsk, of ten houses, and two hundred
souls.

The Quinults, of sixty houses, and one thousand
souls.

The Chillates, of eight houses, and one hundred
and fifty souls.

The Calasthorte, of ten houses, and two hundred
souls.

The Quinnechant, consisting of two thousand
souls.

A particular detail of the characters, manners,
and habits of the tribes, must be left to some future
adventurers, who may have more leisure and a
better opportunity than we had to accomplish this
object. Those who first visit the ground, can
only be expected to furnish sketches rude and
imperfect.

Wednesday, 15. Two hunting parties intended
setting out this morning, but they were prevented

by incessant rain, which confined us all to the fort.

The Chinnooks, Clatsops, and most of the adjoining nations, dispose of the dead in canoes. For this purpose a scaffold is erected, by fixing perpendicularly in the ground four long pieces of split timber. These are placed two by two, just wide enough apart to admit the canoe, and sufficiently long to support its two extremities. The boards are connected by a bar of wood run through them at the height of six feet, on which is placed a small canoe, containing the body of the deceased, carefully wrapped in a robe of dressed skins, with a paddle, and some articles belonging to the deceased by his side. Over this canoe is placed one of a larger size, reversed, with its gunwale resting on the cross-bars, so as to cover the body completely. One or more large mats of rushes or flags are then rolled round the canoes, and the whole secured by cords usually made of the bark of the white cedar. On these cross-bars are hung different articles of clothing, or culinary utensils. The method practised by the Killamucks differs somewhat from this ; the body being deposited in an oblong box of plank, which, with the paddle, and other articles, is placed in a canoe, resting on the ground. With the religious opinions of these people we are but little acquainted, since we understand their language too imperfectly to converse on a subject so abstract ; but it is obvious, from the different deposits which they place by their dead, that they believe in a future state of existence. *

Thursday, 16. To-day we finished curing our meat, and having now a plentiful supply of elk, and salt, and our houses dry and comfortable, we wait patiently for the moment of resuming our journey.

The implements used in hunting, by the Clatsops, Chinnooks, and other neighbouring nations, are the gun, bow and arrow, deadfall, pits, snares, and spears or gigs. The guns are generally old American or British muskets repaired for this trade; and although there are some good pieces among them, they are constantly out of order, as the Indians have not been sufficiently accustomed to arms to understand the management of them. The powder is kept in small japanned tin flasks, in which the traders sell it; and when the ball or shot fails, they make use of gravel or pieces of metal from their pots, without being sensible of the injury done to their guns. These arms are reserved for hunting elk, and the few deer and bears in this neighbourhood; but as they have no rifles, they are not very successful hunters. The most common weapon is the bow and arrow, with which

---

* This fact is much too equivocal to warrant an inference so important. These deposits might have been intended for nothing more than the testimonials of surviving affection. Amongst those savages, where the language was better understood, it does not appear that the Indians intended any thing more by such sacrifices than to testify their reverence for the dead.—AMERICAN EDITOR.

every man is provided, even though he carries a gun, and which is used in every kind of hunting. The bow is extremely neat, and being very thin and flat, possesses great elasticity. It is made of the heart of the white cedar, about two feet and a half in length, two inches wide at the centre, whence it tapers to the width of half an inch at the extremities ; and the back is covered with the sinews of elk, fastened on by means of a glue made from the sturgeon. The string is formed of the same sinews. The arrow generally consists of two parts ; the first is about twenty inches long, and formed of light white pine, with the feather at one end, and at the other a circular hole, which receives the second part, formed of some harder wood, and about five inches long, and secured in its place by means of sinews. The barb is either of stone, or else of iron or copper, in which latter place, the angle is more obtuse than any we have seen. If, as sometimes happens, the arrow is formed of a single piece, the whole is of a more durable wood, but the form just described is preferred : because, as much of the game consists of wild fowl, on the ponds, it is desirable that they should be constructed so as to float, if they fall into the water. These arrows are kept in a quiver of elk or young bear skin, opening not at the ends, as the common quivers, but at the sides ; which, for those who hunt in canoes, is much more convenient. These weapons are not, however, very powerful, for many of the elk we kill have been wounded with them ;

and, although the barb with the small end of the
arrows remain, yet the flesh closes, and the animal
suffers no permanent injury. The deadfalls and
snares are used in taking the wolf, the raccoon, and
the fox, of which there are, however, but few in
this country. The spear or gig employed in pursuit of the sea-otter, (which they call spuck,) the
common otter, and beaver, consists of two points of
barbs, and is like those already described as common among the Indians on the upper part of the
Columbia. The pits are chiefly for the elk, and
are therefore usually large and deep cubes of
twelve or fourteen feet in depth, and are made by
the side of some fallen tree lying across the path
frequented by the elk. They are covered with
slender boughs and moss, and the elk either sinks
into it as he approaches the tree, or, in leaping
over the tree, falls into the pit on the other side.

Friday, 17. Comowool and seven other Clatsops
spent the day with us. He made us a present of
some roots and berries, and in return we gave him
an awl and some thread, which he wanted for the
purpose of making a net. We were not able to
purchase any more of their provisions, the prices
being too high for our exhausted stock of merchandize. One of the Indians was dressed in three
very elegant skins of the sea-otter: for these we
were very desirous of trafficking: but he refused
every exchange except that of blue beads, of which
he asked six fathom for each skin, and as we had
only four fathom left, he would not accept for the

remaining two, either a knife, or any quantity of beads of another sort.

In fishing, the Clatsops, Chinnooks, and other nations near this place employ the common straight net, the scooping or dipping net with a long handle, the gig, and the hook and line. The first is of different lengths and depths, and used in taking salmon, carr, and trout, in the deep inlets among the marshy grounds, and the mouths of deep creeks. The scooping net is used for small fish in the spring and summer season; and in both kinds the net is formed of silk-grass, or the bark of white cedar. The gig is used at all seasons, and for all kinds of fish they can procure with it; so too is the hook and line, of which the line is made of the same material as the net, and the hook generally brought by the traders; though before the whites came, they made hooks out of two small pieces of bone, resembling the European hook, but with a much more acute angle, where the two pieces were joined.

Saturday, 18. We were all occupied in dressing skins, and preparing clothes for our journey home-wards. The houses in this neighbourhood are all large wooden buildings, varying in length from twenty to sixty feet, and from fourteen to twenty in width. They are constructed in the following manner. Two posts of split timber, or more, agreeably to the number of partitions, are sunk in the ground, above which they rise to the height of fourteen or eighteen feet. They are hollowed at the top, so as to receive the ends of a round beam or pole, stretching from one to the other, and forming the upper point of the roof for the whole extent of the building. On each side of this range is placed another, which forms the eaves of the house, and is about five feet high; but as the building is often sunk to the depth of four or five feet, the eaves come very near the surface of the earth. Smaller pieces of timber are now extended by pairs, in the form of rafters, from the lower to the upper beam, where they are attached at both ends with cords of cedar-bark. On these rafters two or three ranges of small poles are placed horizontally, and secured in the same way with strings of cedar-bark. The sides are now made with a range of white boards, sunk a small distance into the ground, with the upper ends projecting above the poles at the eaves, to which they are secured by a beam passing outside, parallel with the eave-poles, and tied by cords of cedar-bark passing through holes made in the boards at certain distances. The gable ends and partitions are formed in the same way, being fastened by beams on the outside, parallel to the rafters. The roof is then covered with a double range of thin boards, except an aperture of two or three feet in the centre, for the smoke to pass through. The entrance is by a small hole cut out of the boards, and just large enough to admit the body. The very largest houses only are divided by partitions, for though three or four families reside in the same room, there is quite space enough for all of them. In the centre of each room is a space six or eight feet square, sunk to the depth of twelve inches below the rest of the floor, and enclosed by four pieces of square timber. Here they make the fire, for which purpose pine bark is generally preferred. Around this fire-place mats are spread, and serve as seats during the day, and very frequently as beds at night; there is, however, a more permanent bed made, by fixing, in two or sometimes three sides of the room, posts reaching from the roof down to the ground, and at the distance of four feet from the wall. From these posts to the wall itself, one or two ranges of boards are placed so as to form shelves, on which they either sleep, or where they stow away their various articles of merchandize. The uncured fish is hung in the smoke of their fires, as is also the flesh of the elk, when they are fortunate enough to procure any, which is but rarely.

Sunday, 20. This morning we sent out two parties of hunters in different directions. Soon after we were visited by two Clatsop men and a woman, who brought several articles to trade : we purchased a small quantity of train-oil for a pair of brass arm-bands, and succeeded in obtaining a sea-otter skin, for which we gave our only remaining four fathoms of blue beads, the same quantity of white ones, and a knife : we gave a fish-hook also in exchange for one of their hats. These are made of cedar-bark and bear-grass, interwoven together in the form of an European hat, with a small brim of about two inches, and a high crown, widening upwards. They are light, ornamented with various colours and figures, and being nearly water-proof, are much more durable than either chip or straw hats. These hats form a small article of traffic with the whites, and the manufacture is one of the best exertions of Indian industry. They are, however, very dexterous in making a variety of domestic utensils, among which are bowls, spoons, skewers, spits, and baskets. The bowl or trough is of different shapes, sometimes round, semicircular, in the form of a canoe, or cubic, and generally dug out of a single piece of wood, the larger vessels having holes in the sides by way of handle, and all executed with great neatness. In these vessels they boil their food, by throwing hot stones into the water, and extract oil from different animals in the same way. Spoons are not very abundant, nor is there any thing remarkable in their shape, except that they are large and the bowl broad. Meat is roasted on one end of a sharp skewer, placed erect before the fire, with the other fixed in the ground. The spit for fish is split at the top into two parts, between which the fish is placed, cut open, with its sides extended by means of small splinters. The usual plate is a small mat of rushes or flags, on which every thing is served. The instrument with which they dig up roots, is a strong stick, about three feet and a half long, sharpened, and a little curved at the lower end, while the upper is inserted into a handle, standing transversely, and made of part of an elk or buck's horn. But the most curious workmanship is that of the basket. It is formed of cedar-bark and bear-grass, so closely interwoven, that it is water-tight, without the aid of either gum or resin. The form is generally . conic, or rather the segment of a cone, of which the smaller end is the bottom of the basket; and being made of all sizes, from that of the smallest cup to the capacity of five or six gallons, answers the double purpose of a covering for the head or to contain water. Some of them are highly ornamented with strands of bear-grass, woven into figures of various colours, which require great labour; yet they are made very expeditiously, and sold for a trifle. It is for the construction of these baskets, that the bear-grass forms an article of considerable traffic. It grows only near the snowy region of the high mountains, and the blade, which is two feet long and about three-eighths of an inch wide, is smooth, strong, and pliant; the young blades particularly, from their not being exposed to the sun and air, have an appearance of great neatness, and are ge-nerally preferred. Other bags and baskets, not water-proof, are made of cedar-bark, silk-grass, rushes, flags, and common coarse sedge, for the use of families. In the manufactures, as well as in the ordinary work of the house, the instrument most in use is a knife, or rather a dagger. The handle of it is small, and has a strong loop of twine for the thumb, to prevent its being wrested from the hand. On each side is a blade, double-edged and pointed ; the longer from nine to ten inches, the shorter from four to five. This knife is carried about habitually in the hand, sometimes exposed, but mostly, when in company with strangers, put under the robe.

Monday, 20. We were visited by three Clatsops, who came merely for the purpose of smoking and conversing with us. We have now only three days' provision, yet so accustomed have the men become to live sparingly, and fast occasionally, that such a circumstance excites no concern, as we all calculate on our dexterity as hunters.

The industry of the Indians is not confined to household utensils : the great proof of their skill is the construction of their canoes. In a country, indeed, where so much of the intercourse between different tribes is carried on by water, the ingenuity of the people would naturally direct itself to the improvement of canoes, which would gradually become, from a mere safe conveyance, an elegant ornament. We have accordingly seen, on the Columbia, canoes of many forms, beginning with the simple boats near the mountains, to those more highly decorated, because more useful, nearer the mouth of the Columbia. Below the grand cataract there are four forms of canoes: the first and smallest is about fifteen feet long, and calculated for one or two persons : it is, indeed, by no means remarkable in its structure, and is chiefly employed by the Cathlamahs and Wahkiacums among the marshy islands. The second is from twenty to thirty-five feet long, about two and a half or three feet in the beam, and two feet in the hold. It is chiefly remarkable in having the bowsprit, which rises to some height above the bow, formed by tapering gradually from the sides into a sharp point. Canoes of this shape are common to all the nations below the grand rapids.

But the canoes most used by the Columbian Indians, from the Chilluckittequaws inclusive, to the ocean, are about thirty or thirty-five feet long. The bow, which looks more like the stern of our boats, is higher than the other end, and is ornamented with a sort of comb, an inch in thickness, cut out of the same log which forms the canoe, and extending nine or eleven inches from the bowsprit to the bottom of the boat. The stern is nearly rounded off, and gradually ascends to a point. This canoe is very light and convenient; for though it will contain ten or twelve persons, it may be carried with great ease by four.

The fourth and largest species of canoe we did not meet with till we reached tide-water, near the grand rapids below, in which place they are found among all the nations, especially the Killamucks, and others residing on the sea-coast. They are upwards of fifty feet long, and will carry from eight to ten thousand pounds weight, or from

twenty to thirty persons. Like all the canoes we
have mentioned, they are cut out of a single trunk
of a tree, which is generally white cedar, though
the fir is sometimes used. The sides are secured
by cross-bars, or round sticks, two or three inches
in thickness, which are inserted through holes made
just below the gunwale, and made fast with cords.
The upper edge of the gunwale itself is about five-
eighths of an inch thick, and four or five in breadth,
and folds outwards, so as to form a kind of rim,
which prevents the water from beating into the
boat. The bow and stern are about the same
height, and each provided with a comb, reaching
to the bottom of the boat. At each end, also, are
pedestals, formed of the same solid piece, on which
are placed strange grotesque figures of men or animals, rising sometimes to the height of five feet,
and composed of small pieces of wood, firmly
united, with great ingenuity, by inlaying and mor-
tising, without a spike of any kind. The paddle
is usually from four feet and a half to five feet in
length ; the handle being thick for one-third of its
length, when it widens, and is hollowed and thinned
on each side of the centre, which forms a sort of
rib. When they embark, one Indian sits in the
stern, and steers with a paddle, the others kneel in
pairs in the bottom of the canoe, and sitting on
their heels, paddle over the gunwale next to them.
In this way they ride with perfect safety the highest
waves, and venture, without the least concern, in
seas, where other boats or seamen could not live an

instant. They sit quietly and paddle, with no other movement; except when any large wave throws the boat on her side, and, to the eye of a spectator, she seems lost: the man to windward then steadies her by throwing his body towards the upper side, and sinking his paddle deep into the wave, appears to catch the water and force it under the boat, which the same stroke pushes on with great velocity. In the management of these canoes the women are equally expert with the men; for in the smaller boats, which contain four oarsmen, the helm is generally given to the female. As soon as they land, the canoe is generally hauled on shore, unless she be very heavily laden; but at night the load is universally discharged, and the canoe brought on shore.

Our admiration of their skill in these curious constructions was increased by observing the very inadequate implements with which they are made. These Indians possess very few axes, and the only tool employed in their building, from felling of the tree to the delicate workmanship of the images, is a chissel, made of an old file, about an inch and a half in width. Even of this, too, they have not yet learnt the management, for the chissel is sometimes fixed in a large block of wood, and being held in the right hand, the block is pushed with the left without the aid of a mallet. But under all these disadvantages, these canoes, which one would suppose to be the work of years, are made in a few weeks. A canoe, however, is very highly prized:

in traffic, it is an article of the greatest value, except a wife, which is of equal consideration ; so that a lover generally gives a canoe to the father in exchange for his daughter.

CHAPTER XXIII.

TUESDAY, 21. Two of the hunters came back with three elk, which form a timely addition to our stock of provisions. The Indian visitors left us at twelve o'clock.

The Killamucks, Clatsops, Chinnooks, and Cathlamahs, the four neighbouring nations with whom we have had most intercourse, preserve a general resemblance in person, dress, and manners. They are commonly of a diminutive stature, badly shaped, and their appearance by no means prepossessing. They have broad, thick, flat feet, thick ankles, and crooked legs : the last of which deformities is to be ascribed, in part, to the universal practice of squatting, or sitting on the calves of their legs and heels, and also to the tight bandages of beads and strings worn round the ankles by the women, which prevent the circulation of the blood, and render the legs, of the females particularly, ill-shaped and swollen. The complexion is the usual copper-coloured brown of the North American tribes, though the complexion is rather lighter than that of the Indians of the Missouri, and the frontier of the United States : the mouth is wide and the lips thick ; the nose of a moderate size, fleshy, wide at the extremities, with large nostrils, and generally low between the eyes, though there are rare instances of high aquiline noses ; the eyes are generally black, though we occasionally see them of a dark yellowish-brown, with a black pupil. But the most distinguishing part of their physiognomy, is the peculiar flatness and width of their forehead, a peculiarity which they owe to one of those customs by which nature is sacrificed to fantastic ideas of beauty. The custom, indeed, of flattening the head by artificial pressure during infancy, prevails among all the nation we have seen west of the Rocky mountains. To the east of that barrier, the fashion is so perfectly unknown, that there the western Indians, with the exception of the Alliatan or Snake nation, are designated by the common name of Flatheads. This singular usage, which nature could scarcely seem to suggest to remote nations, might, perhaps, incline us to believe in the common and not very ancient origin of all the western nations. Such an opinion might well accommodate itself with the fact, that while on the lower parts of the Columbia both sexes are universally flatheads, the custom diminishes in receding eastward, from the common centre of the infection, till among the remoter tribes near the mountains, nature recovers her rights, and the wasted folly is confined to a few females. Such opinions, however, are corrected, or weakened, by considering that the flattening of the head is not, in fact, peculiar to that part of the Continent, since it was among the first objects which struck the attention of Columbus.

But wherever it may have begun, the practice is now universal among these nations. Soon after the birth of a child, the mother, anxious to procure for her infant the recommendation of a broad forehead, places it in the compressing machine, where it is kept for ten or twelve months; though the females remain longer than the boys. The operation is so gradual, that it is not attended with pain; but the impression is deep and permanent. The heads of the children, when they are released from the bandage, are not more than two inches thick about the upper edge of the forehead, and still thinner above : nor with all its efforts can nature ever restore its shape; the heads of grown persons being often in a straight line from the nose to the top of the forehead.

The hair of both sexes is parted at the top of the head, and thence falls loosely behind the ears, over the back and shoulders. They use combs, of which they are very fond, and, indeed, contrive, without the aid of them, to keep their hair in very good order. The dress of the man consists of a small robe, reaching to the middle of the thigh, tied by a string across the breast, with its corners hanging loosely over their arms. These robes are, in general, composed of the skins of a small animal, which we have supposed to be the brown mungo. They have, besides, those of the tiger, cat, deer, panther, bear, and elk, which last is principally used in war parties. Sometimes they have a blanket woven with the fingers, from the wool of their native sheep; occasionally a mat is thrown over them to keep off rain; but except this robe, they have no other article of clothing during winter or summer, so that every part of the body, but the back and shoulders, is exposed to view. They are very fond of the dress of the whites, whom they call pashisheooks, or clothmen; and whenever they can procure any clothes, wear them in our manner: the only article, indeed, which we have not seen among them is the shoe.

The robe of the women is like that worn by the men, except that it does not reach below the waist. Those most esteemed are made of strips of sea-otter skin, which being twisted, are interwoven with silk-grass, or the bark of the white cedar, in such a manner that the fur appears equally on both sides, so as to form a soft and warm covering. The skins of the raccoon, or beaver, are also employed in the same way; though, on other occasions, these skins are simply dressed in the hair, and worn without further preparation. The garment which covers the body from the waist as low as the knee before, and the thigh behind, is the tissue already described, and is made either of the bruised bark of white cedar, the twisted cords of silk-grass, or of flags and rushes. Neither leggings nor moccasins are ever used, the mildness of the climate not requiring them as a security from the weather, and their being so much in the water rendering them an incumbrance. The only covering for the head is a hat made of bear-grass, and the bark of cedar, interwoven in a conic form, with a knob of the same shape at the top. It has no brim, but is held on the head by a string passing under the chin, and tied to a small rim inside of the hat. The colours are generally black and white only, and these are made into squares, triangles, and sometimes rude figures of canoes and seamen harpooning whales. This is all the usual dress of females; but if the weather be unusually severe they add a vest, formed of skins like the robe, tied behind, without any shoulder-straps to keep it up. As this vest covers the body from the armpits to the waist, it conceals the breasts, but on all other occasions they are suffered to remain loose and exposed, and present, in old women especially, a most disgusting appearance.

Sometimes, though not often, they mark their skins by puncturing and introducing some coloured matter : this ornament is chiefly confined to the women, who imprint on their legs and arms, circular or parallel dots. On the arm of one of the squaws we read the name of J. Bowman, apparently a trader who visits the mouth of the Columbia. The favourite decoration, however, of both sexes, are the common coarse blue or white beads, which are folded very tightly round their wrists and ankles, to the width of three or four inches, and worn in large loose rolls round the neck, or in the shape of ear-rings, or hanging from the nose; which last mode is peculiar to the men. There is also a species of wampum very much in use, which seems to be worn in its natural form without any preparation. Its shape is a cone somewhat curved, about the size of a raven's quill at the base, and tapering to a point, its whole length being from one to two and a half inches, and white, smooth, hard, and thin. A small thread is passed through it, and the wampum is either suspended from the nose, or passed through the cartilage horizontally, and forms a ring, from which other ornaments hang. This wampum is employed in the same way as the beads, but is the favourite decoration for the noses of the men. The men also use collars made of bears' claws, the women and children

those of elks' tusks, and both sexes are adorned
with bracelets of copper, iron, or brass, in various
forms.

Yet all these decorations are unavailing to conceal the deformities of nature and the extravagance
of fashion ; nor have we seen any more disgusting
object than a Chinnook or Clatsop beauty in full
attire. Their broad flat foreheads, their falling
breasts, their ill-shaped limbs, the awkwardness of
their positions, and the filth which intrudes through
their finery ; all these render a Chinnook or Clatsop beauty, in full attire, one of the most disgusting
objects in nature. Fortunately this circumstance
conspired with the low diet and laborious exercise
of our men, to protect them from the persevering
gallantry of the fair sex, whose kindness always
exceeded the ordinary courtesies of hospitality.
Among these people, as indeed among all Indians,
the prostitution of unmarried women is so far from
being considered criminal or improper, that the
females themselves solicit the favours of the other
sex, with the entire approbation of their friends
and connexions. The person is in fact often the
only property of a young female, and is therefore
the medium of trade, the return for presents, and
the reward for services. In most cases, however,
the female is so much at the disposal of her husband or parent, that she is farmed out for hire.
The Chinnook woman, who brought her six female
relations to our camp, had regular prices, proportioned to the beauty of each female ; and among

all the tribes, a man will lend his wife or daughter for a fish-hook or a strand of beads. To decline an offer of this sort is indeed to disparage the charms of the lady, and therefore gives such offence, that although we had occasionally to treat the Indians with rigour, nothing seemed to irritate both sexes more than our refusal to accept the favours of the females. On one occasion we were amused by a Clatsop, who having been cured of some disorder by our medical skill, brought his sister as a reward for our kindness. The young lady was quite anxious to join in this expression of her brother's gratitude; and mortified that we did not avail ourselves of it, she could not be prevailed on to leave the fort, but remained with Chaboneau's wife, in the next room to ours, for two or three days, declining all the solicitations of the men, till finding, at last, that we did not relent, she went away, regretting that her brother's obligations were unpaid.

The little intercourse which the men have had with these women is, however, sufficient to apprise us of the prevalence of the venereal disease, with which one or two of the party had been so much afflicted, as to render a salivation necessary. The infection in these cases was communicated by the Chinnook women. The others do not appear to be afflicted with it to any extent: indeed, notwithstanding this disorder is certainly known to the Indians on the Columbia, yet the number of infected persons is very inconsiderable. The exist-

ence of such a disorder is very easily detected, particularly in the men, in their open style of dress;
yet in the whole route down the Columbia, we have
not seen more than two or three cases of gonorrhœa,
and about double that number of lues venerea.
There do not seem to be any simples which are
used as specifics in this disorder, nor is a complete
cure ever effected. When once a patient is seized,
the disorder ends with his life only; though from
the simplicity of their diet, and the use of certain
vegetables, they support it for many years with but
little inconvenience, and even enjoy tolerable
health; yet their life is always abridged by decrepitude or premature old age. The Indians, who
are mostly successful in treating this disorder, are
the Chippeways. Their specifics are the root of
the lobelia, and that of a species of sumac, common
to the United States, the neighbourhood of the
Rocky mountains, and to the countries westward,
and which is readily distinguished by being the
smallest of its kind, and by its winged rib, or
common footstalk, supporting leaves oppositely pin-
nate. Decoctions of the roots are used very freely,
without any limitation, and are said to soften the
violence of the lues, and even to be sovereign in
the cure of the gonorrhœa.

The Clatsops and other nations at the mouth of
the Columbia, have visited us with great freedom,
and we have endeavoured to cultivate their intimacy, as well for the purpose of acquiring information, as to leave behind us impressions favourable

to our country. Having acquired much of their language, we are enabled, with the assistance of gestures, to hold conversations with great ease. We find them inquisitive and loquacious, with understandings by no means deficient in acuteness, and with very retentive memories; and though fond of feasts, and generally cheerful, they are never gay. Every thing they see excites their attention and inquiries, but having been accustomed to see the whites, nothing appeared to give them more astonishment than the air-gun. To all our inquiries they answer with great intelligence, and the conversation rarely slackens, since there is a constant discussion of the events, and trade, and politics, in the little but active circle of Killamucks, Clatsops, Cathlamahs, Wahkiacums, and Chinnooks. Among themselves, the conversation generally turns on the subjects of trade, or smoking, or eating, or connexion with females, before whom this last is spoken of with a familiarity which would be in the highest degree indecent, if custom had not rendered it inoffensive.

The treatment of women is often considered as the standard by which the moral qualities of savages are to be estimated. Our own observation, however, induced us to think that the importance of the female in savage life has no necessary relation to the virtues of the men, but is regulated wholly by their capacity to be useful. The Indians, whose treatment of the females is mildest, and who pay most deference to their opinions, are by no means the most distinguished for their virtues; nor is this deference attended by any increase of attachment, since they are equally willing with the most brutal husband, to prostitute their wives to strangers. On the other hand, the tribes among whom the women are very much debased, possess the loftiest sense of honour, the greatest liberality, and all the good qualities of which their situation demands the exercise. Where the women can aid in procuring subsistence for the tribe, they are treated with more equality, and their importance is proportioned to the share which they take in that labour; while in countries where subsistence is chiefly procured by the exertions of the men, the women are considered and treated as burdens. Thus, among the Clatsops and Chinnooks, who live upon fish and roots, which the women are equally expert with the men in procuring, the former have a rank and influence very rarely found among Indians. The females are permitted to speak freely before the men, to whom, indeed, they sometimes address themselves in a tone of authority. On many subjects their judgments and opinions are respected; and in matters of trade, their advice is generally asked and pursued. The labours of the family, too, are shared almost equally. The men collect wood and make fires, assist in cleansing the fish, make the houses, canoes, and wooden utensils; and whenever strangers are to be entertained, or a great feast prepared, the meats are cooked and served up by the men. The peculiar province of the female is to collect roots, and to manufacture the various articles which are formed of rushes, flags, cedar-bark, and bear-grass: but the management of the canoes, and many of the occupations, which elsewhere devolve wholly on the female, are here common to both sexes.

The observation with regard to the importance of females applies with equal force to the treatment of old men. Among tribes who subsist by hunting, the labours of the chase, and the wandering existence to which that occupation condemns them, necessarily throws the burden of procuring provisions on the active young men. As soon, therefore, as a man is unable to pursue the chase, he begins to withdraw something from the precarious supplies of the tribe. Still, however, his counsels may compensate his want of activity; but in the next stage of infirmity, when he can no longer travel from camp to camp, as the tribe roams about for subsistence, he is then found to be a heavy burden. In this situation they are abandoned among the Sioux, Assiniboins, and the hunting tribes on the Missouri. As they are setting out for some new excursion, where the old man is unable to follow, his children, or nearest relations, place before him a piece of meat and some water, and telling him that he has lived long enough, that it is now time for him to go home to his relations, who could take better care of him than his friends on earth, leave him, without remorse, to perish when his little supply is exhausted. The same custom is said to prevail among the Minnetarees,

Ahnahawas, and Ricaras, when they are attended by old men on their hunting excursions. Yet, in their villages, we saw no want of kindness to old men. On the contrary, probably because in villages the means of more abundant subsistence renders such cruelty unnecessary, the old people appear to be treated with attention, and some of their feasts, particularly the buffaloe dances, were intended chiefly as a contribution for the old and infirm.

The dispositions of these people seem mild and inoffensive, and they have uniformly behaved to us with great friendship. They are addicted to begging and pilfering small articles, when it can be done without danger of detection, but do not rob wantonly, nor to any large amount; and some of them having purloined some of our meat, which the hunters had been obliged to leave in the woods, they voluntarily brought some dogs a few days after, by way of compensation. Our force and great superiority in the use of fire-arms, enable us always to command; and such is the friendly deportment of these people, that the men have been accustomed to treat them with the greatest confidence. It is therefore with difficulty that we can impress on our men a conviction of the necessity of being always on our guard, since we are perfectly acquainted with the treacherous character of Indians in general. We are always prepared for an attack, and uniformly exclude all large parties of Indians from the fort. Their large houses usually contain several families, consisting of the parents, their sons and daughters-in-law, and grand-children, among whom the provisions are common, and whose harmony is scarcely ever interrupted by disputes. Although polygamy is permitted by their customs, very few have more than a single wife, and she is brought immediately after the marriage into the husband's family, where she resides until increasing numbers oblige them to seek another house. In this state the old man is not considered as the head of the family, since the active duties, as well as the responsibility, fall on some of the younger members. As these families gradually expand into bands, or tribes, or nations, the paternal authority is represented by the chief of each association. This chieftain, however, is not hereditary: his ability to render service to his neighbours, and the popularity which follows it, is at once the foundation and the measure of his authority, the exercise of which does not extend beyond a reprimand for some improper action.

The harmony of their private life is indeed secured by their ignorance of spirituous liquors, the earliest and most dreadful present which civilization has given to the natives of the other continent. Although they have had so much intercourse with whites, they do not appear to possess any knowledge of those dangerous luxuries, at least they have never inquired after them, which they probably would have done, if once they had been introduced among them. Indeed, we have not observed any liquor of an intoxicating quality used among these or any Indians west of the Rocky mountains, the

universal beverage being pure water. They, however, sometimes almost intoxicate themselves by
smoking tobacco, of which they are excessively
fond, and the pleasures of which they prolong as
much as possible, by retaining vast quantities at a
time, till after circulating through the lungs and
stomach, it issues in volumes from the mouth and
nostrils. But the natural vice of all these people
is an attachment for games of hazard, which they
pursue with a strange and ruinous avidity. The
games are of two kinds. In the first, one of the
company assumes the office of banker, and plays
against the rest. He takes a small stone, about the
size of a bean, which he shifts from one hand to
the other with great dexterity, repeating at the
same time a song adapted to the game, and which
serves to divert the attention of the company, till,
having agreed on the stake, he holds out his hands,
and the antagonist wins or loses as he succeeds or
fails at guessing in which hand the stone is. After
the banker has lost his money, or whenever he is
tired, the stone is transferred to another, who in
turn challenges the rest of the company. The
other game is something like the play of ninepins :
two pins are placed on the floor, about the distance
of a foot from each other, and a small hole made
behind them. The players then go about ten feet
from the hole, into which they try to roll a small
piece resembling the men used at draughts; if they
succeed in putting it into the hole, they win the
stake ; if the piece rolls between the pins, but does

not go into the hole, nothing is won or lost; but
the wager is wholly lost if the chequer rolls outside
of the pins. Entire days are wasted at these games,
which are often continued through the night, round
the blaze of their fires, till the last article of clothing, or even the last blue bead is won from the
desperate adventurer.

In traffic they are keen, acute, and intelligent;
and they employ in all their bargains a dexterity
and finesse, which, if it be not learnt from their
foreign visitors, may show how nearly the cunning
of savages is allied to the little arts of more civilized trade. They begin by asking double or treble
the value of their merchandize, and lower the
demand in proportion to the ardour or experience
in trade of the purchaser; and if he expresses
any anxiety, the smallest article, perhaps a handful
of roots, will furnish a whole morning's negociation.
Being naturally suspicious, they of course conceive
that you are pursuing the same system. They,
therefore, invariably refuse the first offer, however
high, fearful that they or we have mistaken the
value of the merchandize, and therefore cautiously
wait to draw us on to larger offers. In this way,
after rejecting the most extravagant prices, which
we have offered merely for experiment, they have
afterwards importuned us for a tenth part of what
they had before refused. In this respect they differ
from almost all Indians, who will generally exchange, in a thoughtless moment, the most valuable

article they possess, for any bauble which happens to please their fancy.

These habits of cunning or prudence, have been formed or increased by their being engaged in a large part of the commerce of the Columbia; of that trade, however, the great emporium is the Falls, where all the neighbouring nations assemble. The inhabitants of the Columbian plains, after hav-ing passed the winter near the mountains, come down as soon as the snow has left the valleys, and are occupied in collecting and drying roots, till about the month of May. They then crowd to the river, and fixing themselves on its north side, to avoid the incursions of the Snake Indians, continue fishing till about the first of September, when the salmon are no longer fit for use. They then bury their fish and return to the plains, where they remain gathering quamash, till the snow obliges them to desist. They come back to the Columbia, and taking their store of fish, retire to the foot of the mountains, and along the creeks, which supply timber for houses, and pass the winter in hunting deer or elk, which, with the aid of their fish, enables them to subsist till, in the spring, they resume the circle of their employments. During their resi-dence on the river, from May to September, or rather before they begin the regular fishery, they go down to the Falls, carrying with them skins, mats, silk-grass, rushes, and chappelell bread. They are here overtaken by the Chopunnish, and other

tribes of the Rocky mountains, who descend the
Kooskooskee and Lewis's rivers, for the purpose of
selling bear-grass, horses, quamash, and a few skins
which they have obtained by hunting, or in exchange for horses, with the Tushepaws.

At the Falls, they find the Chilluckittequaws,
Eneeshurs, Echeloots, and Skilloots, which last
serve as intermediate traders or carriers between
the inhabitants above and below the Falls. These
tribes prepare pounded fish for the market, and the
nations below bring wappatoo roots, the fish of the
sea-coast, berries, and a variety of trinkets and
small articles which they have procured from the
whites.

The trade then begins. The Chopunnish, and
Indians of the Rocky mountains, exchange the
articles which they have brought for wappatoo,
pounded fish, and beads. The Indians of the
plains being their own fishermen, take only wappatoo, horses, beads, and other articles procured
from Europeans. The Indians, however, from
Lewis's river to the Falls, consume as food or fuel
all the fish which they take; so that the whole
stock for exportation is prepared by the nations
between the Towahnahiooks and the Falls, and
amounts, as nearly as we could estimate, to about
thirty thousand weight, chiefly salmon, above the
quantity which they use themselves, or barter with
the more eastern Indians. This is now carried
down the river by the Indians at the Falls, and is
consumed among the nations at the mouth of the
Columbia, who in return give the fish of the sea-

coast, and the articles which they obtain from the whites. The neighbouring people catch large quantities of salmon and dry them, but they do not understand or practise the art of drying and pounding it in the manner used at the Falls, and being very fond of it, are forced to purchase it at high prices. This article, indeed, and the wappatoo, form the principal subjects of trade with the people of our immediate vicinity. The traffic is wholly carried on by water; there are even no roads or paths through the country, except across the portages which connect the creeks.

But the circumstance which forms the soul of this trade, is the visit of the whites. They arrive generally about the month of April, and either remain until October, or return at that time; during which time, having no establishment on shore, they anchor on the north side of the bay, at the place already described, which is a spacious and commodious harbour, perfectly secure from all, except the south and south-east, winds; and as they leave it before winter, they do not suffer from these winds, which, during that season, are the most usual and the most violent. This situation is recommended by its neighbourhood to fresh water and wood, as well as to excellent timber for repairs. Here they are immediately visited by the tribes along the sea-coast, by the Cathlamahs, and lastly by the Skilloots, that numerous and active people, who skirt the river between the marshy islands and the grand rapids, as well as the Coweliskee, and who carry down the fish prepared by their immediate neighbours the Chilluckit-tequaws, Eneeshurs, and Echeloots, residing from the grand rapids to the Falls, as well as all the articles which they have procured in barter at the market in May. The accumulated trade of the Columbia now consists of dressed and undressed skins of elk, sea-otter, the common otter, beaver, common fox, spuck, and tiger cat. The articles of less importance, are a small quantity of dried or pounded salmon, the biscuit made of the chappelell roots, and some of the manufactures of the neighbourhood. In return they receive guns (which are principally old British or American muskets), powder, ball, and shot, copper and brass kettles, brass tea-kettles, and coffee-pots, blankets, from two to three points, coarse scarlet and blue cloth, plates and strips of sheet-copper and brass, large brass wire, knives, tobacco, fish-hooks, buttons, and a considerable quantity of sailors' hats, trowsers, coats, and shirts. But, as we have had occasion to remark more than once, the objects of foreign trade, which are the most desired, are the common cheap blue or white beads, of about fifty or seventy to the pennyweight, which are strung on strands a fathom in length, and sold by the yard or the length of both arms: of these the blue beads, which are called tia commashuck, or chief beads, hold the first rank in their ideas of relative value: the most inferior kind are esteemed beyond the finest wampum, and are temptations which can always seduce them to part with their most valuable effects. Indeed, if the example of civilized life did not completely vindicate their choice, we might wonder at their infatuated attachment to a bauble in itself so worthless. Yet these beads are, perhaps, quite as reasonable objects of research as the precious metals, since they are at once beautiful ornaments for the person, and the great circulating medium of trade with all the nations on the Columbia.

Those strangers who visit the Columbia for the purpose of trade or hunting, must be either English or Americans. The Indians inform us that they speak the same language as we do, and indeed the few words which the Indians have learnt from the sailors, such as musket, powder, shot, knife, file, heave the lead, damned rascal, and other phrases of that description, evidently show that the visitors speak the English language. But as the greater part of them annually arrive in April, and either remain till autumn, or revisit them at that time, which we could not clearly understand, the trade cannot be direct from either England or the United States, since the ships could not return thither during the remainder of the year. When the Indians are asked where these traders go on leaving the Columbia, they always point to the south-west, whence we presume that they do not belong to any establishment at Nootka Sound. They do, however, mention a trader by the name of Moore, who sometimes touches at this place, and the last time he came he had on board three cows; and when he left them, continued along the north-west coast, which renders it probable, that there may be a settlement of whites in that direction. The names and description of all these persons who visit them in the spring and autumn are remembered with great accuracy, and we took down, exactly as they were pronounced, the following list: The favourite trader is

Mr. Haley, who visits them in a vessel with three masts, and continues some time. The others are

Youens, who comes also in a three-masted vessel, and is a trader.

Tallamon, in a three-masted vessel, but he is not a trader.

Callalamet, in a ship of the same size; he is a trader, and they say has a wooden leg.

Swipton	three-masted vessel,		trader.
Moore	four	do.	do.
Mackey	three	do.	do.
Washington	three	do.	do.
Mesship	three	do.	do.
Davidson	three	do. does not trade, hunts elk.	
Jackson	three	do.	trader.
Bolch	three	do.	do.

Skelley, also a trader, in a vessel with three masts, but he has been gone for some years. He had only one eye.

It might be difficult to adjust the balance of the

advantages or the dangers of this trade to the nations of the Columbia, against the sale of their furs, and the acquisition of a few bad guns and household utensils.

The nations near the mouth of the Columbia enjoy great tranquillity; none of the tribes being engaged in war. Not long since, however, there was a war on the coast to the south-west, in which the Killamucks took several prisoners. These, as far as we could perceive, were treated very well, and though nominally slaves, yet were adopted into the families of their masters, and the young ones placed on the same footing with the children of the purchaser.

The month of February and the greater part of March were passed in the same manner. Every day, parties as large as we could spare them from our other occupations were sent out to hunt, and we were thus enabled to command some days' provision in advance. It consisted chiefly of deer and elk; the first is very lean, and the flesh by no means as good as that of the elk, which, though poor, is getting better: it is indeed our chief dependence. At this time of the year it is in much better order in the prairies near the point, where they feed on grass and rushes, considerable quantities of which are yet green, than in the woody country up the Netul. There, they subsist on huckleberry bushes and fern, but chiefly on an evergreen, called shallun, resembling the laurel, which abounds through all the timbered lands, particularly along the broken sides of hills. Towards the latter end of the month, however, they left the prairies near Point Adams, and retired back to the hills; but fortunately, at the same time the sturgeon and anchovies began to appear, and afforded us a delightful variety of food. In the mean time, the party on the sea-coast supplied us with salt: but though the kettles were kept boiling all day and night, the salt was made but slowly; nor was it till the middle of this month that we succeeded in procuring twenty gallons, of which twelve were put in kegs for our journey as far as the deposits on the Missouri.

The neighbouring tribes continued to visit us, for the purpose of trading, or merely to smoke with us. But on the 21st, a Chinnook chief, whom we had never seen, came over with twenty-five of his men. His name was Tahcum, a man of about fifty years of age, with a larger figure and a better carriage than most of his nation. We received him with the usual ceremonies, gave the party something to eat, smoked most copiously with them all, and presented the chief with a small medal. They were all satisfied with their treatment; and though we were willing to show the chief every civility, could not dispense with our rule of not suffering so many strangers to sleep in the fort. They, therefore, left us at sun-set. On the twenty-fourth, Comowool, who is by far the most friendly and decent savage we have seen in this neighbourhood, came with a large party of Clatsops, bringing among other articles, sturgeon and a small fish, which has just begun, within a day or two past, to make its appearance in the Columbia.

From this time, as the elk became scarce and lean, we made use of these fish whenever we could catch them, or purchase them from the Indians. But as we were too poor to indulge very largely in these luxuries, the diet was by no means pleasant, and to the sick, especially, was unwholesome. On the 15th of March we were visited by Delashilwilt, the Chinnook chief, and his wife, accompanied by the same six damsels, who in the autumn had encamped near us, on the other side of the bay, and whose favours had been so troublesome to several of the men. They formed a camp close to the fort, and began to renew their addresses very assiduously, but we warned the men of the dangers of intercourse with this frail society, and they cautiously abstained from connexion with them.

During the greater part of this month, five or six of the men were sick ; indeed, we have not had so many complaining since we left Wood river ; the general complaint is a bad cold and fever, something in the nature of an influenza, which, joined with a few cases of venereal, and accidental injuries, complete our invalid corps. These disorders may chiefly be imputed to the nature of the climate.

END OF THE SECOND VOLUME.

Printed by A. Strahan,
Printers-Street, London.

Lightning Source UK Ltd.
Milton Keynes UK
10 December 2010

164139UK00001B/33/P

9 781108 023795